SEÁN LEMASS

THE LOST MEMOIR

SEÁN LEMASS

THE LOST MEMOIR

The autobiography of Ireland's most admired taoiseach

edited by Ronan McGreevy

eriu

First published in the UK in 2026 by Eriu
An imprint of Bonnier Books UK
5th Floor, HYLO, 105 Bunhill Row,
London, EC1Y 8LZ

A CIP catalogue record for this book is available from the British Library.

Hardback ISBN: 978-1-80444-390-3

Also available as an ebook

3 5 7 9 10 8 6 4 2

Design and Typeset by Envy Design
Printed and bound in Great Britain by CPI (UK) Ltd, Croydon CR0 4YY

FSC www.fsc.org MIX Paper | Supporting responsible forestry FSC® C013604

The authorised representative in the EEA is Bonnier Books UK (Ireland) Limited.
Registered office address:
Block B, The Crescent Building
Northwood, Santry
Dublin 9, D09 C6X8
Ireland
compliance@bonnierbooks.ie

www.bonnierbooks.co.uk

There is a tide in the affairs of men
Which, taken at the flood, leads on to fortune;
Omitted, all the voyage of their life
Is bound in shallows and in miseries.

William Shakespeare, *Julius Caesar*, Act 4; Scene 3

CONTENTS

FOREWORD BY GARY MURPHY

On 1 June 1971, Dermot Ryan wrote to Charles Haughey expressing his sympathy on the death of Seán Lemass. In offering his condolences to Lemass's son-in-law, Haughey, his daughter Maureen Lemass, and the whole family, Ryan described himself as being 'very upset indeed' by Lemass's death, and the loss as being 'beyond expression'. He told Haughey that while he was at the hospital and the church on both days – removal and burial mass – he kept in the background as he 'could not bear to meet people or to talk to them'. He added: 'I felt almost as if I had lost a father, he was such a friend and advisor to me and it was because his death came as such a shock to me and affected me so badly that I did not speak to you and to the rest of the family at the ceremonies, but you know that you and all the family have my deepest sympathy.'[1] He forwarded Haughey a resolution of sympathy that had been passed at a meeting of Ryan's Car Hire Limited on Lemass's death.

Haughey replied a few days later thanking Ryan for what he described as his 'kind and generous letter'.[2] He had known

Ryan for years through his business interests and Fianna Fáil connections. Both were members of the party's national executive and of its fundraising arm, TACA. Ryan had been a benefactor of the party offering financial support for years and fleets of cars on election day. He ran as a Fianna Fáil candidate in the 1969 general election in the Dublin North Central constituency but polled a paltry 610 votes on 1.7 per cent of the vote. Next door in Dublin North East, Haughey – Fianna Fáil's Director of Elections – topped the poll with a massive 11,677 votes, some 31.5 per cent of the electorate.

If Ryan's one and only general election outing was a campaign to forget, it was a resounding triumph for Haughey, who masterminded Fianna Fáil's first overall majority since 1957. There was no guarantee Fianna Fáil would be returned to power in 1969. Labour was excited by its raft of high-profile candidates, and its 'Seventies will be socialist slogan'. Fine Gael, although it was wracked with internal divisions, had a new young leader in Liam Cosgrave, who fancied his chances against Fianna Fáil's own first-time leader Jack Lynch. While Lynch had been taoiseach since 1966, he was untested in electoral battle as leader, and Fianna Fáil's revolutionary elite was off the stage. The party entered the election without Seán Lemass on the ticket for the first time since its foundation some forty-three years earlier in May 1926.

Lemass had topped the poll and been elected on the first count in all fourteen of the general elections he had fought as a Fianna Fáil candidate. With the old guard disappearing, Lemass's old intellectual foe, Seán MacEntee, also chose not to fight the election, it was feared by many in the party that Fianna Fáil was losing not only experience but a little part of its soul. Haughey was seen by many as part of the *nouveau riche* who, with their gauche ways, were at odds with the party's traditions and indeed its history. He was particularly suspicious to the founding elite, given that his father was a pro-treatyite, Michael Collins man. But Haughey had the advantage of being an electoral victor, and more than anything else Fianna Fáil was interested in winning elections and being in power. The 1969 overall majority copper-fastened the view of the younger generation in the party that it was in safe electoral hands with Lynch and Haughey.

What that generation did not foresee was the Arms Trial held in September of the following year. This was a very traumatic time for Lemass's daughter, Maureen, Haughey's wife, and mother to their four children. It must have been equally so for Lemass given that the liberty of his son-in-law was at stake, and the consequences of a guilty verdict for his daughter and grandchildren. Yet Lemass never said anything about the trial beyond supposedly telling Lynch to do what he had to do as taoiseach. The enmity which Maureen Haughey held towards Lynch was seen in its fullest expression on Lemass's death, when Lynch attended the family home to pay his respects but was met coldly by the Lemasses, and not at all by Maureen Haughey, who refused to speak to him when she answered the door to his knock. Close to four and a half decades later, when I interviewed her in 2014 to discuss her life and times with both her father and husband, she summed up Lynch as being a weak man. Even then she had not forgiven him for what she considered his role in an essentially unjustified and sham trial that attacked not only her husband but her wider family.[3]

Just over six months after Haughey was acquitted in the arms trial, Lemass succumbed to a short illness from a collapsed lung and died in May 1971. On his retirement he stated that his general health was quite good. But the truth was his lungs were in poor shape. His health then began to decline remorselessly once he left public life. The great fascination that persists around Lemass revolves around his extraordinary pragmatism. He was at the heart of Irish politics for four decades when big ideas dominated political discourse. The establishment and settling of a new state, the thirst to regain the fourth green field and reunify the national territory, and the quest for the country to take its place amongst the nations of the earth were big issues but also somewhat esoteric to how ordinary people lived their lives.

While these ideas obsessed Éamon de Valera, Lemass was more concerned with the mundane issue of how Irish people would prosper economically. He, of course, wanted the country to be unified, and for Ireland to be accepted as a prosperous, independent country fully able to participate in global affairs. But he was also fully aware that more than anything, Irish people needed to provide in the first instance for their families. This was the issue that mattered to ordinary citizens. The four changes of government between 1948 and 1957 showed Lemass that the Irish people were dissatisfied with their lot in a state that was barely three decades old. He had little truck with de Valera's view that there were more important things than economic development. What was the point of reunification and global participation if the state could not look after its own people, and the only foreign question those people asked was what country should they emigrate to? At a political level the evidence was clear that if a government could not make economic progress, then the electorate would look elsewhere.

Lemass was the essential Dublin jackeen with little understanding of rural Ireland, but he was aware of the importance agriculture was to the wider population and economy, and indeed the success of Fianna Fáil. His real passion, however, lay in his mission to build up native industry to provide jobs for Ireland's people. He was essentially the man who built the protectionist house in the 1930s, and then knocked it down two decades later, when it had outlived its usefulness. He replaced it by building a newer house based on free trade and membership of a European bloc, although he would not live to see the day that Ireland entered the EEC. The architect of protectionism became the apostle of free trade precisely because de Valera was so far removed from the reality of the lives of those who lived in the state he did so much to create. And de Valera, unlike Lemass, was oblivious as to why some 600,000 people left Ireland in the 1950s. His continuous calls for emigrants to return home drove Lemass to despair. By 1959 Lemass was desperate to be taoiseach. He had things to do and little enough time to achieve his goals.

For Lemass, the Irish state was nothing without its people, and that's why The Lemass tapes are of such value. Here is the real Lemass. He is the impatient, gruff, all-business character that history records. But he is also thoughtful, always questioning, always thinking, always wanting to do the right thing. He has an admirable and touching desire not to let anybody down. The nature of politics, however, is that people always feel let down. In that context it is remarkable that Lemass – perhaps uniquely amongst Irish political leaders – is not associated with failure. In his drive, work ethic, pragmatism and indeed dreams, Lemass became the embodiment of the people. These tapes ensure that we know why that was the case and why his legacy endures.

FOREWORD BY SEÁN HAUGHEY

The publication of this book based on The Lemass tapes has been a long time in the making.

Seán Lemass retired as taoiseach in 1966. Correspondence with the businessman Dermot Ryan on a project to record his memoirs commenced the following year and all 23 interviews were completed by early January 1969.

Ryan very kindly handed over the tapes and transcripts to Lemass's grandson Seán D. Lemass and, following careful consideration, the Lemass family decided to donate the material to the UCD archives for safekeeping and for further research.

Throughout his life, Seán Lemass placed great value on loyalty. Dermot Ryan was a long-time friend and supporter and there is no doubt that Lemass trusted him implicitly. This is evidenced by the honest and forthright answers he gave to the comprehensive set of questions put to him by the interviewer.

The Lemass family are extremely grateful to Dermot Ryan for undertaking this work and for taking the necessary steps to ensure that the interviews would be made readily available in the future.

In doing so, he has done a great service to all those with an interest in Irish history and in politics generally.

Seán Lemass was self-educated and widely read. His comprehensive knowledge and wisdom on a wide variety of issues are very evident from his answers. The tapes and transcripts are a treasure trove of history and give us an extraordinary insight into the political events of the time but also into the personality of the man.

Like many of his contemporaries, Lemass was reluctant to talk about his activities during the 1916 Rising, the War of Independence and the Civil War, and this period of his life was not the subject of the interviews. However, he does outline in detail his views on many of the national and international issues of the day. He explains the background to the establishment of Fianna Fáil in 1926 and his thinking behind the many initiatives to promote the economic development of the country. In addition, he gives us a behind-the-scenes look into the workings of cabinet government as well as a blunt assessment of some of his Oireachtas colleagues. It will also come as a surprise to many to read of his apprehensions about succeeding Éamon de Valera and becoming taoiseach for the first time. Finally, his reflections on his family life, including his relationship with his loving wife Kathleen and their four children, are particularly interesting and allow us to see for the first time more of Seán Lemass, the private man.

It is true that Lemass had a reputation of being somewhat impatient and a little blunt at times, but to his family he was a warm and friendly man, who was not aloof or austere, who softened in retirement, who was aware of family events and personalities, and who was affectionate to his grandchildren.

RONAN McGREEVY

Seán Lemass is widely acknowledged as Ireland's most successful taoiseach and he has left us an extraordinary legacy. These interviews are in effect his only political memoir. This book is ground-breaking, thoroughly researched, and long overdue. It ensures that important historical material will now be accessible to a much wider audience. The Lemass family are absolutely delighted that the tapes and transcripts are finally seeing the full light of day.

FOREWORD BY THE RYAN FAMILY

The Lemass Tapes Will Reshape Irish History

This was the headline of the 2018 *Irish Times* article revealing the existence of the 22 interviews that businessman Dermot Ryan had conducted with Seán Lemass almost half a century earlier.

Dermot Ryan, the man behind the tapes, was one of Ireland's most successful businessmen of his time. With wealth equivalent to a billionaire by today's standards, financial incentive was the driving force in the many ventures he pursued.

Aiming to write Irish Taoiseach Seán Lemass's political memoir, however, was a clear exception to Ryan's usual impetus. Ryan admired Lemass immensely, precisely because he was a man who thought deeply and was of strong conviction, yet driven by ambitions opposite to Ryan. Ryan wanted to explore the inner thinking of someone he felt was a great man. He was motivated by a desire to share Lemass's view of the world with an Irish audience.

As readers are brought on this journey, it is interesting to consider the relationship between these two men. Lemass, the older, wiser and values-driven politician; Ryan, the younger, vibrant and ambitious businessman. Connected by something fundamentally similar in their character.

Ryan was visionary. He had bold ideas and many of them brought him great fortune. He took up poetry, won awards and published his work. He began horse-riding at age 27, his walls soon covered in show-jumping cups and rosettes. He pursued sculpting with his home and other homes decorated in his art. Ryan constantly found ways to succeed beyond his businesses. The Irish press were curious about Ryan, and often featured him with his wife and five children.

In February 1969, an article in the *Daily Mirror* described Ryan as the 'reluctant millionaire'. Another article on the tapes in the *Irish Times* in 2018 was titled 'Lemass, a reluctant Taoiseach'.

Lemass talked to Ryan about how his freedoms ceased when he became taoiseach, and when he was to give up office, he felt he would be free of his responsibilities 'at last'. In the 1969 *Daily Mirror* article, Ryan is quoted as saying 'I often think of my first year at university. No money, no power, no status, no authority and a great deal of freedom. Today, I have much less freedom.'

Despite his determined character, Ryan never completed his project of documenting Seán Lemass's reflections on his time running the country. That 2018 headline was precisely what he had aimed for.

To leave such a legacy, with no financial strings attached – simply a gift to the Lemass family and to Ireland – is truly his greatest professional achievement.

The Ryan family is profoundly grateful to the Lemass family for handing the tapes to UCD archives and to Ronan McGreevy for fulfilling Ryan's vision.

Enough is never enough

Enough will never be enough
If the criterion is achievement.
We'll always reach one peak to sight another,
A crest that makes the place we are
seem lesser.
Rather than strive to bear the unbearable strain,
Rather than think that success will relieve
the pain.
It is better to be what we are,
And content to have gone thus far,
To accept that we'll never be great,
To live life before it is too late.

Poem by Dermot Ryan
Published by Des O'Connell Printing

INTRODUCTION

In April 2022 a *Sunday Independent*/ Ireland Thinks poll to mark the centenary of the Stateasked the Irish public who they believed to have been the best taoiseach. The clear winner was Seán Lemass, with 25.8 per cent of the vote. His nearest challenger was Fine Gael's Garret FitzGerald at 14.2 per cent.

His record as taoiseach from 1959 to 1966 was such that even political opponents wondered what kind of Ireland would have emerged had he ascended to the role earlier in his career. The Labour Party leader Brendan Corish thought Lemass should have become taoiseach ten or fifteen years prior to 1959. 'It might have been a somewhat different Ireland' – a view shared by the Fine Gael leader Liam Cosgrave when Lemass died in 1971.[1]

For all his achievements Lemass left no memoir or authorised biography in his lifetime. Neither did he donate his papers to a university, as many politicians have done. It was assumed he had no interest in giving his own version of events for posterity. This assumption is confounded by these recordings, which arose out of a series of 23 interviews between 22 April 1967 and 9 January

1969 with the businessman Dermot Ryan. They are and were intended to be Lemass's own take on his life in politics.

Ryan, who was born in Dublin to a family from County Limerick, founded the Ryan Group, which had substantial interests in hotels, caravan parks, car hire and insurance in the 1950s and 1960s. He was also a member of the Fianna Fáil national executive and TACA, the party's fundraising arm. He stood for election for Fianna Fáil in Dublin North-Central in the 1969 general election, but was unsuccessful. In a profile that year in the *Irish Times* his wealth was estimated at IR £2.5 million (€35 million today).[2] He was a long-time admirer of Lemass and made him a member of the board of Ryan Tourism Holdings after Lemass retired as taoiseach in 1966. Ryan described Lemass as a man who could have been 'a millionaire many times over if he had devoted his talents to business, but he and his contemporaries did not seem to care about money. I have never known a man with such intelligence, judgement and integrity as Lemass and who made such little money from his activities.'[3]

Correspondence between Lemass and Ryan reveals the purpose of the interviews. Ryan wrote to Lemass in January 1967, three months before the recordings started, outlining his plans. Ryan was reading biographies of major political figures including Éamon de Valera, Winston Churchill and Charles de Gaulle as possible templates and asked for background material that Lemass could recommend.[4] Lemass suggested Dorothy Macardle's *The Irish Republic*, a book published in 1937 about the Irish Revolution told from the anti-Treaty side. Another was Lord Longford's *Peace by Ordeal* about the Anglo-Irish Treaty negotiations. Lemass could recommend no books from the time of Fianna Fáil's time in government after 1932.

The pair continued to correspond long after the recordings were completed. Ryan gave Lemass sight of his work. He envisaged a biography of Lemass being partially a transcript of his questions and answers (as in this book) and partially his own commentary based on Lemass's answers. Lemass was evidently pleased with what he saw, contributing photographs from his own archive.

Their last correspondence dates from 9 November 1970, when Lemass told Ryan: 'It seems to be turning out much better than I had expected so far. Needless to remark I will be very willing to cooperate with you in any further work you may decide to go into.' Three months later Lemass was rushed to the Mater Hospital with a collapsed lung. A lifetime of heavy smoking – his pipe was his constant companion – had caught up with him and he died on 11 May 1971 at the age of 71.

It is clear these interviews were intended to be Lemass's account of his political life from his own perspective. He was given sight of the material and his handwritten annotations were included. It was, in effect, his political memoir, as Ryan explained to Lemass's grandson Seán Haughey in 2009.

> Seán Lemass felt that he would like to leave an account of his endeavours for posterity. He was emphatic that it would be his story from his point of view. It was agreed that I would be free to publish the resultant work at my discretion in such form as I might decide, but, in particular, as a book with the aim – … in the long-term perspective of history – that a version of the events of his life which was accurate and had the clear stamp of his personal perceptions and interpretations would be available.

The tapes consisted of 22 hours of interviews and 1,200 pages of typed transcripts, amounting to 273,000 words. Had the book Ryan envisaged appeared, as it was supposed to, in the early 1970s, much of its content would have been toned down or even omitted because of the risk of libel proceedings. Lemass had little time for politicians who sued for libel, and never did so himself, but not every politician was possessed of his thick skin.

> Any politician taking a libel action against a newspaper is always very foolish. Juries feel that the politician shouldn't be soft-skinned and they are always against the politician who says he is libelled and wants to collect damages.[5]

Ryan invested time as well as money in his project. Recording equipment in the late 1960s was difficult to come by and expensive. Reel-to-reel tapes were unreliable. He employed assistants to help him with his research, booked a studio for his recordings and had a stenographer on site. He envisaged an ambitious programme to recoup his investment including serialisation rights and a feature film.

The book, he believed, would showcase Ireland's 'greatest leader' and would be bought by 'every Fianna Fáil household at least'. Lemass had given him 'carte blanche which surprised me at the time' to do as he saw fit with the tapes.

> He agreed to give me answers to the advance questions and such supplementary questions as I would ask with permission to quote him, particularly in a book I would produce. The narrative would be created in a series of interviews. His importance made me aim much higher. I considered Lemass

> to be Ireland's most important historical figure and I had adequate funds to publish independently.

Ryan's plans were derailed by the outbreak of the Troubles in the North. His role as the executive chairman of the Northern Ireland Inter-Denominational Distress Organisation (NIDO), which was set up in the late 1960s to help the nationalist community who had been burned out of their homes, consumed much of his time.

Then his tourism business collapsed as a result of the oil crisis in 1973, which made travel to Ireland prohibitively expensive. Ryan moved to London and spent the rest of his life there. 'Work needed all my time and the easy availability of funds was gone. It seemed better to defer publication in the belief that the situation would change. I would do it properly at a later time,' he told Seán Haughey. There never was a later time for Ryan.

The Ryan family handed the tapes and the transcripts over to the Lemass family, and in turn the Lemass family donated the tapes and transcripts to the University College Dublin (UCD) archives, which already has the papers of several taoisigh on site. Lemass's great-grandson Aidan O'Connor approached me about covering the tapes for the *Irish Times*. My newspaper published a supplement entitled 'The Lemass Tapes' on 2 May 2018.[6] In the introduction to the supplement, Professor John Horgan, whose 1996 biography *Seán Lemass: Enigmatic Patriot* is the most authoritative to date on the man, identified the tapes as a unique political memoir.

> There are a number of reasons why these transcripts – and Lemass's hand-written annotations on them – are of extraordinary value. For one thing, political memoirs

> highlight achievements and obscure defeats. By contrast, Lemass's frankness is noteworthy. He all but dons sackcloth and ashes at his inability to get unions and managements to agree on national budgetary policy, for example. Meanwhile, his insights on contemporary European leaders are sharp and perceptive, and quite novel in Irish historiography, while his concerns about the problems of party management and leadership are as relevant today as when they were recorded. His judgment on some of his contemporaries (including cabinet colleagues) ranges from the benign to the acerbic with a frankness that few politicians have had the courage to apply, before or since. And – most palpable of all, perhaps – there is his growing sense of frustration, fuelled by a combination of loyalty and impatience, at the length and increasing immobilism of de Valera's last two periods in office. All in all, this is a more complete – and a compelling – portrait of a man in high office, of his difficulties, his achievements, and his mindset, as we are ever likely to get, one of universal relevance to students of politics.[7]

Ryan died in London in 2023 at the age of 95 having lived long enough to see the publication of his tapes, albeit in truncated form, in the *Irish Times*. Ryan was a diligent and knowledgeable interviewer. In the pre-internet era, it was a considerable feat of scholarship to assemble questions covering such a huge range of subjects.

Lemass is one of the few figures in Irish political history who is universally admired. Lemass's successor as taoiseach, Jack Lynch, thought 'the manifold results of his endeavours for the nation will constitute an enduring monument to his name'.[8] Other Fianna

Fáil taoisigh have praised his transformational impact on the country's fortunes. His son-in-law Charles Haughey saw him as a confident man who transmitted that confidence to the country. Bertie Ahern thought of him as 'like me, a practical socialist. He knew you had to generate money before you could distribute it'. For Micheál Martin his decision to commit Ireland to a European future was the 'foundation upon which we have achieved dramatic and sustained progress in employment, in standards of living, in education levels and in our ability to be heard in the international community'.[9]

Lemass's reputation transcends party loyalties. Fine Gael taoisigh Garret FitzGerald, John Bruton and Leo Varadkar have all expressed their admiration for him. Varadkar believed Lemass's optimistic vision for Ireland has been vindicated.

> He brought an optimism to politics and that helped lift our country out of long-term decline and open it to the world. He was a moderniser whose idealism encouraged him to find pragmatic solutions to long-standing problems. Critical of what he felt was an Irish 'disposition to be sorry for ourselves', he told the Dáil that 'once you start feeling sorry for yourself, you are finished'.[10]

In the public mind Lemass's impact on Ireland can be summarised in the title of a 2009 RTÉ Television documentary, *Lemass: The Man Who Made Modern Ireland*.[11] Before him there was poverty, emigration and closed-mindedness; after him there was prosperity, population growth and open-mindedness, or so the conventional wisdom goes. Lemass does not deserve all the credit for this undoubted transformation of Ireland in the late 1950s and 1960s; neither can he be absolved of the underachievement that preceded it, having been a minister for more than 20 years.

He could not have affected the changes that were made without the support of like-minded individuals, notably the Minister for Finance James Ryan and the senior civil servant Thomas Kenneth (T.K.) Whitaker. Many others too had come to the same conclusion that Ireland in the 1950s was a state without a viable future in the absence of drastic change.

Though he did not become taoiseach until 1959, Lemass was effectively in charge of economic policy from 1957, when Fianna Fáil returned to office, and he was the prime driver behind Whitaker's First Programme for Economic Expansion in 1958, which reversed the fortunes of a struggling Irish state. Whitaker and Lemass, two men impatient for change, were bonded by a mutual regard. 'I greatly admired his good sense and his decisiveness,' Whitaker said of Lemass. 'His intelligence was a shield against error, making his life an active learning process.' Whitaker was chosen as Ireland's Person of the Century in an RTÉ poll in 2001.

Lemass brought political will to the first programme, which abandoned the principles of protectionism, opened up the country to foreign capital and eased the profound existential despair wrought by decades of economic underachievement. He began the process of preparing Ireland for entry into the European Economic Community (EEC). Through no fault of his own, Ireland was unable to achieve that goal in his time as taoiseach because of Charles de Gaulle's opposition to Britain's entry, which he first vetoed in 1963. Lemass was uncannily prescient about Britain's attitude to Europe at the time.

> I do not think they had any other idea initially in relation to the Common Market, except to destroy it. Even when they recognised they were not going to succeed in breaking it up, their application for membership was probably inspired by the idea that they could slow down its development in some way and perhaps change its character.[12]

Lemass saw the importance of government investment in education, health and infrastructure, and if the Irish public wanted better public services they had to pay for them. The introduction of a very modest turnover tax (an early forerunner of VAT) of 2.5 per cent in 1963 almost brought down his government, but Lemass was not for turning. Lemass believed a rising tide would lift all boats, as he frequently said. He correctly forecast that a more prosperous economy could see tax revenue rise without making the public feel poorer as a result.

> I am saying that if the total national income is a thousand million pounds, which it will be, the government takes twenty-five per cent of that. It is the total cost of all the services provided by the government including the paying of interest and debt and all this. In other countries it would be thirty, thirty-five and forty per cent of whatever the total income is and it will be here in that way also at some stage, because, as our national income rises, as the income per head rises, not merely will the government expenditure grow in line but it will grow faster than the national income and this in itself is a good thing.[13]

In 1951 Lemass gave an interview to the *Irish Times* in which he observed that 'our people have an inferiority complex still; that is historically understandable'.[14]

He transmitted his own self-confidence to the country when he assumed office. The population, which in 1961 hit an all-time low of 2.82 million people, began to grow again and emigration reached more manageable levels. The changes set in train by Lemass continue to this day. At the time of writing the population of the state is set to reach 5.6 million by the end of the decade, double what it was in 1961.

Many independent commentators have noted Lemass's role as a transformational taoiseach in the 1960s. In his seminal work *Ireland: 1912–1985: Politics and Society*, Professor Joe Lee concluded it was not Lemass's 'manner of gaining power, nor his manner of holding it, that distinguished him uniquely among Irish prime ministers. It was his manner of using it.'[15]

Lee documented the manner in which optimism returned to Ireland on Lemass's watch. Living standards rose by 50 per cent, emigration dropped from 14.8 per 1,000 in 1951 to 3.7 per 1,000 in 1971, the number of families rose by 48,000 between 1961 and 1971, the number of marriages went from 14,700 per annum in 1957 to 22,000 by 1971. All these indices reversed a century of demographic decline.

Brian Girvin noted in his 1989 book *Between the Worlds* that Lemass's governments 'initiated the most comprehensive attempt at modernisation which has occurred in Ireland. Ireland acquired "modernity" in this decade, becoming increasingly industrialised, secularised, urbanised and bureaucratised.'[16]

Writing in 1969, the journalist Vincent Browne thought that when Lemass had been in office for just seven years, 'the country had recovered its self-confidence and economic health and other objectives looked plausible rather than the makings of a bad joke'. Presciently, he suggested that in the fullness of time 'history may judge him our greatest patriot'.[17]

Lemass's biographer Tom Garvin believed his legacy was 'profoundly cultural: the collective imagined project of a successful and modern Irish nation-state'.[18]

The German Nobel Prize-winning author Heinrich Böll wrote his *Irisches Tagebuch* (*Irish Journal*) travelogue in 1957. He was charmed by Ireland's intimacy and economic backwardness, which he thought of as the antithesis of post-war industrialised Germany. The book was a huge seller in Germany. By the time the English language translation came out ten years later, Böll did not recognise the country he thought he knew. It had 'caught up with two centuries', he suggested, 'and leaped over another five'.[19]

This book, which has now been published six decades later, amounts to the frankest memoir from any significant Irish political figure. Lemass was famously blunt. When asked a straight question, he gave a straight answer. He suggested minor edits to many of his answers but left the substance intact. His oral answers are far more revealing than had he committed his observations to paper, where he could later reflect and edit what he said.

His unfiltered assessment of many of his contemporaries, not least de Valera, but others such as his successor as taoiseach Jack Lynch, former cabinet colleagues Seán MacEntee and Paddy Smith and the former Minister for Health Dr Noël Browne, could have done reputational damage to these men, who were still alive when Lemass recorded the tapes. He damned Lynch with faint praise, stating that he was somebody who could provoke 'feelings of trust rather than admiration'.

Lemass has been the subject of at least six biographies, but the first, by Brian Farrell, was not published until 1983, so Ryan had no preceding book to call on as a reference guide. Ryan acknowledged in the first sentence of the first interview that Lemass insisted that we 'shouldn't go into depth in the period earlier than 1925'. Ryan stuck diligently to that request and Lemass does not address his role in the Easter Rising, the War of Independence or the Civil War except tangentially.

A less compliant interviewer might have pushed Lemass more on his involvement in the Irish Revolution, but there is no guarantee that Ryan would have coaxed anything revelatory out of his subject from that period. Lemass was never one to overplay or valorise his role.

In 1969 he sat down for a series of interviews with Michael Mills, the political editor of the *Irish Press*. Lemass told Mills that during the War of Independence he had been involved in 'quite a number of active engagements. I don't like talking about it because individuals were killed.'[20] And, as for the Civil War, 'terrible things were done by both sides. I'd prefer not to talk about it.'[21]

Seán Lemass is among the most scrutinised of Irish lives. The first full-length analysis of his political life was Paul Bew and Henry Patterson's *Seán Lemass and the making of Modern Ireland 1945–66*, published in 1982. This was followed a year later by Farrell's short biography, entitled *Seán Lemass* and published by Gill & Macmillan. *Seán Lemass: A Biography* by Michael O'Sullivan, published in 1994, was followed two years later by Horgan's biography. Robert Savage's *Seán Lemass* (Life & Times series) published in 1999 was more an analysis of

Lemass's policy choices than a straightforward biography. *The Lemass Era: Politics and Society in the Ireland of Seán Lemass* by Brian Girvin and Gary Murphy was published in 2005 and followed in 2009 by *Judging Lemass*, a fully illustrated appraisal of his life by Tom Garvin, published by the Royal Irish Academy (RIA). This was followed two years later by Dr Bryce Evans's iconoclastic *Democratic Dictator*, which concluded that Lemass's contribution to Ireland had been overpraised.

Yet none of the authors of these books, with the exception of Farrell, whose book contained a short excerpt from one of Ryan's interviews, had access to these tapes. Neither did they have complete access to the digitised material from the military archives which have transformed our understanding of the revolutionary period. The new information addresses many of the questions which Lemass left unanswered in his lifetime. They are set out here in the opening chapter.

Lemass's determination to foster better relations between North and South began with his visit to meet the Northern premier Terence O'Neill in January 1965. Successive taoisigh had indulged in rhetoric about the evils of partition, but this was the first meeting between the two premiers since 1925. It raised premature hopes of better times for the North. By the twentieth interview, which occurred just after the civil rights march in Derry on 5 October 1968, Lemass was already confronting the realisation that his efforts had amounted to nothing as the North slid into a vicious conflict that lasted 25 years.

Lemass confounded the oft-quoted political adage that all political lives end in failure. He was able to go at a time of his choosing, November 1966. His adult life from the age of 24 had been consumed by politics. He had, he believed, on balance done a good job in the circumstances. He cared little for the verdict of future historians who would judge his shortcomings as his generation had judged the shortcomings of previous generations.

Few politicians with such long careers could have left office with so few regrets. The passing years have not diminished Lemass's reputation. If anything, it has been enhanced. At the time of writing, a bill to change the name of Dublin airport to Seán Lemass Dublin International Airport was progressing through the House of the Oireachtas. His can-do spirit is often invoked in relation to Ireland's contemporary problems, most notably that of housing, but they are problems of the prosperity that Lemass did so much to create and not the problems of poverty.

Editor's note

This book is based on the hard-copy transcripts of the interviews between Dermot Ryan and Seán Lemass, which have been transcribed digitally partially by UCD and by myself. Ryan sought to schedule each interview to follow a chronology in time. The first interview covers Lemass's early years in politics and subsequent interviews follow a roughly chronological order, each picking up from the previous one.

The pair would often digress into some other issues and there was much repetition. Ryan intended to edit the tapes himself and provide a commentary, much as I have done here. He was unable to complete the task. Editing the tapes would have been a considerable challenge in the pre-internet era, such is the range of subjects covered.

Lemass had an impressive memory, but he would mention

individuals just by their title or their surnames. Take this passage about the Department of Industry and Commerce when he took over in 1932.

> You see Ferguson doesn't talk to the man who was director of statistics at the time, Lyon,[22] and he doesn't talk to Riordan[23] who was the director of industry, and Riordan and Lyon did not talk to one another so they would not come into the same room together.

It is possible now to determine who all these men were. When Lemass spoke of political events, he assumed Ryan knew what he was talking about and did not feel the need to elaborate for a wider audience.

> The only time in my life that I ever got an enormous vote, the highest ever accorded to any candidate in a general election was when I was having a full-scale row with the Bishop of Galway and this was dominating the political scene.

Which bishop? What row? What election? Lemass does not say, but it is possible now to determine that he was speaking about his row with the Bishop of Galway, Dr Michael Browne, in 1945.

In editing these tapes, I have endeavoured as far as possible only to provide context to the material and footnotes to explain the cast of characters that Lemass mentions using mostly the online *Dictionary of Irish Biography* where possible.

As a member of Fianna Fáil and a businessman, Ryan was principally concerned with issues of economics and politics and less with social issues. Lemass's government was responsible for much reforming legislation on social issues, which I have included for context. Nevertheless, Lemass and Ryan were men of their time and their use of gendered language (a politician is always a 'he') reflected their world view. The role of women in the Ireland of Lemass's time was not discussed in these interviews.

I have used the phrase 'the Irish Free State' to describe the state between 1922 and 1937. I have used the term 'Ireland' as a reference to the state on the international stage.

Ronan McGreevy, January 2026

PART I

THE LONG APPRENTICESHIP

SEÁN LEMASS:
THE EARLY YEARS
(1899–1923)

The origins of the Lemass name are uncertain. Biographers of Seán Lemass have concluded that it is an anglicised corruption of the French Le Maistre, a common name among the Huguenot refugees who fled to Ireland in the late seventeenth century. Tolerance of the Protestant faith in France turned to persecution in 1685 after King Louis XIV revoked the Edict of Nantes which had guaranteed freedom of religion to those of the Protestant faith.

Rather than renounce their faith, hundreds of thousands of Protestants fled abroad to countries where the Protestant religion was tolerated – Ireland among them. The Huguenots were industrious and practical minded. They had an influence on Ireland much greater than their numbers. Along with the Lemasses, the La Touche family, founders of the Bank of Ireland, the well-known architect James Gandon and the writer Samuel Beckett are descended from Irish Huguenots.[1] Lemass often remarked that he never met another Irish person with his surname outside his own family. This is a characteristic he shared with Éamon de Valera, the other totem of Irish nationalism with a foreign name.

Many contemporaries attributed Lemass's personality and even his leonine appearance to his Huguenot Protestant background. 'Sean Lemass, a reticent, pragmatic planner called "The Quiet Man" is by temperament and ancestry more Gallic than Gaelic and represents a wholly new species of leadership for Ireland,' a flattering portrayal from *Time* magazine in May 1963 observed.[2]

John Francis Lemass was born on 15 July 1899 in Ballybrack, County Dublin in a summer cottage his family rented. Lemass's father, John Timothy (John T.), ran a successful hatter and outfitter shop at No. 2 Capel Street. Seán's mother, Frances Phelan, was the daughter of a Kilkenny horticulturist, and she managed a florist's shop in Wicklow Street. Seán was the second oldest of seven children. His brother Noel was two years older than him. Seán was known as Jack to distinguish himself from all the other Johns in the family. He gaelicised his name to Seán after 1916.[3]

As Christopher 'Todd' Andrews, a near-contemporary and friend of Lemass (born 1901), remembered, Ireland at the turn of the nineteenth century was a country that had lost its 'consciousness as a separate identity'.[4] The death of Charles Stewart Parnell in 1891 and the poisonous split that followed fractured the unity of Irish nationalism. Andrews thought his native Dublin was a 'British city and accepted itself as one' and it was a society divided on distinctly British class lines.[5]

Four months after Lemass was born, the Second Boer War began. The conflict between the British and the breakaway Boer republics of the Transvaal and the Orange Free State galvanised Irish nationalist opinion on the side of the Boers. At the same time thousands of Irishmen served in British uniforms, many of them cheered and showered with flowers along the quays of Dublin as they embarked for South Africa. The convulsions around the war would presage the even greater schisms in Irish society that occurred during the First World War that would eventually lead to an independent Irish state.

Lemass's grandfather, John Lemass Sr, was a Parnellite member of Dublin Corporation who refused a loyal address to the Prince of Wales on his visit to Dublin in 1885.[5] Lemass's father, in turn, was active in the Irish Parliamentary Party. Lemass recalled a meeting at the back of his father's shop in Capel Street in which prominent local members of the party rejected a candidate foisted on them by party headquarters. It was an early lesson in the machinations of party politics.

> They all went out of the shop in a group, like aristocrats walking to the guillotine, with their faces set and their fists clenched, pale and drawn-looking, determined to do this thing which was a mortal sin for anybody involved in politics in those days. But they did it; they voted against the party. That was in 1906 or 1907 and it is the earliest political experience I can remember.[7]

During Lemass's childhood, nationalist Ireland was fixated on the tantalising promise of Home Rule. The cause of Irish independence, the complete separation from the United Kingdom, was a minority pursuit. The December 1910 general election saw the Irish Party holding the balance of power in Westminster and the party seized the moment to pursue Home Rule.

The introduction of the Home Rule Bill into the House of Commons in April 1912 marked the beginning of a period of tumult without parallel in modern Irish history. Lemass's life too took an irrevocable turn. The formation of the Ulster Volunteer Force (UVF) in 1912 to oppose Home Rule was followed a year later in 1913 by the Irish Volunteers, set up as an armed nationalist counterpoint to the UVF. There were now two armed militias in Ireland with contrasting visions of the country's future. The prospect of a sectarian civil war was a real possibility until the outbreak of the First World War in August 1914.

Lemass attended the Sisters of the Holy Faith at Haddington Road national school and from 1908 the Christian Brothers at the O'Connell School off the North Circular Road. The Brothers had a reputation for inculcating their pupils with Irish nationalist fervour, in contrast to many more expensive Catholic secondary schools that had made their peace with the British Empire and prided themselves on producing imperial functionaries.[8] Lemass was a bright pupil who particularly excelled at mathematics and was ranked as one of the top ten students in the country in the subject when he sat the Intermediate Certificate. His intelligence was obvious, and his father sent him to Rosse College in St Stephen's Green, a crammer school, with a view to him becoming a lawyer, but events intervened.[9]

Lemass was a year underage when he joined the Irish Volunteers in 1915. His recruiter was Pat Mullen, who worked in Lemass's father's shop. Lemass, along with his brother Noel, became a member of A Company of the 3rd Battalion of the Volunteers.[10] The battalion commandant was de Valera. They would forge the most significant political partnership in the history of the Irish State, between them holding the office of taoiseach for almost 30 years. 'My impression of him was of a long, thin fellow with knee breeches and a tweed hat. But he had, of course, enormous personal magnetism,' Lemass recalled of his first meeting with de Valera.[11]

Lemass's early introduction to firearms would have the most tragic consequences. On 28 January 1916, he accidentally shot and killed his 21-month-old brother Herbert with a revolver at the family home in Capel Street. Quite what Lemass was doing with a loaded revolver in his home is not clear. Herbert was being minded by his older sister Clare while Seán was sitting in an armchair playing around with the weapon. Clara had her back to Herbert and recalled hearing a loud bang. She turned around to see her baby brother dead at her feet. Herbert Lemass had died from gunshot wounds to the head. The inquest jury suggested that 'something should be done to prevent young boys getting possession of firearms'.[12]

Reports of the tragedy were published in the *Irish Independent*, the *Sunday Independent* and the *Irish Times*. Many of his contemporaries in the Irish Volunteers must have known about what had happened. Lemass's company commanding officer before the Easter Rising, Joseph O'Connor, told the Bureau of Military History in 1951 that Lemass, 'owing to an accident in the family had ceased parading for some time' and was not mobilised during the Easter Rising. He went no further than that in explaining the nature of the accident.[13]

The first historian to address the Lemass family tragedy was Trinity College Dublin Professor of Contemporary Irish History Eunan O'Halpin, who wrote about it in the pages of the *Irish Times* in 2013. The realisation that Lemass had killed his own brother was news to his immediate family.[14] His eldest daughter, Maureen, knew nothing about it until O'Halpin published his account. So thoroughly had Herbert Lemass been erased from the family annals that his name was absent from the family headstone in Glasnevin Cemetery until 2016.[15]

The realisation that he had killed his own infant brother, albeit accidentally, must have had a traumatic impact on Seán. His biographer Bryce Evans has speculated that Lemass's ceaseless endeavour in the service of the country may have been partially driven by this particular tragedy:[16]

> It arguably imbued Lemass with a restless desire to atone – not in an overtly Catholic sense but in service to the nation. In the revolutionary period, this meant taking up arms in pursuit of the republican ideal. In the post-revolutionary period, this would take the form of a workaholic commitment to national regeneration.

Seven years later, Noel Lemass's mutilated body was found in the Dublin Mountains. He had been murdered by Free State forces. Did these two tragedies contribute to Lemass's famed reticence about the past and his capacity to forgive and forget, O'Halpin asked.

> One distinctive aspect of Lemass's political persona was his disinclination to [harp] on about the past ... Lemass was notable for his refusal to attack opponents in terms of their 'national records' or alleged Civil War misdeeds.[17]

In 1916 another Herbert Lemass died. Lemass's first cousin Lieutenant Herbert Lemass was killed at the Battle of the Somme on 23 October while serving with the Royal Dublin Fusiliers. Herbert's brother Edwin Lemass also served in the war with the Royal Army Service Corps and went on to join the British Colonial Service as an administrator in Egypt. Their father, Peter Lemass, was the secretary of the Board of Education in Ireland, a 'Castle Catholic' as those who worked for the British administration were contemptuously called in nationalist Ireland.[18]

Fifty years later, in marking the centenary of the Easter Rising, Lemass may have had his own relatives in mind when he spoke of those Irishmen who had served in British uniforms during the First World War.

> In later years it was common – and I was also guilty in this respect – to question the motives of those who joined the new British armies at the outbreak of the war, but it must be said in their honour and in fairness to their memory that they were motivated by the highest purpose.[19]

The tragedy of having killed his infant brother did not thwart Lemass's revolutionary ardour and he and Noel returned to drilling and training. Neither knew about the Easter Rising until after it started. On Easter Monday morning 1916, they encountered Eoin MacNeill cycling out to Rathfarnham from the city centre in an agitated state. MacNeill, the putative head of the Irish Volunteers, had issued a countermanding order to the Rising, fearing there was no chance of military success after Sir Roger Casement was apprehended at Banna Strand on Good Friday and the *Aud*, which carried 20,000 German rifles and ammunition, was intercepted by the Royal Navy and scuppered by its crew.

He failed to deter the Lemass brothers from what he believed, not unreasonably, was a doomed enterprise. 'For myself I was so excited, so full of enthusiasm of the whole idea, that the thought of the consequences never entered my head at all,' Lemass remembered.[20]

Having been turned away from both Jacob's Factory and the

Four Courts, the brothers were admitted into the GPO by a friendly sentry. Lemass was sent to the roof of the building with a shotgun and a basketful of home-made bombs in anticipation that British troops would try to storm the building. 'I fired a few shots from the GPO, but, whether they hit anybody, I don't know,' he told Michael Mills in 1969.

The GPO garrison fled the burning building and made a last stand in Moore Street. Lemass and other hapless volunteers were told to fix bayonets and wait to charge the British troops. It would have been a death sentence, Lemass realised, but the order never came. Worn out with the excitement of it all, Lemass fell asleep on the ground in an alleyway off Moore Street. He woke up to be told by Seán Mac Diarmada that the rebels had surrendered. He was marched, along with his defeated colleagues, to Richmond Barracks and spent a month in a crowded prison cell, but was released home on account of his youth.

At the 50th anniversary of the Rising in 1966, when he was taoiseach, he was called upon by many people to give his own account of his involvement. Lemass, somewhat reluctantly, wrote an account for the spring 1966 edition of the Jesuit magazine *Studies*.[21] The account is strictly a factual one, shorn of any sense of melodrama. Lemass carried the wounded James Connolly on a stretcher, but, typically for him, he adds that many other people did too. He told Dermot Ryan:

> I was very reluctant to write that article. It was the editor of *Studies* who pressed me to do it. I tried to keep it as factual as possible and it was really an account of my personal experience, and I intended that it should have no significance of any sort other than that.

Lemass's desire to underplay his role in the Rising extended to eschewing any mention of the leg wound he received in the fighting. According to one volunteer, Lemass was so badly injured that he had to be carried to the toilet in Richmond Barracks.

Lemass had just turned 17 years of age. He and Noel returned to their father fearful of the reception they would get. Their fears were unfounded. John T. walked into their bedroom the following morning with a green, white and orange celluloid button in his lapel, 'which was his way of telling me he had come over to our side'. Lemass's father recognised the change in attitudes to Irish independence that occurred after the execution of the leaders of the Easter Rising. Nevertheless, he encouraged his son to go back to school to matriculate and study to be a barrister. Lemass, with the heedlessness of youth, ignored his father's wishes. 'I mean, you couldn't expect a young fellow who had been through the Rising, actively engaged in that type of operation, to sit down seriously to study. I didn't do it, so I gave up that idea.'[22]

Lemass's lack of formal schooling never hindered his political career; neither did he appear to suffer from a lack of self-confidence as a result of it. He compensated by being a dedicated reader and autodidact from a young age, amazing his contemporaries by reading economic journals while incarcerated in Ballykinlar camp during the War of Independence. His friend Ernie O'Malley remembered Lemass's breadth of reading while the two were incarcerated together during the Civil War.

> He read aloud Carlyle's explosive sentences; quoted Kropotkin; sketched with enthusiasm the plots of Upton Sinclair's novels; and recited Kipling's spattered word rhymes; the latter possibly because he thought they would annoy me.

In the years between 1916 and the outbreak of the War of Independence, Lemass took on a training role with the Volunteers. His youth was no bar to him giving military training to men much older than himself. The British attempt to introduce conscription to Ireland in March 1918 gave a timely fillip to the Irish Volunteers and thousands rushed to join the ranks. Keeping them trained and enthusiastic took up much of Lemass's time.

Lemass's involvement in the War of Independence has provoked a mountain of speculation, especially as he himself was so reticent about it. He was in charge of C Company of the Dublin Brigade on Sunday 21 November 1920 when the IRA assassinated 14 suspected British agents.

Did Lemass kill a man on Bloody Sunday? In 2014 his application for a military service pension, which he made in 1942, was released as part of the process of the digitisation and release of the state's massive military pensions archive.[23] It is a measure of the straitened circumstances Lemass found himself in, even as a government minister in 1942, that he felt the need to apply for a military pension to top up his meagre ministerial salary. Men and women who participated in the Irish Revolution had to account for their actions in order to qualify for a pension. Even in the privacy of the pensions board, the Irish revolutionary equivalent of the confession box, Lemass could not bring himself to elaborate about his activities on that day.

Could you amplify Bloody Sunday?

I was in the command of the Company who were operating.

Lemass said no more than that and the board members never thought to question him further. Yet, in his written application, Lemass elaborates on what he told the board. He scribbled the words 'Baggot Street' and 'Baggallay'. The Baggallay in question is Captain Geoffrey Baggallay (29) from Wimbledon, south London, who was a pre-war veteran of the British Army attached to the Machine Gun Corps. He was wounded twice during the war before losing his leg at the Battle of Cambrai in November 1917. He trained as a barrister specialising in court martial law and was employed as a courts-martial officer under the Restoration of Order in Ireland Regulations (1920). These military courts were sentencing IRA men to death during the War of Independence. Furthermore, Michael Collins had been told that Baggallay had tipped off the Royal Irish Constabulary (RIC) about the presence in a Dublin hotel of a solicitor and Sinn Féin councillor John Lynch who had been raising funds through the National Loan which was funding the Dáil and its activities. Lynch was shot dead on 22 September, 1920 in the Royal Exchequer Hotel in Dublin.[24] Baggallay was regarded as a legitimate target for execution.

On Bloody Sunday morning, at around 10 a.m., a three-man team consisting of Lemass, Matt McDonnell and James 'Jimmy' Brennan brought a hammer to break down the door of 119 Baggot Street, but they did not need it. A maid let them in. They rushed upstairs and found their target in his pyjamas. Baggallay assumed they had come for his weapon, which he reached for. According to McDonnell, 'Lemass and Jimmy and I fired 2 in the head from the 3 guns. I heard a maid screaming afterwards but I was told she was alright.'[25]

In their own applications for military pensions both

McDonnell[26] and Brennan[27] confirm they shot Baggallay, and their files contain letters from Lemass vouching for their service.[28] In Brennan's file there is a letter from the ex-commandant of the Dublin Brigade's second battalion, Thomas Burke, in which he states that Brennan was 'on the Bloody Sunday job with Mr Seán Lemass in charge'.

In a letter in Lemass's file, his commanding officer in the Dublin Brigade, Frank Henderson, was more forthcoming. 'Among his activities were the raiding parties of British officers for arms and numerous similar "jobs". He was engaged on "Bloody Sunday" in the execution of an enemy intelligence officer at Lower Leeson Street.'

Lemass never admitted to the shooting, though he is unlikely to have had much sympathy for his victim. There was nothing heroic about shooting an unarmed man in his bed, even if the exigencies of the war demanded it. He may have felt guilt too as another IRA volunteer, Thomas Whelan (22), was apprehended and hanged for the murder of Baggallay though he credibly claimed to have been at mass at the time of the shooting.[29]

Lemass was picked up a month after Bloody Sunday. A letter in the family files from Dublin Castle to Lemass's father confirmed his son had been arrested and was 'on (Michael) Collins' list and is graded as a lieutenant IRA'. Lemass was incarcerated in Ballykinlar internment camp, where he became noted for his impiety in refusing to recite the Rosary each evening. He was released along with all the other detainees after the signing of the Anglo-Irish Treaty on 6 December 1921. Lemass got drunk on the special train carrying the released prisoners back to Dublin.[30]

De Valera, for reasons that remain unclear to this day, did not participate in the Anglo-Treaty talks that set up the Free State and was shocked when the Irish delegation signed the Treaty without him. After a fractious debate, the Dáil passed the Treaty by 64 votes to 57. De Valera took his followers out of the Dáil.

Now Lemass was in a dilemma – should he side with the members of Dáil Éireann or with his IRA comrades who had wrought from the British a measure of independence unthinkable a decade previously? Lemass was not doctrinaire at the beginning about the Treaty. 'Everybody was debating and arguing, many of them trying to convince themselves that this could be acceptable and would work as a solution to the problems between ourselves and Britain.'[31]

Joe Lawless, who went on to become a colonel in the Irish Army, recalled a conversation he had with Lemass early in 1922 after the Treaty was signed. Lawless suggested to him that Michael Collins was right in viewing the Treaty as the 'freedom to achieve freedom'. If he and Lemass were to quit over some 'abstract argument against the Treaty'[32] they would simply be replaced in the new Irish Army by 'ex-British officers and opportunists of all kinds'. Lemass, according to Lawless, agreed with him, yet within weeks he had taken the anti-Treaty side.[33]

Lemass acknowledged that the Irish treaty negotiators were never going to get everything they wanted, but what they got was inadequate. Lemass was particularly agitated about the Oath of Allegiance to the British monarch, which every member of the Dáil was supposed to take. Like all republicans he believed there could be no Irish republic nor the prospect of one as long as the oath remained in place.

In early 1922 Lemass took up a role as a training officer in the grounds for the Royal Dublin Society (RDS) for the nascent Irish police force that was to replace the Royal Irish Constabulary

(RIC). He resigned when he realised his first pay cheque came from the Provisional Government.[34]

He later reported to anti-Treaty IRA leader Rory O'Connor, who was then occupying some buildings in Gardiner Row that were used as an anti-Treaty HQ. In March 1922 a new anti-Treaty IRA was created. O'Connor hosted an infamous press conference in which he was challenged as to how they would respond in the event of the public supporting the Treaty.

> 'That is a matter of policy for the executive of the army to consider.'
>
> 'Do we take it we are going to have a military dictatorship then?'
>
> 'You can take it that way if you like.'[35]

Yet, according to Lemass, O'Connor declined to attack the pro-Treaty forces. 'Rory said if the Civil War was going to start, we were not going to start it.'[36] Both Lemass and de Valera would find out the hard way that the attempted usurpation of the people's will as expressed through the Dáil by self-appointed military cabals could not be tolerated in a democratic society. It is a lesson neither forgot when they were in power.

During the Easter recess of 1922 O'Connor took his followers, including Lemass, into the Four Courts, which they occupied in defiance of the Provisional Government. An unreal stand-off ensued. The Provisional Government (memorably described by one of its own, Kevin O'Higgins, as 'eight young men in the City Hall standing amidst the ruins of one administration, with the foundations of another not yet laid, and the wild men screaming through the keyhole') felt it lacked the authority to evict the rebel garrison.[37]

Lemass was selected as adjutant to Commandant Paddy O'Brien, the officer in charge of the Four Courts garrison. Lemass gave passes in and out of the Four Courts and the rebels came and went as they pleased. Ever the planner, Lemass sought to reconnoitre the sewers as a potential means of escape and fell in. 'He smelled to heaven,' Ernie O'Malley recalled.[38] Lemass was present when O'Brien said he would rather blow up the Four Courts then surrender it to the 'Staters', as he called them, and they set about putting barrels of paraffin and petrol in the headquarters block of the courts complex.

On 16 June 1922 the first general election held in the new Irish State delivered a profound electoral rebuke to the anti-Treaty side. De Valera's anti-Treaty Sinn Féin got just 21.9 per cent of the vote. The Irish public, having endured eight years of conflict, going back to the outbreak of the First World War, were tired and wanted to get on with their lives. The abstruse and vitriolic debates over the merits of the Treaty were irrelevant to their struggles.

Any attempt at post-election reconciliation between pro- and anti-Sinn Féin was brutally pre-empted by the assassination six days later of Field Marshal Sir Henry Wilson, the former head of the British Army turned Unionist MP. The assassination by two London-born British Army veterans of the First World War turned IRA gunmen, Reggie Dunne and Joseph O'Sullivan, was erroneously but conveniently blamed on the anti-Treaty rebels by the British government. The British, who still retained a substantial military presence in Ireland, threatened to intervene if the Provisional Government did not remove the Four Courts garrison. Six days later the newly established National Army shelled the Four Courts using British guns, beginning the Irish Civil War.

For the second time in six years Lemass found himself part of a garrison which had been hopelessly outgunned and surrounded. Lemass and his comrades surrendered after three days. On the last day garrison commander Paddy O'Brien warned Lemass of an impending massive explosion. Lemass was in a room just off the Dome of the Four Courts when the Public Records Office went up in a catastrophic explosion, destroying centuries of priceless archives.[39]

Lemass was injured by flying glass. Once again he was rounded up, as he had been after the Easter Rising, but the Free State gaolers were not as assiduous as the British and approximately 50 prisoners escaped through an unlocked door of a house in Stoneybatter. Lemass fled south to continue the fight. In Enniscorthy O'Brien was killed during their doomed attempt to storm the castle where the National Army troops were based. Lemass escaped to Baltinglass in Co Wicklow and then walked all the way back to Dublin, a distance of 55 kilometres.[40] He was arrested on Bachelors Walk in November 1922 and interned in Curragh camp along with hundreds of other anti-Treaty prisoners.

Beaten militarily and having lost what public support they had, the anti-Treaty IRA called a ceasefire on 30 April 1923, followed by a 'dump arms' order. 'Further sacrifice on your part would now be in vain and the continuance of the struggle in arms unwise in the national interest. Military victory must be allowed to rest for the moment with those who have destroyed the Republic,' de Valera told them.

Thousands of republican prisoners remained incarcerated at

the end of the Civil War. Lemass and others attempted to tunnel their way out of Curragh camp and were caught. He was taken to the Glasshouse, the notorious military prison, where he was handcuffed to a rack on the wall and left hanging with his toes barely touching the ground for several hours.[41] Lemass feared he would be executed by the Free State government, but he was saved by the end of the war. Lemass learned many lessons from the Civil War, the importance of public opinion being one of them.

> The IRA in the Civil War made the tremendous mistake – the fundamental mistake – of forgetting the importance of public opinion. They were being told by the papers that the people of the country were all in favour of the Treaty, which wasn't true, but having accepted this, they began to adopt an attitude of hostility or indifference to the people and certainly an indifference to public opinion – to keeping public opinion on their side.

There was no surrender, no peace treaty, no sense of finality. The Civil War did not end; it petered out, leaving resentments that lasted for decades. Many within the new Free State security apparatus were emboldened by victory in the Civil War and set about settling scores.

Noel Lemass was two years older than Seán, a leader of men, and the more dominant of the two. Many of the brothers' contemporaries would have picked Noel as the one most likely to succeed in post-independence Ireland. During the Civil War he escaped from Gormanstown camp and fled to England. He returned to Ireland in the summer of 1923 after hostilities ended with a reasonable expectation of returning to normal life.

On 3 July 1923 he walked out of the Wicklow Hotel at the junction of Wicklow Street and Exchequer Street in Dublin, having had lunch with a friend, John Devine, the superintendent of the Dublin Corporation Cleansing Department. The pair were accosted from behind by armed men. Devine was taken to the Criminal Investigation Department (CID) headquarters in Oriel House, Westland Row, but was released when he established his identity. Noel Lemass's disappearance shocked a country which hoped it had left the traumas of the Civil War behind. The *Irish Times* observed: 'Dublin has now returned to virtually normal conditions and the kidnapping of a man in broad daylight in one of the city's busiest streets ought to be impossible.'[42]

Noel Lemass's remains were found on the Featherbed Mountain near Rathfarnham on 12 October 1923. The coroner, Dr J.P. Brennan, noted that Lemass's teeth had been 'brutally forced from his jaws – something the most pitiless savage would be ashamed of'. His head had been severed from his body. The inquest jury at Rathmines Town Hall found he had been 'brutally and wilfully murdered' and that the 'armed forces of the State' had been 'implicated in his removal and disappearance'.[43]

The extended Lemass family commissioned a study of the evidence pertaining to the case, which was carried out by Supreme Court judge Adrian Hardiman before his death in 2016. Hardiman concluded that the man who killed Noel Lemass was Captain James Murray of the Free State Army intelligence department. Murray had been called as a witness to the inquest, but the National Army refused to release him – he was already in military custody for other crimes. Murray was eventually convicted of the murder of Joseph Bergin, a military policeman.

In 1925, the English journalist Cyril Bretherton wrote a

book, *The Real Ireland*, in which he stated that Noel Lemass was known to have ambushed a Ford car at Leeson Street Bridge on the first day of the Civil War, 28 June 28 1922, killing three Free State officers. He named Joe McGrath, then the head of the Free State military service, as the man who ordered the revenge killing of Noel Lemass.

In 1927 McGrath won a celebrated libel action against Bretherton. The £3,700 award, a colossal sum at the time, allowed McGrath to set up the hospital sweepstakes and become one of the new state's first indigenous millionaires. In his review, Hardiman concluded that it *was* McGrath, in his status as head of the Free State's military secret service, who ordered the killing of Lemass and that Murray carried it out.[44]

Lemass was still in state custody when he heard about his brother's abduction. He feared the worst. 'For some reason my parents thought of advertising in the "missing persons" columns of the newspapers but it was quite obvious to all of us that he must have been killed.' Lemass was released to attend his brother's funeral, one of the largest seen in Dublin since that of Michael Collins the previous year. The funeral coincided with the first day of the Sinn Féin ard fheis in the Mansion House. The confluence of these two events would propel Seán Lemass into one of the longest and most successful political careers in Irish history.

CHAPTER 1

ACCIDENTAL POLITICIAN

'If you have 200 men and assume that each of them went out to vote illegally 10 times, it's 2,000 votes, which was of little significance, but if you had 200 men who were really prepared to work an election campaign, they could get out thousands of votes and this is what I set out to do.'

On 17 October 1923, the day of his brother's funeral, Seán Lemass was elected to the ard chomhairle of Sinn Féin at the party's ard fheis.

SL: Now when I was elected to the ard chomhairle of Sinn Féin at this ard fheis, this I knew was just an emotional response. My brother's funeral took place during that ard fheis, you see, and the ard fheis adjourned so that the delegates could attend the funeral. All these delegates were up from the country.

There were a lot of people like Mary MacSwiney[1] who were wrapped up in their own little personal intrigues; my first reaction was one of disgust. What was I doing here, they were not doing anything but talking? This was a bad period in our history. We were beaten as a national movement and as a political party. Well, it was my first effort into what would be regarded as politics. Until then the Irish Republican Army (IRA) regarded themselves as having nothing to do with these politicians in Sinn Féin. There was even a certain suggestion of contempt for these politicians in Sinn Féin.

At that time I think I was director of intelligence in the Dublin brigade of the IRA[2] and I could reconcile my membership of the ard chomhairle of Sinn Féin with my job as director of intelligence, which was to know everything that was going on. And this I remained, I think, until I became elected to the Dáil and then of course it had to stop. What I read in the paper was that I was elected as a member of the ard chomhairle of Sinn Féin. I had no problem in deciding to take it.

Lemass found himself involved in a party that was acting as a shadow government with a shadow cabinet and an army (the IRA), but with no power. Having absented themselves from the Dáil, morale was low, though anti-Treaty Sinn Féin had performed credibly in the August 1923 general election, increasing its number of seats from 36 to 44 and its percentage of the popular vote from 21.9 per cent to 27.4 per cent.

SL: At that time, of course, we weren't in the Dáil, but you'll have to understand the constitutional theories that were prevalent in Sinn Féin at that time and which were becoming increasingly unrealistic as the years passed by. The theory was that the Second Dáil[3] was the only legitimate government of the country and that the surviving members of the Second Dáil were, in fact, custodians of the only lawful authority of the country. I, of course, was not elected to the Second Dáil and I think there was some question as to my status, although in fact when the members of the Second Dáil used to meet as the lawful authority in the country, they quickly adjourned into another body, which was the Comhairle na dTeachtaí (Council of Deputies).[4]

The Council of Deputies is where my status was fully established. This was all, as I said, becoming increasingly unreal and more and more people were beginning to recognise that we had argued ourselves into an untenable position and that we'd have to get back to some base from which real political work could be done.

We were all becoming increasingly conscious of the fact that if we wanted to achieve anything through political action, we'd have to have a more realistic programme relating to immediate objectives rather than merely proceeding like the Jacobins asserting our status but doing nothing effectively to maintain it.

There was no effective plan of action at all and even the minor activities, such as the boycott of British goods, were so insignificant as to constitute no alternative, no substitute for a political policy. Increasingly, I suppose, de Valera began to rely upon a few of us for advice in these matters: Frank Aiken,[5] Gerry Boland,[6] myself, Seán MacEntee[7] and Jim Ryan.[8]

Six days after Noel Lemass was buried, the Cumann na nGaedheal TD Philip Cosgrave died at the age of 38 from nephritis (kidney inflammation). Cosgrave was the brother of the President of the Executive Council (effectively taoiseach) William T. Cosgrave. His death precipitated a by-election in the Dublin South constituency scheduled for 12 March 1924. Lemass, then just 24 years old, was nominated to stand against James O'Mara, a successful businessman more than twice Lemass's age who had been an Irish

Party MP and then a Sinn Féin TD. O'Mara won the seat with 49 per cent of the vote, seven points ahead of Lemass, who polled credibly in his first election. It would be the only time in his career that Lemass was not elected.

DR: How were you selected as a Dáil candidate?

SL: I was down at Webbs Bookshop on the Quay – I was buying some second-hand books when a newsboy came along selling the *Evening Mail* and I bought the *Evening Mail* and just looked through it and here I saw, 'Sinn Féin candidate – Mr Seán Lemass has been selected as a candidate.' Well, that by-election was lost pretty largely because of an ineffective organisation, as well as because the whole political atmosphere was against us at the time. Confusion existed at the time in the whole republican movement. The Dublin Brigade of the Irish Volunteers rallied to my help, but their conception of fighting elections was to impersonate voters. The idea of asking people to vote for you or to do the normal work of a political party didn't occur to them at all. They organised an impersonation operation, with rescue squads for anybody who was arrested impersonating others, as a sort of military campaign, which was in my view a complete waste of time and effort.

Another opportunity presented itself in the same constituency six months later when Cumann na nGaedheal TD Hugh Kennedy resigned to take up a position as Chief Justice. Lemass had learned from his previous outing and was better prepared, but it was a close-run thing. In a straight fight Lemass won the by-election with 51.4 per cent of the vote against his Cumann na nGaedheal opponent Séamus Hughes.

SL: This time I oversaw the operation. In the second election campaign I decided that all this business of impersonating and all this organisation for impersonating – and it involved a lot of organisation – lists of people – names on the wall of people who were known to be away or sick or dead – was such a waste of time. If you have 200 men and assume that each of them went out to vote illegally 10 times, it's 2,000 votes, which was of little significance, but if you had 200 men who were really prepared to work an election campaign, they could get out thousands of votes and this is what I set out to do. We were able to run a campaign against the Cumann na nGaedheal candidate,[9] who had been involved in some of the nastiness of the Civil War, and by concentrating on this aspect of it they were able to create a situation where the Cumann na nGaedheal supporters would not go out to support him and didn't go out to support him. The result was that we got a majority vote. Not a very large majority – 1,000 or so.[10]

In March 1925 de Valera appointed Lemass as Minister for Defence in his shadow government. Lemass took over from Frank Aiken, who had been both chief of staff of the IRA and Minister for Defence. A nonplussed Lemass wrote to Aiken immediately after his appointment: 'I am not sure as to what my duties and powers are to be.'

SL: The surviving members of the Second Dáil had nominated a government and very shortly after I was elected to the Dáil I was appointed to this government as Minister for Defence by Éamon de Valera. This did involve some real administrative work – there was, of course, the Irish Republican Army at the time, which in 1925 continued to give its allegiance to this Second Dáil, and which in any event got its money to maintain itself through the Minister for Finance of the Second Dáil, who was a man named Michael Colivet,[11] a Deputy for Limerick, and at that time there was a fair amount of money coming in, through America mainly.

My recollection is that the expenditure upon the army organisation came to some hundreds of pounds a week. This money dried up very suddenly. Suddenly it stopped. One day Colivet came along and told me there was no more money and I remember summoning a meeting of the army council at that time to tell them there was no more money. Now the army council had some money left. This weekly subvention which they were getting from the Minister for Finance had exceeded what it was actually spending. Various economies had been achieved and there was some money left, you know, which enabled the process of running down the army expenditure to be completed less abruptly than the cutting off of the funds would suggest.

In June 1925 de Valera dispatched Gerry Boland, Seán Russell and Pa Murray to Russia to elicit support for the anti-Treaty side. They travelled via London, Hamburg and Leningrad (now St Petersburg). Murray had made Russian contacts in London during the War of Independence. Russell, the most senior IRA figure on the trip, was joined by Boland, who was sent by de Valera to keep an eye on things. Murray, travelling under the name Patrick Hughes, met Joseph Stalin, who wanted to leverage the Irish diaspora against the British. Boland recalled being asked by one Cheka (secret police) agent whether or not they had hanged bishops. When he responded in the negative, the Cheka agent responded: 'Ah, you people are not serious at all.'[12] The Soviets refused to give weapons, but they did agree to send £500 a month for the IRA, a considerable sum at the time, in return for IRA help in spying on the British. The Soviets quickly reduced the sum of money to £100 per month, citing low-quality intelligence.

SL: The idea of going to Russia was to procure some supply of armament, not to establish any type of political arrangement with the Russians. There was an assumption that the Russian government would be hostile towards the British government and that as a hostile government they might be prepared to lend support in the way of a shipment of arms. It was found out that they wouldn't do this at all. The delegation which went to Russia, which consisted of Gerry Boland, Pa Murray and Seán Russell, disagreed considerably among themselves over the line which they should take with the Russians – whether to discuss some sort of political agreement, or to be content to enter into no political agreement of any sort, saying to them, 'If you want to supply arms to somebody who might use them against Britain, OK, we'll take them.' Indeed, the three members of the delegation divided into three separate sections, and they each returned from Russia by a separate route. They wouldn't even come back together, and I had the job after the return, not merely of trying to find out what happened, but of trying to reconcile the three members of the delegation who by this time were hardly talking to each other. That was a botch, but it cost a fair amount of money.

In November 1925 de Valera's shadow government faced the greatest threat to its authority. The IRA, which had always resented being under civilian authority, staged a convention, broke away and declared it would take no instruction from the elected officials.

SL: During 1925 there was this sense of unreality of the whole business, the recognition that, although we were claiming there was a lawful government in existence, that government had no effective power. There was the growing sense of objection in the IRA towards the idea of political control of activities, [which] created a situation where the army council met and decided that they were no longer accepting political control.

A convention was held in Bullock Castle, Dalkey, and a resolution was passed to the effect that henceforth the only lawful authority over the IRA and the sole authority in the army was to be the army council. This was, of course, only a recognition of the reality of the situation, but I think it did have influence on the subsequent development of events because insofar as this government had any function at all, any executive power which it could use, it was solely through the army. Once they had withdrawn their allegiance to it, then of course it became even more theoretical in its existence than it was before.

By this time, of course, all the discussions were directed towards the idea of finding a base for effective political action and this led to the conclusion that the attack should be upon the oath in the Free State Constitution.[13] There was a conviction that if the attack was concentrated on the oath, that the oath could be broken down and this would be the beginning of the process by which other objectionable features of the Treaty would be attacked. The conviction began to grow that a really sustained assault on the oath could succeed, first of all because it was unpopular with everybody, even those who had to take it, and it was something that the average person could understand as being objectionable. It involved no great problem of explanation as to what we were objecting to. This ultimately produced the idea which led to the establishment of Fianna Fáil – namely the idea that we should agree to accept our seats as members of the Free State Dáil if the oath were removed.

After the Treaty was signed, when you had this situation where the pro-Treaty members of the Second Dáil were one day acting as the government of the Dáil and one day acting as the Provisional Government, the proposition was carried that the IRA would cease to give recognition to the authority of either of these governments and recognise only the authority of its own army council. That took place during the truce period between the signing of the Treaty and the outbreak of the Civil War.[14]

They were willing to surrender their independence of action to get out of the Civil War when the Civil War was obviously over and they'd been beaten, but the hankering to get back to the situation where they didn't have to accept any sort of political control, the control of politicians was still there, and, of course, was increasingly justified by the ineffectiveness of the Sinn Féin political section and the obvious ineffectiveness of the Second Dáil and of the government that had been appointed. It was this growing sense of futility and frustration which also led to the situation that ultimately created the formation of Fianna Fáil. The belief was growing that we were achieving nothing and would ultimately just fade away and disappear perhaps only as a nostalgic memory like the Jacobeans unless we could get some firmer base for political action.

CHAPTER 2

NEW PARTY, NEW BEGINNINGS

'Sinn Féin had collected all the cranks in the country and there were people making speeches in favour of vegetarianism and the single tax, all sorts of queer sorts of cranks, who were certainly confusing the public mind.'

The foundation of the Fianna Fáil party came against the background of increasing frustration within Sinn Féin about the policy of abstentionism. The limitations of the policy were starkly exposed in December 1925 when the Cumann na nGaedheal government rushed through legislation giving effect to the Boundary Commission settlement agreed between the Irish and British governments. Nationalist Ireland had anticipated that Article 12 of the Anglo-Irish Treaty, which set up the commission, would transfer the majority nationalist counties of Fermanagh and Tyrone, Derry city and South Armagh to the Free State, thus rendering Northern Ireland an unviable state. It proved to be a naive belief.

A leaked copy of the report published in the *Morning Post* on 7 November 1925 envisaged only piecemeal changes to the border and, worse still, recommended the transfer of East

Donegal to the North. The leaked report led to the resignation of the Free State's representative on the commission, the Minister for Education, Eoin MacNeill, who admitted far too late that he was never suited to the role.

The Irish government rushed to London and agreed a deal with the British to keep the border as it was in return for Britain writing off the Free State's share of the imperial debt, which at the time amounted to 80 per cent of the Free State's annual GDP. The Boundary Commission legislation was passed by 71 votes to 20 on 10 December 1925. Sinn Féin then had 48 seats. Had it been there, it would not have been able to overturn the vote, but it could have made it much more difficult for the government. Lemass had already made up his mind by then that abstentionism was a dead-end policy and set out his views in a series of coruscating opinion pieces in *An Phoblacht* between October 1925 and March 1926. At the November 1925 Sinn Féin ard fheis a motion was proposed to end the 'insidious rumours that Republicans will enter the Free State parliament if the oath be removed'. Instead, elected TDs would only enter a 'Republican parliament for all Ireland'. De Valera, sensing a trap which would bind him, did not accept the motion.

The increasingly fractious debate was finally resolved at the Sinn Féin ard fheis on 9 March 1926 in Rathmines Town Hall. De Valera's motion that entering the Dáil was a 'question not of principle but of policy' should the oath be abolished was narrowly defeated by 223 votes to 218. De Valera returned the following morning to tender his resignation as Sinn Féin president and walked out with his followers.

De Valera accepted Lemass's suggestion that they start a new party. With his characteristic energy and sense of certitude, Lemass threw himself into the building of a new party, convening the first meeting of what would become Fianna Fáil on Good Friday (2 April) 1926. Lemass wanted to call the new party The Republican Party; de Valera preferred the more mystical Fianna Fáil (Soldiers of Destiny). Fianna Fáil (The Republican Party) was launched on 16 May 1926 at La Scala Theatre in Dublin.

SL: I'm trying to emphasise the effect of the Boundary Commission upon the development of the Fianna Fáil party. There was this apparent situation when the Boundary Commission reported about the dissenting members of Cumann na nGaedheal, the Labour Party, the National League and Fianna Fáil. If we were in the Dáil there would have been a majority against this thing and of course the pressure then began to come upon us to go into the Dáil and take the oath and take our seats. And we had a meeting in the Shelbourne Hotel where this course was advocated, and it was advocated by Hugh O'Flynn and others.[1] There were some members of the party of that kind, who had been associated with Fianna Fáil, but who had not been sort of actively involved in the Fianna Fáil movement, but we decided against it. At that time, it looked like being a wrong decision, but we decided to stay out even if by going in we could defeat what appeared to be a national disaster. In fact, it didn't work out that way. When the motion was put for its approval in the Dáil, the majority in favour was larger than our total vote and if we had gone in, some of those who voted against it would have voted for it.[2] But it does in fact mark the point of time at which the necessity to take a new political position began to be fully realised by not merely the members of the Sinn Féin party who were elected, but by the members of the Sinn Féin party of the country.

Now this Boundary Commission had a very distinct bearing on the whole business, because it came at the time when we were in this process of changing step, when the policy was introduced into the Dáil. You see here the ultimate financial settlement which involved the abandonment by the British of their financial claims in consideration of the government accepting partition.[3] When this came back there was tremendous feeling about it as there would be today. The people will accept the fact that the Border is there, but to give recognition to the fact that it is going to remain there is a different thing altogether and this agreement appeared to involve the government accepting it. It looked at the time as if there would be a majority to reject this if we were in the Dáil and we weren't in the Dáil and a large part of the pressure which ultimately was to change the policy of the Fianna Fáil party started at this time.

Here we were, living in this dream world, when quite suddenly a practical issue has come to the point in the form of an agreement with Britain which has to be approved by the Dáil, which it seemed we had the power to stop if we decided to use that power, and the decision not to use it was taken. But it was taken with a great deal of misgiving amongst our people in the country – the people who were, if not actively supporters of Sinn Féin at the time, the potential supporters we had to get if we were ever to hold a majority. They felt that we were letting them down by not overcoming our emotional scruples by going in to stop this business in the Dáil. So I would say that this particular event did have in the ultimate development of the situation a very considerable significance.

There was more or less a general agreement that there should be a special ard fheis to settle this question one way or the other. And, of course, that financial settlement – 'the big nought' as it was called – was also the origin of what was known as the 'land annuity dispute' because it was contended that this didn't apply to the land annuities – the land annuities which were paid by the farmers to the Irish government were still being transmitted to the British Land Commission.[4]

DR: Was there a feeling then that there was a tendency to fade at this stage?

SL: Oh yes; a feeling that we were up in the air – we hadn't our feet on the ground at all. Now this would naturally vary from person to person. You'd have people who were so committed to this purely theoretical existence of the Republic and its government that they'd resent anything which would cast any doubt on it. To the younger people, like myself, who wanted to find some firmer basis for political organisation and political action it had not the same significance. Mary MacSwiney,[5] Art O'Connor[6] – these people would never have accepted that anything else but this purely theoretical conception that the Republic had never been dissolved. They became so deeply involved in this idea that many times discussions about it were like discussions in fairyland.

The vision was that at some stage in some election the people of the country would vote by a majority to say the Treaty never existed, and to put everything back to where it was before the Treaty was signed and Dáil Eireann, the legitimate government, re-established. Other ideas were being discussed – de Valera was certainly responsible for the idea of concentrating on the immediate objective – the oath. He saw this was a fundamental point and began to discuss this idea of a public pledge to participate in the work of the Dáil and taking our seats then, provided that this political test on the oath was removed. The idea of what we called an intermediate objective developed gradually. You see, we saw the futility of expecting the people at one election to vote for the whole Republican position in toto, and we began to realise that we would have to get them to do this piecemeal, the oath being the first step. When I say the oath being the first step, this was de Valera's idea, that this was the obvious first step to try to get rid of the oath.

The first time that the idea of making this public announcement that we'd take our seats in the Dáil if the oath were removed, didn't emerge until 1925. This was the proposition that ultimately was discussed by the Sinn Féin ard fheis, and you'll notice that there were two Sinn Féin ard fheiseanna held in 1925. I think the decision to hold the extraordinary ard fheis, which was held the following spring, was concurred to by everyone – by those who were opposed to the idea as much as by those who were in favour of it, as a way of getting a decision on the point anyway.

DR: Yes, 223 to 218 was the actual vote itself.

SL: A very confused vote. There was no proper time for serious debate or major policy change. Emotion was far more effective than common sense, do you understand? Of course, there were a lot of emotional speeches made there which produced this adverse vote. To this day I'm not sure whether de Valera wanted an adverse vote or not. He certainly wasn't upset by the fact that he'd lost the vote. He probably saw advantages in having a clean break and a new party. He also saw advantages in continuing with Sinn Féin, in view of the traditions of Sinn Féin and the possibility of financial support from America. It wasn't all black and white. There were advantages both ways, and I must say that I personally felt rather happy that we had a clean break and had to start a new organisation.

Mind you, at the time, I tried very hard to produce the other result; but when it was over there was a certain feeling of relief as there was a lot of nonsense associated with the old Sinn Féin organisation. Sinn Féin had collected all the cranks in the country and there were people making speeches in favour of vegetarianism and the single tax, all sorts of queer sorts of cranks, who were certainly confusing the public mind as to what Sinn Féin stood for and trying as it were to link us in with their own queer ideas. By having a clean break, we got clear of a lot of this confusion that had grown up around the old Sinn Féin organisation. I'd say this was de Valera's greatest achievement. I mean, look over the whole of his career, 1916 to 1921, a lot of it would have happened if de Valera hadn't been there at all. The same would apply from 1932 on, the first Fianna Fáil government, and in keeping neutrality during the war; others could perhaps have done these things, but I'd say nobody but him could have got the republican movement, in the atmosphere of the 1920s, back to a state of reality so effectively that within a few years we were elected by the people as a government, by a majority. He alone could have done this.

DR: Bearing in mind his position up to that time, a man of his idealism must have had a considerable internal struggle?

SL: He had many struggles with his own conscience and even during all this period was still intellectually committed to the idea that the Second Dáil had never been dissolved, and that the legitimate authority of government somehow resided in the members of the Second Dáil. It took him a long time before he began to forget about this notion, and not until 1932 did he finally accept that these old theories and notions had no relevance to the circumstances at the time. Naturally there was a desire to try to conceal the magnitude of this split in the republican movement, and I suppose a hope that ultimately it would be healed in some way. But in fact, I think I'm correct in saying that the need for it soon disappeared, because there was no real split, do you see? As soon as Fianna Fáil got started it was soon the only political organisation left in the Republic beside the Sinn Féin organisation, and the remnant of Sinn Féin disappeared with extraordinary rapidity. This feeling of unreality, frustration, ineffectiveness, was far more widespread amongst the ordinary rank and file members than it was amongst the leaders. They couldn't follow all this theorising about the Second Dáil and the legitimate government, they weren't greatly concerned about it.

The ard fheis was by no means representative of the real feeling of the movement. I'd say by 1932 Sinn Féin as a political organisation had ceased to exist altogether, and the only effective republican political organisation was Fianna Fáil.[7] Now, as soon as we broke with Sinn Féin and developed a definite programme that could be explained – now we had our feet on the ground and knew that whatever the future might bring we had signposted the road we were going to take. Many of these people themselves showed their lack of conviction in the reality of this position, by coming into Fianna Fáil.

The Fianna Fáil name – there was a lot of argument about it. In a sense it was an attempt to avoid using the term 'Republican Party', because de Valera had this idea that the objective was not only to re-establish the Republic, but that to get to this objective he had to proceed on a step-by-step basis, and we would be handicapping ourselves by calling ourselves the Republican Party, or something of that kind, so we stuck to Fianna Fáil. He picked that name and he forced it on us, not having any doubts about its highly poetic connotation, and with 'the Republican Party' in small print underneath it.

That was another factor which had to be borne in mind. By the end of 1924/1925, American money had dried up altogether and, whatever money Sinn Féin had, I don't know whether they had very much revenue; it had remained with Sinn Féin, you see.[8] When Fianna Fáil started, there was no money at all – Dev got some subscriptions from individuals, I suppose. A doctor – this friend of his, a doctor man in Merrion Square – went round to a few friends to get some money.[9] But after Fianna Fáil was founded, after the organisation was finally launched, he went off to America.[10]

Irish American opinion always had a tremendous significance for de Valera. He was always very much concerned to ensure that what he was doing here would be understood by the Irish Americans. He came back from America with a fair amount of money, so for a time we didn't have this problem of no way to pay postage or notepaper and that sort of thing, although it wasn't enough to run a political organisation on. We had to get up and organise the national collection, which has been the mainstay of Fianna Fáil ever since.

After Fianna Fáil was founded, when I became the chief

organiser, this was when it became utterly impossible to follow any other type of business. You see, Fianna Fáil had no money. I'd no money, except what I could earn, and it didn't become possible for me to relinquish the job of earning money until we got into the Dáil – until we actually took our seats in the Dáil in 1927. I began to draw the Dáil allowance as a deputy, and this was supplemented by some amount from Fianna Fáil headquarters and I then became whole time in politics, organising Fianna Fáil as secretary – had an office in their head offices – ran the whole place and participated in the Dáil work. From then on I was a whole-time politician.

CHAPTER 3

ENTERING THE DÁIL

'You just had to announce that the republic still lived and that anybody who didn't accept this was a so and so, and that was all there was to it'

SL: I found myself getting more and more interested in the work the Dáil was doing, the legislation, which often had no political significance, that was coming along. I found, I suppose, that I had some facility for talking, also that people began to listen to what I had to say in the Dáil – all this helped, of course, to maintain interest in it too.

I used to have to speak at public meetings during the Sinn Féin period. At one by-election I was the candidate myself. What I was like, I don't know – I'm sure I was awful. You just had to announce that the republic still lived and that anybody who didn't accept this was a so and so, and that was all there was to it. So that I've no conception of what the speeches sounded like, but I'm sure they were at least no worse than the others. There was no political message in it except nationalism. Everybody was involved deeply in politics in those days, to an extent that they are not involved now. I mean the deep political issues that have been debated and decided – in that everybody was politically conscious and those who were against the Treaty were committed as to a religion so that the effort of the organisation wasn't so much to convert people to the cause we were advocating as to get them active in that cause. Bit by bit, as the despondency or despair began to disappear, this became easier and easier, once you began to show that you could achieve results; hope began to be born again and, one by one, people who had nothing to do with you in the earlier years began to come along and help and ultimately became as deeply involved as myself.

I always tell the story of Neil Blaney's father, Neal. Neal Blaney was the key man in north Donegal. He was the battalion commander in the northern Donegal area during the Black and Tan war period and Civil War, and I felt that I could make no progress in north Donegal until I got Neal Blaney and I went up to see him. He was a small farmer in one of the peninsulas up there. I took the train to Letterkenny and I met a middle-aged man there called Conal Carberry. He had a small, licensed pub there and he was the only man I could get to come with me to show me where Neal Blaney lived. I didn't know his exact address and Conal agreed to come with me and all the way he kept telling me about the ferocious parish priest who was in this parish (Neal Blaney's parish), and that as soon as he heard we were in the parish he would be out with bell, book and candle. We had to pass through two or three villages on the way from Letterkenny to Neal Blaney's farm, and each time he'd say, 'Come in and have a drink.' We'd go into the local pub and he'd ask for two whiskeys and I'd say, 'No, I don't want any' and he'd drink the two himself.

But then we arrived at Blaney's village. By this time poor Conal had six whiskeys in him and he said, 'Before we go to see Neal Blaney, I'm going to have a word with this parish priest' and he went over and started banging on the parish priest's door.

Before that he was afraid of his life of what was going to happen to him – but anyway, fortunately, the parish priest wasn't in. I went out to see Neal Blaney and young Neil tells me he remembers this since he was a young fella of four or five playing in his bare feet (it was midsummer). Blaney wouldn't even come down off the rick of hay. I told him what I was there for, but he'd have nothing to do with it. 'I want to spend the rest of my life working my farm – I've given as much as I intend to give to Ireland.' I kept arguing and arguing with him for an hour and I remember after some time, he stuck the fork in the hay and he came down off the rick and he picked up his coat. 'Come on', he said, 'we'll talk to some of the lads.' And from then on, of course, there were no further problems left in the area. We had a cumann formed in that town before we left it and within a matter of weeks we had the whole place fully organised because once Blaney said 'You're to form a Fianna Fáil cumann in your area' it was formed.

The general election held on 9 June 1927 was the first contested by the new Fianna Fáil party. The party achieved 26.2 per cent of the vote and 44 seats. It was a bad election for Cumann na nGaedheal. Its percentage share of the vote fell from 39.0 to 27.4 per cent and its seats from 63 to 47 out of a 153-seat Dáil. The Sinn Féin vote collapsed from 44 seats to 5. A significant player in the election was the short-lived National League party founded in the same year as Fianna Fáil by Major William Redmond, the son of the former Irish Parliamentary Party leader John Redmond. The party, somewhat surprisingly, won eight seats.

Cumann na nGaedheal returned to government without an electoral mandate, but it was able to govern with the support of the Farmers' Party, which won 11 seats, and some independents. Fianna Fáil turned up on the first day of the new Dáil on 23 June 1927, but its deputies were refused entry because they would not take the oath. The assassination of Kevin O'Higgins on 10 July changed everything. Cosgrave described O'Higgins's murder as the 'political assassination of a pillar of the state'. O'Higgins was shot dead on his way to mass in Booterstown, Co Dublin. The shooting appears to have been more opportunistic than planned. He was killed, according to later accounts, by three former anti-Treaty IRA men – Bill Gannon, Archie Doyle and Tim Coughlan, who were on their way to a football game in Wicklow in a stolen car when they spotted O'Higgins without a bodyguard. The government moved swiftly to introduce the Public Safety Act, which allowed for stringent powers of arrest and detention and banned the IRA. The Electoral Amendment Act required in future that all Dáil candidates would have to commit to taking the oath, otherwise they could not stand for election. O'Higgins was loathed in republican circles as one of the members of the government who had sanctioned the execution of 81 republican prisoners during the Civil War, including, famously, his own best man, Rory O'Connor. Lemass's lack of concern or pity, as elicited here, can be seen in that context.

DR: [Cumann na nGaedheal] lost 16 [seats] – you went up from 36 to 44.

SL: Yes, that's right. That's all. Well, then, of course, there came the announcement by Cumann na nGaedheal that they were going to introduce legislation to deprive us of our membership of the Dáil and to prevent candidates being elected to the Dáil who refused to take the Oath of Allegiance. Of course, this was what forced the decision to go into the Dáil eventually. I remember I was speaking at a meeting in Leitrim and when I was driving home to Dublin, I passed through Enfield in County Meath, when a garda stopped the car and he said, 'Somebody's shot O'Higgins.' They had been told to check all the cars. I was, of course, shocked at the news. This was a big event, you know. But the one thing that struck me was how completely indifferent the Gardaí were to this business. He was the Minister for Justice, he was the man who was supposed to have formed the force, but there was certainly no personal sympathy with O'Higgins. I don't know, now this could have been an act put on for my benefit, you know what I mean – they knew who I was as I hadn't to identify myself. How completely unemotionally these men who were supposed to be O'Higgins's men accepted the fact that somebody had shot him that day in Dublin.

The government immediately went to arrest persons who were associated with Fianna Fáil, against whom they had no evidence at all, to instil into the mind of the public that Fianna Fáil was associated with it. They let them all out in a few days as there wasn't the slightest evidence. However, this event did have a very profound political consequence. We were already, I suppose, beginning to feel that we were on another policy of frustration. We'd been elected – 44 of us – on the grounds that we'd take our seats in the Dáil if the oath was abolished. We had gone to the Dáil to demand our seats and been refused admission and we were asking where the hell do we go from here and it wasn't at all clear where we would go from here. It was at that stage that de Valera decided (actually, he'd probably had it in mind all the time) that we'd find a way of getting over this difficulty and get into the Dáil. There's something there about declaring the oath to be an empty formula. Now what happened was that J.J. Walsh, who was a member of the Cumann na nGaedheal government,[1] said, 'Why do these people refuse to take this oath, which is only an empty formula, which I take as an empty formula? I don't regard myself bound by this oath, which is only an empty formula. I regard it as something I must do in order to exercise my rights as an elected deputy.' It was then that Dev said, 'If that's so, if what you say is correct, then it's no problem for us either', and that is the proposition he got the party to accept, that we would say that we do not regard this as an oath. We won't have anything to do with it as an oath; we're signing a declaration because we're told that it is a formula of no significance, with which we must conform in order to get our seats in the Dáil. We all went through this ritual. Now, there were a couple of by-elections pending and then there came the Jinks business.

Fianna Fáil entered Dáil Éireann on 10 August 1927. The Dáil arithmetic changed at a stroke and Fianna Fáil was determined to bring down the minority Cumann na nGaedheal government. De Valera decided to support a minority Labour government; although that party had won only 22 seats to Fianna Fáil's 44, it was a means of getting Cumann na nGaedheal out. A vote of no confidence in the government was scheduled for Tuesday 16 August. Redmond agreed to support it. The *Irish Times* speculated that the motion would be carried by 73 votes to 69 and Labour would form a government supported by Fianna Fáil. In reality, two Labour TDs were missing, narrowing the vote. The stage was set for the Jinks affair, one of the most infamous and celebrated episodes in Irish politics. John Jinks was a National Party TD for Sligo.

SL: We were now into the Dáil and there was now a situation where the Cumann na nGaedheal party was in a minority in the Dáil, if you count the Redmondite party [National Party], the Labour Party and ourselves together. This is what induced [Tom] Johnson of the Labour Party to put down his motion of no confidence. There was no intention to form a coalition government. We had decided that we would put in a Labour Party government, or a Labour Party government with Redmondite members, and support it. They'd be the government. But we wouldn't be in the government and this of course led to the famous division where Bryan Cooper[2] got John Jinks[3] intoxicated and Jinks couldn't turn up to vote and ultimately you got this even division.

DR: [The vote was] 71:71.[4] This is a fact, that Jinks was in fact drunk?

SL: Oh yes, Bryan Cooper could drink anyone under the table. He got Jinks into the bar and they drank away, and by the time he was finished Bryan Cooper was still able to walk, but poor Jinks couldn't.

In August 1927 W.T. Cosgrave called a snap general election following O'Higgins's death. Fianna Fáil advanced further, going from 44 to 57 seats, but Cumann na nGaedheal, standing on a law and order platform, did even better, going from 47 seats to 62. It was able to form a minority government with the support of the Farmers' Party, which had won six seats, and a number of independent TDs.

DR: The June 1927 election – was that your first as director of elections?

SL: I was director of elections. Of course, an election in those days was very different from now. You didn't have the mass media which you have now – we didn't have any newspapers. An election campaign was very much a matter of organising public meetings, an enormous number of public meetings, and posters and leaflets, which were printed by the million. You had no radio, you had no television and, of course, the newspapers had very limited circulation. No newspapers gave you any coverage and those few newspapers which existed didn't circulate at all outside the towns, because the present-day motor distribution of newspapers didn't exist. So the only way that you could get into the rural areas was by word of mouth – and perhaps the local paper. And it involved a great deal of work in the production of printed material, as well as in the holding of public meetings, and there again you'd be doing the five or six meetings a night. In fact, we didn't have much of a staff, so you had to do all the work, even to the point of parcelling up the bundles of leaflets and sticking the stamps on them from time to time.

Fianna Fáil found itself as the main opposition party and Lemass busied himself building up the party. In 1928 Lemass made a much-commented-on statement in the Dáil when he described Fianna Fáil as a 'slightly constitutional party'. He explained: 'We have adopted the method of political agitation to achieve our end, and because we believe, in present circumstances, that method is in the interests of the nation as a whole and of the republican movement and for no other reason.' The constitution Lemass was referring to was the Free State Constitution of 1922, which included the oath. The phrase has been interpreted as a veiled warning that Fianna Fáil still retained the threat of violence if it did not get its way. In reality, Fianna Fáil, as events would show, completely abandoned militarism.

SL: This was probably the busiest time in my life. I never worked as hard in my life as I did from that period, '26/'27 until the election of 1932. This was a time where every spare moment of my time was completely involved. Of course, I became whole-time on the job. I was fully occupied with this work. Every evening, we had a meeting of some sort or the other in Dublin or down in the country. I achieved by the end of the year the particular target I set myself in the number of registered Fianna Fáil cumann, the activities, the membership, the capacity to undertake various activities and so on. It wasn't so hard. The nucleus of the organisation was there.

In the organisation of Fianna Fáil, I believed everything turned upon maintaining the widest possible area of personal contact. Meeting the people personally and from then on writing to them periodically and asking their opinion on things – asking them to help you out with some of the problems. In this way you got them involved in the work of running the organisation as closely as yourself and of course there was growing enthusiasm. They were tremendous people; they were working as hard as I was and completely dedicated and some of them without any personal ambition at all. The anti-Treaty elements were still predominantly the basis of our organisation. Now, during these years, we began to realise the political truth that we couldn't get a majority unless we converted to our support people who had voted for the Treaty, whatever their motives may have been for doing so, and therefore the emphasis in propaganda began to shift from asserting that those who had supported the Treaty were traitors and blackguards and everything else to saying that they were all decent men who had been misled. And that was all that was possible during these years. It was much later that you could say, 'no matter what side you were on in the Treaty argument', this is what has to be done now and we want your help in doing it, because to have said that earlier would have antagonised a lot of people on whose activity we were relying. At every stage there are some quotations from me which marked this process of moving away from the strict anti-Treaty attitude. And always there was some criticism from somebody of any departure from this strict line. Now, in a sense, politics were in the doldrums – you see, the most remarkable thing about that period is that the Cumann na nGaedheal government at the time had lost any sense of direction, they had no aims of any sort, they had no objective to realise, they had no clear policy to communicate. Their only argument for being allowed to continue was that they had won the Civil War, restored peace and order and that if they disappeared disorder would start up again. This was a purely negative policy approach. They had no economic or social policy. There was nothing that they could rally people to, except the idea that their removal would mean another deluge of disorder and fighting.

DR: To what extent do you think this arose from the death of [Arthur] Griffith and [Michael] Collins?

SL: Well, that's very hard to say. It would be almost impossible to answer that. I suppose they must have been a tremendous loss to the pro-Treaty side in the sense that they were the men who had emerged as the leaders of that side and who had the greatest capacity to develop a policy, but it was more than that, it was a sort of acceptance of defeat; I mean there was ... they were more concerned with what they had just done than what they were going to do and I should say a feeling, which they probably didn't admit to themselves but which was there nevertheless, that they were going to go out eventually and that the republican idea – the anti-Treaty – would become successful.

They didn't have the leaders because they didn't have the convictions. I said this before, that a very high proportion of those who were in support of the Treaty were so because they assumed it meant peace, but were nevertheless dissatisfied with the Treaty as a settlement and there was no policy. [Arthur] Griffith did try to do it and I think [Kevin] O'Higgins did try to develop the idea that membership of the Commonwealth was itself a policy, a worthwhile policy, which could be defended, but they were getting no response at all from either their own supporters or even their colleagues in the government. Men like J.J. Walsh[5] and the rest of them, you see, they would be sort of apologising for any deterioration in their republicanism; that's what the Treaty implied for them, and I should think that Collins would have come to this view also. Collins, as you know, was the man who in many ways secured the acceptance of the Treaty.

We take this Treaty, we tell the British we are satisfied with it but in fact we are going to use it to move forward from there, a stepping stone to obtain freedom – and this, as you know, began to produce troubles for the Cumann na nGaedheal government because by 1924 and 1925 you had people who had been induced into this position and who were saying 'What about it, when do we step off the stepping stone, when do we use the freedom to achieve freedom?' This was complicated by a lot of personal differences which emerged as well and it led to the Army Mutiny,[6] it led to the growing discontent in the ranks of Cumann na nGaedheal, particularly in the army, with the inactive policy that they followed in this regard since the end of the Civil War.

And, of course, they missed out very badly by not trying to identify themselves with Irish nationalism. Now [Ernest] Blythe[7] himself was a fanatic for the language, but he wasn't able to get any of the others to follow him at all and, even on the idea of industrial protection – which Griffith would presumably have been arguing for – they pursued a policy of doing as little as possible. If they had used the Treaty position after the Civil War to achieve all the aims that had been talked about during the republican period in economic, social and cultural policy, which they were free to do without any variation of the Treaty position, then they could have justified the Treaty to an extent, which they never attempted to do. This could have been [due to] lack of leadership, lack of administrative capacity. But it's very hard to know what the real explanation is. The fact was that in all this period they were just merely content to govern, doing the minimum that was necessary to carry on government.

Lemass showed an enormous appetite for economic planning and an attempt at coherent thinking from the earliest stage. In 1929 he submitted a paper to the Fianna Fáil party which would be the basis of the party's policy before the Second World War. Unless Irish agriculture modernised and investment was made in industry, the recurring cycles of economic depression and emigration would continue, he argued. He advocated a policy of tariffs and customs duties to protect Irish industry, curbs on foreign industrialists owning Irish industry and a central bank to manage credit flows in and out of the state.

DR: Well, can I ask you one thing here, Mr Lemass? What was the internal process by which this policy, this economic policy, came into being in 1929? Were you shadow minister for Industry and Commerce?

SL: No. We hadn't shadow ministers at that time and indeed I had a vague idea that if we formed a government, I might be Minister for Finance rather than Minister for Industry and Commerce. While at that time, Finance was just the accountancy sector of the government I had a feeling all the time that this was all wrong – that Finance should be the dominant department of the government and should be the formulator of economic development policies. In the end I didn't mind this. Industry and Commerce offered such enormous scope for development and activity I never regretted having taken Industry and Commerce. Remember the great international and economic slump began to develop in 1929 and 1930. All the countries were reverting to protectionism – either protection by exchange control or by tariffs or quotas. World trade was developing at an enormous rate and it would, I think, certainly have been impossible to have any sort of public confidence in the viability of an industrial policy without protection. The system we operate now of government grants and taxation and all this would not have been strong enough, I think, to have got any move at all going.

Lemass's industrial policy was defined as import substitute industrialisation (ISI). Irish industry would be protected from foreign imports by quotas on foreign goods entering the country and tariffs. Theoretically, this would allow Irish industry sufficient protection to provide goods for the domestic market.

DR: There were some limitations in the whole concept of industrial development in those days.

SL: In those days the idea of industrial revival was limited by the idea of supplying the home market with goods which were capable of economic manufacture in the country which the home market would take and which were previously imported. Boots and shoes, shirts, clothes, all consumer products of that kind. We were thinking ahead to a stage where capital goods could be made, where these consumer goods had reached a stage where we were capable of exports – at that time it appeared to be so far ahead that you didn't really have to make any current plans which related to that possibility at all. I always give as an example of the process of industrial development that one of the first taxes we imposed was the Package Tax. … It was the subject of a great deal of political discussion and frivolity and sarcastic remarks and so on – it was a tax on packages, 2d, on any package, which was so comprehensive that if you sent a box of sweets wrapped in silver paper, each sweet was a package.

I tried to explain the idea behind this, but it wasn't easy to get it understood – the political debate at the time was lost in ridicule. But, of course, by eliminating the package you now began to require the manufacturers of these goods to bring them in in bulk and once they started bringing them in in bulk, they began to conceive of the economy of having the goods manufactured here instead of imported. You began to develop the printing and package-making industry, you began to show that there was considerable scope in the manufacture of tin cans, and ultimately you hoped, of tin plate. Indeed, many of the industries of the country had their origin in the recognition of certain importing firms that they couldn't continue … bringing in everything already packed from abroad. You had to start at the very lowest point, where the consumer operated, and you had to go back from that to the ultimate stage of manufacturing the capital goods, the basic raw materials and all the rest of it, and you can only do that when your market for these things has been created. You couldn't set up leather tanneries until you had got the boot industry established; you couldn't set up the chemical industries to treat the leather until the tanneries business was established.

DR: And if I may take up one other point there. In April 1929 you referred to the orgy of petty terrorism which the government had been carrying on in Dublin.

SL: At that time the IRA were again carrying on some occasional activities and there were a number of incidents which led to this type of police activity[8]... I'd say probably exaggerated by the government at the time ... again to get back to the basic position I have described that their only policy, the only coherent attitude was 'We're the government who can maintain law and order and without us there'd be no law and order.' They were disposed not merely to incite some of these activities but to exaggerate them when they occurred.

DR: Going right back to the foundation of Fianna Fáil, you'd have no problem on these?

SL: You'd have no problem on these, these are all things we had decided. There was another event took place – one of the things we were arguing about in the Dáil was a national economic council, which is an attraction to all parties in opposition, it still appears today from time to time, and to our astonishment on one occasion the idea got accepted by the government, and this economic council was formed comprising of some members of Fianna Fáil and some members of the public. I was on it, Paddy Hogan[9] was the chairman, and I remember George O'Brien[10] was on it.

But this council, after a few preliminary and general discussions, got down to one question, the desirability of encouraging the growing of wheat in this country and there was a report published on this – a majority report and a minority report – a complete disagreement, of course, between the two sides and that was the last time it met; they never went on from that at all.

Now as a definition of the different approach of the two parties to the question of the economic problem, the reports of that council are interesting. You see, Fianna Fáil started off with a proposition that the function of Irish agriculture is to grow food to feed the Irish people and Fine Gael put forward the view that the function of Irish agriculture is to produce nothing in particular except profit for the farmer – two entirely different approaches, and everything else that was said about it followed on from this. They were irreconcilable, you couldn't make the two concepts meet. Insofar as it's the duty of Irish agriculture to produce food for the Irish people and bread is the basic food, therefore we must produce wheat and if we can't produce wheat at a market price, OK, then it must be given a price at which we can produce it and that's where the argument started over a guaranteed minimum price which caused such a lot of controversy.

In 1929 Fianna Fáil voted at its ard fheis for party members not to attend receptions held by the government for foreign dignitaries. This policy received little attention until the papal nuncio Archbishop Paschal Robinson took office in 1930. He was the first in Ireland since 1645 and the Cumann na nGaedheal government trumpeted his arrival as one of the many benefits of an independent Irish state. Fianna Fáil's decision to boycott the reception did not go down well with the hierarchy in Ireland. De Valera was absent from Ireland at the time, so it was given to Lemass to explain the Fianna Fáil decision.

SL: This of course pinpoints another very difficult issue for us. We started off stating that the Free State government was an illegal government. It was set up in usurpation of the powers of Dáil Éireann and there was no moral authority to it. When we became members of the Free State parliament ourselves this situation became a little illogical, as you can see. We argued that this is the effective source of government power, and we can therefore try to influence the use of that power without accepting the reality of the government and its functions but the situation became more and more unreal for us, and one of the first real tests was this question: what was our attitude to international representation accredited to it?

I think the papal nuncio [Paschal Robinson] was the first. Now he was accredited to the Free State government – to the Crown as head of the Irish Free State – and were we going to take that further step of going to meet him as the pope's representative accredited to an illegal government? And we decided not to do it. Again, none of us was very happy about this decision but we felt that while change was undoubtedly taking place – change in our attitude towards things – this was pushing the pace a little too hard. I was very unhappy about the political implications in terms of votes of not being present at the reception for the papal nuncio. I'd have wished that we could have found some formula which would enable us to get there. I have a recollection of making a few faux pas myself. I used some phrase when the press came along to me and said are you going? 'We in Fianna Fáil have no objection to meeting the representative of the pope.' Well, you see, this was putting it the wrong way around, the fact that we would presume to have an objection to meeting the representative of the pope got some play in the papers at the time. I kicked myself afterwards, you know, because I said that. Of course I had no objection to meeting the representative of the pope. An American minister also arrived about that time and it was the same situation as with the nuncio, a man named Sterling,[11] but he took it differently because within a few days of his formal introduction as minister I was sitting in the office – we had an office in Abbey Street at the time – when I was told that the American ambassador was downstairs and wanted to see me. He wanted to find out what it was all about, do you see? So, I had the job of explaining it all to him that there was nothing personal in this that it was merely a question of an ambiguous position as far as we were concerned regarding the legitimacy of the government. Strange to say, the first function we went to which involved personal contact with Free State ministers was the reception for Colonel (James) Fitzmaurice and his German associates after flying the Atlantic.[12]

Of course, all our attitudes regarding legitimacy began to change very rapidly when we ourselves became the government. Although we would have still said, I suppose, in that period from 1932 to

1937, that we are the government under the powers created by the Treaty, in the position created by the Treaty, we had effective power but questionable moral right. But we would have avoided saying it if we could because this was the position on which we were challenged from the IRA side, but after the enactment of the constitution, we had no doubt at all about our moral and legal right to do everything under that constitution.

The *Irish Press* newspaper was founded by Éamon de Valera in 1931. The money to start it was raised in the United States, during the War of Independence, for the purpose of financing the First Dáil, but 60 per cent of it never made it to Ireland. Instead, de Valera used it as share capital to start the newspaper. He remained the paper's managing director. The *Irish Press* was set up as a counterpoint to the *Irish Independent*, which was perceived to be pro-Cumann na nGaedheal.

SL: It gave us a medium by which speeches made on our side could be reported at some length, but it also ensured that these speeches would be reported, even in a shorter length, in the other papers. Now that was the main effect. The real influence in the election of 1932 was of course the appalling economic conditions, the acute depression, the sense of impending doom and the complete inability of the government to produce any sort of policy to cope with it. It was this which ultimately broke through the fear of resumption of the Civil War, this stratification of political positions due to the Treaty, and so on. This might never have happened if the depression hadn't happened, or if the Cumann na nGaedheal government had a more active policy, initiated some campaign of any sort for industrial protection or agricultural development.

CHAPTER 4

1932: FROM GUNS TO GOVERNMENT

'The British government was trying to drive us by economic pressure, by starving our people, by destroying our economy to do what we think is wrong and, of course, we are not going to do it.'

The February 1932 Irish general election was the most critical in the history of the state, marking the transition from the victors of the Civil War to the defeated and confirming the primacy of the ballot box in the election.

The election was scheduled for 16 February 1932, though both Fianna Fáil and Fine Gael had been anticipating it for years and had prepared accordingly. The backdrop was the Great Depression, which affected Ireland as it did countries across the world. It caused a large drop in agricultural prices. Irish exports fell by 20 per cent between 1929 and 1931. Commodity prices for Irish farmers halved in those years. The Cumann na nGaedheal government responded by cutting the pay of public servants and reducing social welfare benefits, which increased its unpopularity.

Cumann na nGaedheal had a foreign policy triumph that it could not exploit at the ballot box. The Balfour Declaration of 1926 and the Statutes of Westminster in 1931 enshrined in law the autonomous nature of the dominions within the British Empire: the Irish Free State, Australia, New Zealand, Canada and South Africa. Yet Cumann na nGaedheal was seen by its critics as too deferential to the British. It was relentlessly pilloried as a party of west Brit toffs. The association in the minds of its opponents of Cumann na nGaedheal with privilege was encapsulated in Fianna Fáil's 1932 general election poster slogan paraphrasing Abraham Lincoln: 'Government by the rich for the rich'.

Cumann na nGaedheal countered by attempting to smear Fianna Fáil as a party in thrall to sinister forces. Its most famous election poster, 'The Shadow of a Gunman – keep it from your home' sought to portray Fianna Fáil as a party with a legacy of violence that could not be trusted to uphold law and order. It was in thrall to communists and its policies were 'un-Irish and un-Catholic' – the decision to boycott the papal nuncio two years previously had not been forgotten.

SL: By the time of the general election of 1932, we had a first-class organisation and we've never ceased to have one since – a really first-class and soundly based organisation. There was no parish in the country, no townland, no district that hadn't got an active cumann in it. They may have handled their job wrongly, they may have been over-enthusiastic or insufficiently active, but nevertheless, you felt that the organisation was nationwide in the fullest sense of the term and that in every district, even if you couldn't get round to it yourself, there was somebody there who would do what had to be done.

The 1932 general election was a success for Fianna Fáil, which increased its Dáil seats from 57 to 72, while Cumann na nGaedheal lost four seats. Fianna Fáil fell five seats short of an overall majority and formed a government with the support of the Labour Party, which won seven seats in the election. This was the start of 16 years of unbroken Fianna Fáil rule, but first there were febrile rumours of a coup by Free State officers who did not want the party to take power.

SL: There was a long interval between the election and the re-assembly of the Dáil. One reason was that there was an interval fixed in the order – three weeks, I think. And then there was a man named Patrick Reynolds[1] who was shot up in Leitrim – a Cumann na nGaedheal candidate – it wasn't a political shooting, but he was shot anyway, which meant another election there, you see.[2] And during that period there was undoubtedly a very strong sentiment amongst some of the army officers and guard officers that they shouldn't allow themselves to be run out of office.

They thought they were going to be sacked straight away. Ernest Blythe, I think, was to some extent involved in this – at least, Blythe would have gone along with it, if they had decided to set up a government by force.[3] Blythe, I think, would have taken the presidency of it; Cosgrave wouldn't. It was Cosgrave, I'd say, Cosgrave and Paddy Hogan,[4] who killed it, but it was certainly strong enough to cause real concern. The danger developed after the election, when it was clear that we were to become the government. Whoever was responsible, we all had our own armed guards given to us straight away. We were far more afraid of the armed guards than we were of the people who were likely to attack us, I can tell you that. But it was an indication that they knew there was a danger of some attempt on us.

There was an officer in the army by the name of Paddy Daly[5] – Paddy Daly was an army colonel who had been involved in a lot of the worst events that happened in Kerry, and probably felt that he had a lot of revenge due to him from people who would not hesitate to resort to it if they got the opportunity. He had circulated a document to all these army officers urging them to organise, asking were they going to allow themselves to be sacked and of course their pensions – there were pensions in all this. We had as part of our pre-election policy the abolition of military service pensions and indeed one of the large propaganda posters which we were using. There was an enormous double crown poster with the list of all the pensioners and the amount they were getting, published under the heading 'What price glory?', which was a very personal attack on the individuals concerned, and in this circular Paddy Daly issued there was the question: 'Do we really want to lose our pensions?' Well, almost after the change of government, de Valera said 'We're not going to do this.' There were two ways of handling the inequalities created by the introduction of military pensions to anybody who took the pro-Treaty side. Instead of abolishing the pensions we decided to give pensions to those who took the anti-Treaty side, and that levelled it up, but it must have been touch and go, I think, for some time as to whether in fact those who wanted to would have been able to organise some sort of military coup. Once they failed they failed completely, because you have to remember that the Blueshirt movement,[6] which developed later on, had very much the same origin and the same sentiments; but when the showdown came it was a question of the army coming out to stop the Blueshirts, and they showed no hesitation over it, although there had been changes in the army personnel and we had supplemented the Gardaí at that time.

Lemass was made Minister for Industry and Commerce in the first Fianna Fáil government, a post he was to hold for most of the next 16 years, with the exception of the war period, when he was briefly Minister for Supplies. At 32 he was the youngest minister in a European government at that time. Lemass was determined from the beginning to implement the protectionist policies that he first proposed to Fianna Fáil in 1929 and were the basis of the party's economic platform when it assumed office in 1932. The department he inherited was the biggest in the state with a thousand civil servants.

SL: I could do a lot of work then that I could not do now. Indeed, in that regard, the surprising thing to me was that after the election of 1932, after the election campaign was over, I was completely exhausted. Within a matter of weeks I was minister, and by that time this fatigue had disappeared. It disappeared within a day. There is a photograph of the first Fianna Fáil government and you can see me there with all the signs of fatigue and strain and yet, within a day or two, the novelty of the new work, the enthusiasm of having to get on with this work made me forget all about this sense of tiredness and fatigue. I suppose this would be true of everyone – a change of occupation does also tend to give you new sources of strength and energy. All through that period I have a recollection of being exceedingly busy – busy in the political sense because of the realisation that, with a minority government, the next election would not be five years hence.

DR: When Fianna Fáil formed the government in 1932 the policy which you put forward, which I understand you had developed over the previous years, was all-round protection (in order to strengthen home industries), relief for the farmers from rates, and the abolition of the oath. Perhaps I could ask you how you found your first hundred days.

SL: Well, it was not really hard to settle into the routine of administration – at least I did not find it so. This could be partly due to the fact that I had to reorganise the Department of Industry and Commerce. The then secretary was Lord Glenavy,[7] who had resigned, but was carrying on until his successor was appointed, and the rest of the department had been inactive for a long time. [Patrick] McGilligan[8] had been minister before me and also Minister for External Affairs – he appears to have had very little interest in Industry and Commerce and gave most of his time, I gather, to the Department of External Affairs. After some consideration, I invited Johnny [John Leydon][9] to become secretary and that was the beginning of our association, which lasted all his official career.

It will help you to understand the situation if I tell you the things that happened on the first day. Glenavy brought me over to the department to meet all the other officers of the department. He said, 'I'll bring them all in one by one' and he mentioned the name [Robert] Ferguson.

Anyway, I said to Glenavy, 'There's no good spending the whole day seeing them one by one – bring them all in together'. 'Well,' he said, 'there is a bit of difficulty about that. You see Ferguson doesn't talk to the man who was director of statistics at the time, Stanley Lyon,[10] and he doesn't talk to [Edward J.] Riordan',[11] who was the director of industry, and Riordan and

Lyon did not talk to one another, so they would not come into the same room together.

This indicated a completely disorganised state in the department. After lunch, I was to meet Riordan ... and the private secretary who had been McGilligan's private secretary began to wheel in trays carrying files – I suppose about 50 files – and began to stack them up on the floor of the department. I said: 'What is this all about?' He said: 'Well, Mr Riordan has a lot of grievances about the department and he wants all these files, to establish his case.'

This Riordan was not, of course, very competent. He had not been a civil servant before – he had been a director of the National Industrial Development Association in Cork and had been appointed to this job of director in the Department of Industry and Commerce and, of course, not being an established civil servant – being a person brought in, as it were, to show the civil servants how to do their job – he was getting no co-operation from those above him or below him and he was completely incapable of handling the situation himself.

When Leydon was appointed secretary, I told him that this was the situation in the department – that it was just impossible and that it was his job to clean it up and he did in a matter of hours. He got them all in together and said that anybody who was not prepared to work in full co-operation, to forget all this damn nonsense, he would take his resignation now, and within a very short time, Leydon had the department running as it should be.

Now of course, for the first time, the department began to have work to do. In the first budget of 1932 an enormous number of new duties were imposed. This involved putting on the department the operation of these duties; … examination of the situation which justified the duties and drafting the necessary legislation for them. In a very short time this involved a great deal of promotions in the department. Men were given responsibilities which were inappropriate to their grade and they had been brought up to another grade. I remember particularly two who proved to be the most useful officers I had for all that period. One was a man named J.B. Connell,[12] who ultimately left the department. He was then only a principal officer, but he left the department to become managing director of the Sugar Company some years later. For the first time they were no longer going into the office and reading their papers and dealing with complaints. They now had to work out policies and to recommend decisions. They had to get things organised so that the work we were trying to do could be done. In a very short time, the department changed altogether.

So far as I was concerned, after a few initial changes and removals of people who were obviously incapable of doing work because they had not been doing any for a long time, the department began to work, and work with me, and work very enthusiastically. A large part of the success in the Department of Industry and Commerce was with John Leydon. He was the man whose job it was to get it done. As the department grew, as new activities came in – the development of the air services, Irish Shipping, and all these things – he took on a tremendous burden himself, but of course his department had to grow in size also. Eventually, it developed into two deputy secretaries, and four assistant secretaries. This was something unknown in 1932 and represented a hierarchy of very competent people.

Major industries in Ireland such as the tobacco, soap and confectionery industries were mostly owned by British multinationals such as Imperial Tobacco and Lever Brothers. This became a political problem because indigenous manufacturers could not compete. It was also a priority for the incoming Fianna Fáil government and a key piece of legislation introduced by Lemass – the Control of Manufactures Act 1932, which was designed to minimise foreign ownership of Irish businesses.

DR: One rather major thing you undertook very quickly after that tiring 1932 election was that – the election took place in February – by June you introduced the Control of Manufactures Act.

SL: Yes, this was an exceptional time in that the effort to get industry established would not be successful in the prevailing conditions of the economic slump, mainly by the imposition of tariffs alone. You also had to protect those who might embark upon the establishment of industry here, against the inevitability of competition coming from outside, from the English firms that had been supplying the Irish market. They had this sense that we were only a flash in the pan as a government, that whatever we did in this regard would be undone again in a very short time by the Cumann na nGaedheal government when they came back into office.

There was no enthusiasm at all on the part of any of the British firms that had been involved in the market here to risk themselves here, partly because of the political set-up and partly because of the world economic slump, which deprived them of resources for investment. We felt therefore that the only prospect of getting industry off the ground at that stage was to rely upon

Irish-owned firms, by giving them the assurance that if they did put their money into building factories and so on, that they would not then be faced with the competition of the old suppliers to the market who could come in after them. There was also this idea of trying to decentralise industry. This was the first attempt we had to devise means of encouraging the decentralisation of industry from Dublin and that Act did contain [a] provision that … an exclusive licence could be given to manufacture goods where the minister directed. My recollection is that the only case in which that was exercised was in connection with the manufacture of sewing cotton in a factory in Westport.[13]

They got this exclusive licence, but even that did not stick. Sunbeam, I think, subsequently started manufacturing sewing cotton, and what could we do about it? Nobody shuts down Sunbeam just because of this! That particular policy was a failure – that effort to try to get the decentralisation of industry by compulsion in that way by giving exclusive manufacture licences. It exposed the firms that got an exclusive licence – a monopoly, as it were – to a great deal of hostility in the trade. Ultimately the only successful method for decentralisation came much later when the industrial grants were established – and that was to give larger grant to the persons who went west, to say to him that the further west he went the larger the grant he would get. That produced some result.

DR: Was the main disapproval of proposals of foreign persons establishing industries in Ireland because it was felt that local industry could not stand up to foreign …

SL: That it wouldn't start. Many people came in to discuss projects with me to set up the manufacture of clothing, footwear and things of that kind, but they all said: 'we won't do this if the firm that previously was supplying the market and has the goodwill of the retail trade are going to come in and set up a factory as they would get the trade and we would be out of business'. There was tremendous hostility to the whole policy of industrial development from the buyers of the big houses. These people were the key men in it. They presumably had some personal advantage in maintaining the old situation where they went to London and did their buying for the year and so on. It would be certain that if they got the chance of going back to the old supplier as distinct from an Irish firm, they would do so.

DR: Could one say that the Control of Manufactures Bill in respect of foreign persons entirely arose from this – there was no, as it were, policy of preventing ownership of Irish sources of production from lying in foreign hands.

SL: There was to some extent. I would say that the primary reason was to get Irish people interested in the idea of investing in industry by giving them this further protection – protection not only against the importation of goods, but protection against those who were making them previously coming in and setting up to their detriment. This developed to a later stage where the ideal of maintaining control on Irish firms was related to the planning of industrial growth, because it was quite clear that many of the industries we wanted in Ireland would require foreign ownership or foreign participation of some sort and this gave us a measure of control over them. We were able to influence their development, location and the type of business they did. There was at this time, of course, no thought at all of exports. The idea of Irish goods being exported, with some limited exceptions, was hard to promote, in the circumstances of the world depression which existed. There was an effort made to restore the export trade which Irish woollen manufacturers had previously – at one time they had a very successful export trade. When they got their protection from the government they just transferred this export trade to the home market. Their overall production remained much the same and they were exporting nothing and just supplying the home market, which was now an easy market for them. Perhaps protection in the home market may not have been a good thing because they all just settled down to the easy business of producing the goods that they wanted to produce, selling them to the home market, giving the home market, even, no choice in respect of designs.

One of the key provisions of the Control of Manufactures Act 1932 was that foreign-owned companies had to apply to the state for a licence to operate. Fianna Fáil believed protectionism for Irish industry was pointless unless there was also Irish control of the industries involved. He hoped that such a provision would ensure that native rather than foreign-owned industry thrived in the state.

DR: To some extent, in adopting a policy subsequently on the introduction of foreign capital you had a difficult decision to make. Did you find that change-over …

SL: Ah this was after the war. This fundamental change in policy took place after the war. By then we had recognised all the weaknesses of the 1930s policies. I might add that the circumstances of the 1930s had changed also. It is very difficult to envisage nowadays a situation in which factories in Britain were closing down by the hundreds, unemployment in Britain had risen to five or six million, in America you had the same situation and world trade was diminishing.

To try to develop new industrial capacity, new industrial production in these times – it was very difficult to try to get people to undertake it. They would have been much wiser doing so. Capital goods were cheap, so the capital cost of setting up new industry was at the lowest point of the century and firms that did set up in those days started off, ultimately, with tremendous advantages because of the very low initial outlays they had to undertake. Also in my period in Industry and Commerce I came up against this problem of people coming along with a proposition to set up some important industry with no very definite intention of doing so. It was a matter of taking an option on the right to do so. This was a problem with a lot of these Irish-owned groups in the 1930s and then immediately after the war, after the first Labour government took office in Britain, we were flooded by English firms making propositions of this kind, most of which never developed at all, and this, I felt, was what they were doing.

The first Fianna Fáil government lasted less than a year. Its dependency on the Labour Party became an irritant to de Valera, although it backed him on the two major issues of the day. The first was the non-payment of the land annuities to the British government and the second was de Valera's pledge to abolish the Oath of Allegiance. Matters came to a head at the end of 1932 when de Valera proposed cutting civil servants' wages because of the economic downturn. Labour promised to fight the cuts with every means at its disposal. De Valera took the party at its word and brought down the government before Labour Party leader William Norton got the chance to do it. The general election was scheduled for 24 January 1933.

SL: The fact was that we were in office with the support of the Labour Party and by January of 1933 a situation arose in which it was obvious that the Labour Party could not support us or would not support us or would not continue to support us on a particular bill. This arose out of what was then the established practice in regard to the civil service.

The civil service remuneration was related to the cost of living – it went up and down with the cost of living – and that time the cost of living was going down and going down fairly rapidly in the economic slump of the time so that by January of 1933 a considerable cut in civil service salaries, and this went right down to postmen,[14] was automatically due to take place and this was obviously something that the Labour Party would find it difficult to support. We decided rather than compromise on this arrangement or make it obvious that our withdrawal from it was due to Labour Party pressure, that we would have another election. That was the main reason for it. I doubt if the election would have taken place then if it had not been for this inevitable Dáil crisis as soon as the Dáil reassembled at the beginning of that year.

There were no negotiations. They had announced their intention to support the Fianna Fáil party as the largest party before the Dáil met. There was an arrangement made by which a weekly meeting between [William] Norton and some other members of the party and members of the government took place just to discuss events to make them familiar with intentions regarding legislation and that sort of thing. This did not work out very well. If I told this conference that I was going to introduce the Unemployment Assistance Act,[15] within a few days there would be a speech from Norton demanding the government should produce the Unemployment Assistance Act. In other words, he was trying to exaggerate the influence of his party on government policy and to take the credit in advance for everything the government did that would be popular from his party's point of view.

The 1933 general election vindicated de Valera's decision to call a snap election. Fianna Fáil got an overall majority of one (77/153) and almost exactly half the vote (49.7 per cent). Cumann na nGaedheal, fighting its last election under that banner, lost eight seats and ended up with 48. The short-lived National Centre Party won 11 seats and merged with Cumann na nGaedheal and the Army Comrades Association (ACA) to form Fine Gael in September 1933.

SL: The election took place in the middle of winter, in the coldest winter in living memory. The most hazardous part of it was travelling in the country on icy roads. But nevertheless, the political situation at the time was such that you could still count on enormous crowds at meetings, notwithstanding the fact that it was freezing. There would be a great turnout of people at public meetings which you would not get at all now, but of course there was no other means of communication except public meetings and no television service and radio was very inadequate, if used at all for political purposes.

I think we were fairly confident in the outcome of the election.

But you want to remember what had happened was that we were the outlaw party, the anti-Treaty party, the party about whom it was said in 1932, when we came into power, that the streets of Dublin would run red with blood and we would be out for revenge and the Civil War would start all over again. A year later nothing of that kind had happened. A lot of useful legislation had been enacted and some effort to develop a national economic plan had been apparent and consequently therefore we could go to the electorate in January 1933 fairly certain that all the old type of campaign against us would no longer be paid any attention to.

The Fianna Fáil government of the 1930s is most associated with the Economic War. It arose out of de Valera's unilateral decision in June 1932 to cancel annuity payments to the British government. These were payments made by Irish farmers who had bought land through the various land acts put through by the British pre-independence. They were a source of resentment within Irish nationalism because of the perception that Irish farmers were paying for land that had once been owned by Anglo-Irish landlords who had no right to it in the first place. Fianna Fáil also argued that the terms of the settlement of the Boundary Commission in 1925 absolved the Irish state from handing over the annuities to the British.

The £3 million paid to the British government every year was a serious drain on Irish resources at the time. The British immediately retaliated by putting a 20 per cent tariff on all imported Irish goods and hit Irish farmers hard by imposing quotas on livestock. The Irish Free State, in turn, imposed import duties on goods from Britain. The Economic War caused serious hardship in Ireland and was resented by industrialists and the larger farmers, but it was popular with the public in general. De Valera made it a key platform for himself in the 1933 general election, contrasting his stance with the outgoing government, which insisted the annuities must be paid. Lemass was sceptical and told de Valera bluntly that the economic pain involved was threatening a 'crisis as grave as that of 1847'. He felt Ireland was not ready for an economic war against a much bigger adversary.

SL: There was, of course, a doubt for a while as to the consequences of the Economic War on the electoral results. There was real hardship. Farmers were in a really desperate situation. All the benefits of the policy which we followed had been experienced mainly by urban workers – the housing drive, the new industries, and all the rest of it, the Unemployment Assistance Act – all these were of benefit to urban workers and not to farmers. While something had been done for farmers – the guaranteed price for meat had been introduced, a minimum price of threepence per gallon for milk had been established – threepence per gallon, believe it or not – and even at that we used to have to sell it at a loss. Things of that kind had been done. But I suppose our main lines were that we were in battle with the old enemy and we could not accept his dictation. The British government was trying to drive us by economic pressure, by starving our people, by destroying our economy to do what we think is wrong and, of course, we are not going to do it. This effort, of course, was very strong.

The 1930s was a time of fractious politics between right and left, fascism and socialism/communism across Europe. In the Irish Free State, the new Fianna Fáil government lifted the ban on the IRA in

March 1932. The Army Comrades Association (ACA) was set up by former Free State army officers following the electoral defeat of Cumann na nGaedheal. It quickly attracted some of the leading figures in the party. In February 1933 Éamon de Valera dismissed the Garda Commissioner Eoin O'Duffy, whom de Valera rightly suspected of planning a coup against him. Five months later, O'Duffy was offered and accepted the role of president of the ACA. By that stage the ACA had already adopted the blue shirts which gave rise to one of the most infamous monikers in Irish history – the Blueshirts. The organisation was banned on 8 December 1933.

SL: Remember we are now in an overall majority. It is obvious that there will not be another election for five years. The Cumann na nGaedheal party is deeply divided between the Blueshirts and the non-Blueshirt elements. The Blueshirt people were very active, but active in a way which was not getting them public support. They were blocking the roads, not paying rates and shooting at cars and that sort of thing, which was not winning any support for the Cumann na nGaedheal party. The other element of the Cumann na nGaedheal party were inactive and when the Blueshirts ultimately disappeared, Cumann na nGaedheal was very much in decline. They had lost even the enthusiasm for political action and their Dáil opposition was minimal. In many sessions of the Dáil they were quite short and an enormous amount of legislation went through with very little debate.

The opposition had lost heart, so you did not have the same political worries at all or the same need for political action until the election of 1937 began to appear on the horizon, which came at the full efflux of time. So, apart from the by-elections, there was no need to pay great attention to political work at that time. We were on the ascendant. Our organisation was growing of its own accord because all the people who had hesitated to come with us because of these policy disagreements between the mere assertion of the institution of the living republic and the acceptance of the Treaty to work to a policy – all that had disappeared and many of those who had been opposed to it began to come in and to be active and ultimately emerge as Fianna Fáil deputies, and that sort of thing, so we did not have to work hard to maintain our organisation at that time. It was in full strength, and growing in strength, rather than anything else.

One of the many significant problems faced by the Irish state was the attitude to it shown by the banking sector. The feeling existed that Irish banks remained oriented to London and were reluctant to support the government in building up Irish industry. The de Valera government established two banking commissions in the 1930s – one in 1934 and another in 1938. Their remit was to examine the 'system in Saorstát Éireann of currency, banking, credit, public borrowing and lending and pledging of State credit on behalf of agriculture, industry and the social services'. The commission met against the background of the publication of John Maynard Keynes's theories on the role of the state in Western economies. Keynes argued that government should borrow during times of recession to stimulate the economy. He also advocated borrowing for investment in the economy. His theories made a big impression on Lemass.

SL: The banking commission was one of [Seán] MacEntee's ideas. We were all pressing for fundamental revision of financial policy. We all felt that we were a way behind the rest of the world in this area becoming aware of our own deficiencies in understanding the implications of this policy. We felt it was Finance's obligation to come forward with ideas for change in this regard. Keynes had been published. Keynes was unorthodox at the beginning, but he had been influencing opinion in other governments. A great deal of newspaper comment and books were being published dealing with this new conception of economics which Keynes had started at this time and we were way behind the rest of the world in this area and felt that we should be finding out how these new ideas applied to our circumstances. But nothing was happening, we were not doing anything about it. Ultimately under pressure that something should be done, MacEntee came up with this idea for this banking commission.

The commission was appointed by him and it was probably unfortunate that those who had the understanding that there was a different approach to these problems in Ireland were mainly slightly headcases. We got no breakthrough in the banking area until John Leydon left the government and went into the banking world – he is now chairman of the National Bank.[16] He was the first man to introduce any sort of innovation into banking practice here, but once he did, the others began to follow suit and there has been a complete change of outlook ever since then. The various investment operations that banks are now undertaking and the combinations they have achieved for various purposes are things that would have been inconceivable then. At that time their job was to take in their clients' money and invest it in England.

DR: Eventually, by the beginning of 1935, trade agreements had been made with 18 countries.

SL: Yes, during the Economic War we naturally tried to develop trade with countries other than Great Britain, but of course it was a difficult, almost an impossible operation in times of economic crisis. Every country's trade was going down. Every country was enhancing its trade barriers. Where they did not stop trade by trade barriers, they stopped it by currency restraints of one kind or another. Nevertheless, we did try to pursue negotiations for trade agreements with countries other than Britain. The practical result was not very much; the political result was more obvious. The public saw us trying to promote trade elsewhere, but we did not get much trade.

CHAPTER 5

THE MUNICH BOTHER

'This was real political genius of the highest order which nobody else would have been capable of – anyone else would have put a foot wrong, or would have been tough, when it was unwise to be tough or weak, when it was unwise to be weak.'

In the mid-1930s Éamon de Valera mostly busied himself with constitutional affairs while Lemass tended to a struggling economy. In 1936 de Valera took advantage of the constitutional crisis in the UK to swiftly pass the External Relations Act. It abolished the officer of the governor-general, the British monarch's representative in Ireland. However, as Ireland remained part of the Commonwealth, the British monarch retained the prerogative of accrediting Irish representatives (ambassadors) abroad. This was done by de Valera in the forlorn hope that retaining some connection with the Crown would make it easier to persuade unionists of the benefits of a united Ireland. In 1937 de Valera introduced Bunreacht na hÉireann (the Irish Constitution), which was passed by the Irish public in a referendum on 1 July that year. A general election was held on the same day; Fianna Fáil fell short of an overall majority by one seat, though the party retained power. Lemass topped the poll once again in Dublin South with nearly 16,000 first preference votes. In January 1938 de Valera began negotiations with the British to try to bring the Economic War to an end.

DR: In 1938 there were the important negotiations with Britain?

SL: 1938, of course, was the year of the British negotiations. I do not remember who took the initiative. We had been leading up to negotiations for a settlement of that dispute for some years past. There had been a modified agreement under which we agreed to exchange coal for cattle[1] and the possibility of settling it was always being mentioned, but I suppose the real initiative came from the British and came because of the deterioration in the international situation – the assumption of the inevitability of war with Germany, the desire to protect their western flank by buying peace from Ireland and possibly, of course, by buying Irish participation in the war when it came. This, I think, was the main attraction. They hoped that they would secure not merely a neutral Ireland, which would be a good thing in the case of war, but actual Irish participation in the war. This opened the negotiations. I was not personally concerned in the political end of the negotiations. De Valera used to discuss these with us and when we sat in on the preliminary sessions of the negotiations all the talking was done by de Valera. If we had any comment to make upon the course of the discussion, or any suggestion to make, we wrote it down and passed it up to him.

Every evening the delegation as such would sit in conference and discuss the events of the day, discuss the arguments that had been used pro and con different propositions, and generally acted as a conference on our own behalf, in that regard. This related mainly to the purely practical things – financial settlement, the trade agreement, and I think de Valera told us fairly fully the outcome of his private conversations with Neville Chamberlain, but you could not be quite sure as de Valera played his cards very close to the chest in these matters and was probably pressing Neville Chamberlain for something that was impossible, that the British prime minister could not undertake by himself.

But I will say this for him – he developed a tremendous respect for Chamberlain and was always ready to move to his defence in subsequent years when he appeared to be in disgrace. He never missed the opportunity to pay a tribute to him in public, when this could be done appropriately. He had for Neville Chamberlain quite a considerable personal respect and was probably, more than anything else in the world, regretful of events which not merely put Chamberlain out of power, but created the misconception where he appeared to be in disgrace, or something like this.[2] I will say that there was a lot of unfair criticism of Chamberlain on the grounds that he tried to keep peace with Hitler and Mussolini, and he probably was unwise to come back from Munich waving his bit of paper and saying, 'This means peace in our time.' But, in fact, Britain was not prepared for war at the time, neither physically nor morally, and a lot of the criticism of Chamberlain and his lack of preparations for war and of this Munich agreement came from people on the Labour side in Britain, who had been fiercely opposing the rearmament programme. He did gain them a year in which they were able to improve their armaments, particularly their air force, which made it possible for them to win the war.

To gain time he had to pretend to be satisfied with his talks with Hitler and his agreement with Hitler and to pretend to believe that Hitler was going to keep his word. Whether he did or not, I do not know. This will probably never be known until he reveals, if he ever did reveal, his own particular thinking. It could be that he genuinely believed that Hitler was sincere in giving him these assurances, but of course that belief could only have lasted a few months, because Hitler was in the Sudetenland a few months afterwards and marshalling his armies along the eastern frontiers of Germany, so that any private assurance he got from Hitler, any undertaking as regards the Germans being satisfied with their existing frontiers, was soon proved worthless. In no time Britain was frantically building up her armaments, and the very fact that there was no diminution, but rather an acceleration of their re-armament programme, would suggest that not all of them – perhaps not even Chamberlain – believed that any reliance could be put on Hitler's undertaking. It could be that without saying, 'This means peace in our time', coming back from Munich, he would not have got that time.

Chamberlain was a type of prime minister who wanted to keep everything in his own hands. He himself did not appear to have any capacity to delegate. He handled all the foreign affairs aspects of government and apparently disregarded the views of colleagues and all the rest of it, and often took action without consulting them, or without getting their concurrence. He was a queer type of person. He started life as a social reformer and still had that reforming zeal and was a stubborn character, though he did not look it.

DR: In fact, he was a single-minded type of man; whereas Churchill gave the impression of being tremendously dictatorial and single-minded, in fact Chamberlain was equally so?

SL: I think so, and even more so because I think he often irritated his cabinet colleagues by his failure to consult with them and bring them along with him in their own areas. I remember Chamberlain well. He was a dry sort of character, but he had a sense of humour – you could get a spark of humour out of him, even though he did not look like a man who had a sense of humour until you probed deeper.

There were quite a number of conferences between de Valera and Neville Chamberlain, the prime minister – the two of them by themselves, with nobody else present. We knew that de Valera was trying to get Chamberlain committed on the subject of partition and he made considerable progress with Chamberlain. He got a private undertaking from Chamberlain that he would endeavour to bring about a change of attitude in the British government and in the British people towards partition and shortly after that, in the British House of Commons, Chamberlain, for the first time, said what we wanted him to say – namely that the British government will not oppose the reunification of Ireland if the Irish people wanted it, if the two sections of Ireland could come together in direct negotiation, and agree upon something. Whatever they agreed to, the British government would accept.

It soon became clear that the British wanted a settlement, that this settlement was going to be comprehensive, that they were hoping that it would lead to some form of military agreement, whereas de Valera was trying to extend it to cover partition in some form. There were one or two interesting things that I remember at the time. The big question for the British was the extent to which German submarines might be facilitated in Ireland and make British defence impossible. This had been argued for some time in the course of the preliminary negotiations – how important it was, in the event of a war, that Britain should have protection against submarines from the west, should have facilities for an anti-submarine campaign there. All this ended when a man named [Thomas Inskip],[3] who was Minister for Coordination of Defence in the British government, came in and said that this was something which was no longer a menace as the new sonar device[4] which they had installed enabled a submarine to be located underwater. This meant the elimination of the submarine as an instrument of war, so they were no longer concerned about their anti-submarine defences or their possession of ports in Ireland or the danger to them of Germans getting re-fuelled in Irish ports, and so that was that. Of course, this proved to be completely wrong in the end. Radar certainly was a useful device but the German submarine still became the greatest menace they had during the war. They were in a negotiating position from which they had to withdraw in the sense that it was obvious that they were not going to get from us facilities at Irish ports for anti-submarine war. This was one way of withdrawing.

The trade negotiations went on simultaneously with the political negotiations and it was almost the only time, in my lifetime, that we entered into trade negotiations with the British having bargaining advantages in the sense that the prime minister, the head of the government [Neville Chamberlain] had said to the Board of Trade and the Commonwealth relations man – Malcolm MacDonald,[5] that there had got to be a trade agreement. This meant therefore that we could bargain with the knowledge that the other people could not hold out unreasonably against any propositions that were put before them. We got a good trade agreement: we got this free access to Great Britain, the right to maintain protection here, subject to a preferential rate for the British, and, on the agricultural side, acceptance of the principle that the Irish farmer had the same right of access to the British market as the British farmer and that there could be no arrangement in Britain which would give the British farmer an advantage in British markets over Irish farmers. This did not last very long.

The war came a year later; controls were introduced and they lasted for ten years after the war and by then the British had established their subsidy system, so that, in fact we never really got the benefit of that trade agreement as far as agriculture was concerned, but it was the principle we set out to establish that the Irish farmer selling to the British market did so on completely equal terms with the British farmer. The conclusion of the trade agreement was regarded as being satisfactory.

The British estimated that Irish farmers still owed £78 million in annuity payments, but they decided to settle for a one-off payment of £10 million. In return the British agreed to return the ports of Berehaven, Spike Island and Lough Swilly to Ireland. Britain and Ireland removed all duties that had been placed on each other's goods, though Ireland was allowed to impose duties on a number of imports from Britain to protect its new industries. De Valera did not make the same catastrophic mistake he had made during the Anglo-Irish Treaty negotiations by staying away. From beginning to end he was front and centre of the talks that ended the Economic War. He won praise at home and abroad for his diplomatic breakthrough, yet he still had only a minority government. Once again, he decided to call a snap general election in pursuit of an overall majority. Despite the pain resulting from the Economic War, the Irish public backed him. He won 77 seats (a majority being 70) and 51.9 per cent of the vote, the highest percentage vote

ever given to a single party in an Irish general election. This was not reflected in Lemass's first preference vote, which actually decreased, but he still topped the poll in Dublin South with ease.

SL: The payment of the lump sum of £10 million to get rid of the land annuities was of no importance; the restoration of the ports – ports which were still occupied by the British and fortified by them – to Irish sovereignty was regarded as a tremendous achievement, which it was and, of course, it had a very definite significance in relation to the war which began twelve months later, and the trade agreement was good. We came back here and got defeated on some trivial business in the Dáil.[6] We had not got a majority in the Dáil after the 1937 election and, of course, with considerable enthusiasm, the Dáil was dissolved. Another election was then held which gave us a fairly substantial majority.

It could not have been more perfect and in fact those of us who were concerned with that aspect of affairs were looking for a pretext to have an election. Then we got one handed to us on a plate by a snap vote in the Dáil! That was the big event in 1938 and it had tremendous significance in relation to the subsequent war situation. Of course, it would have been much more important if there had been no war, because then you could have sat down at once to build up a tremendously strong development programme. The sort of political antagonism to Irish industrial development and all the rest of it, which had been holding us up vis-à-vis Britain would have disappeared, agriculture would have benefited enormously, so in every sense the war was a disaster for us.

No doubt de Valera had in mind at that time, having got this reorientation of British policy on partition, and the promise of Chamberlain to be forthcoming on it, to open some direct line of contact with the North. But the whole thing was knocked down because of the IRA campaign, the bombing campaign.

Lemass is referring to Operation Sabotage, which arose out of a decision by the IRA Army Council in January 1939 to declare war on Britain on behalf of the Irish people, who, naturally, were never consulted about the decision and would never have agreed to it. Though its declaration was met with universal derision, the IRA was in deadly earnest. Operation Sabotage involved more than 300 attacks in Britain in 1939. Power plants, London Underground tunnels and railway stations were targeted, culminating in the deaths of five people on 25 August 1939, when bombs went off in Coventry, just a week before the start of the Second World War.

SL: Indeed, this was so contrary to Irish interests at the time that I always suspected that the British secret service was behind it, that the IRA had been infiltrated by some secret service man who was opposed to this idea – some ultra-conservative section of the British secret service – and that they had perhaps inspired the idea and perhaps were even facilitating it. I was deeply suspicious of the whole business, and indeed both then and for quite a long time afterwards, I held the idea that the IRA was undoubtedly being influenced by some hostile element of that kind. It always seemed to become active whenever it suited this ultra-conservative element in Great Britain that it should become active or did the very things that were going to destroy whatever hopes were emerging from our political activities. Certainly, at that time it was the most disastrous thing that could have happened.

During 1938 these ports – Cobh and Swilly – were taken over with a great deal of ceremonial. The surprising thing about that whole business was the opposition of the Labour Party to the agreement – opposition to the taking over of the ports on the grounds that their maintenance was going to cost the Irish taxpayer money. This could have been just politics, but it was very stupid politics and I was sure they would live to regret it.[7] Here was the Economic War ended, here were the full normal trade relations restored, the prospect of economic progress considerably advanced by reason of the trade agreement, and it caused a surprising amount of opposition in the Dáil. Of course, there was no opposition in the country – it led to the big electoral success of 1938, where we went up from 69 to 77 seats and Fine Gael and Labour went down by reason of their opposition. That was an easy election. You knew the tide was with you; you knew that public opinion was with you; you knew you had a clear issue, namely for or against this settlement with England, and there was no special difficulty in the election campaign at all.

DR: You were saying there, Mr Lemass, that it was de Valera's problem of reconciling the changes. To what extent did you accept his views unquestioningly? And did you, as a younger man, say, 'What he decides'.

SL: Oh, completely in these political issues and that was true all the time. I always felt that in these areas of main political activity he was far superior to anyone I know. He had a capacity for longsightedness and understanding of the situation. In that area I was completely in subordination, but when we came down to talk about economic policies we used to have furious arguments and I wouldn't subordinate my judgement at all, but in this wide area of general policy confidence in his leadership was increasing all the time by the enormous success of that first Fianna Fáil government in finally demolishing the Treaty altogether – only a matter of three or four years, and at the end of it the British government accepted the whole business in the early part of 1938. This was real political genius of the highest order which nobody else would have been capable of – anyone else would have put a foot wrong, or would have been tough, when it was unwise to be tough or weak, when it was unwise to be weak.

He was able to walk the middle course all the time, to take advantage of every opportunity that emerged and eventually created a situation where five years after he became head of the government again the Treaty was dead and without any ill effects, even in the matter of relationship with Great Britain. As I say, he alone was capable of that and I accepted that, and, in these areas, I just sat and heard what he had decided and rarely attempted to argue with him.

CHAPTER 6

SECOND WORLD WAR: MINISTER FOR SUPPLIES

'I said at one time in the Dáil that if the necessity arose for me to make an order prohibiting men wearing trousers, the public would accept this until the day they saw one man wearing trousers. Do you follow me?'[1]

The 1938 agreement was a relief for Lemass, who could now concentrate on his role in the Department of Industry and Commerce without having to deal with the imposition of punitive tariffs on Irish goods, but the relief was short-lived. The outbreak of the Second World War on 1 September 1939 would prove to be the sternest test of the Irish state's sovereignty. For the next five and a half years Éamon de Valera resisted ferocious pressure from the Americans and the British to join the fight against Nazi Germany. There was also a real threat in 1940 of a Nazi invasion of Ireland. Immediately after war was declared, Lemass resigned his position as Minister for Industry and Commerce to take up the newly created role as Minister for Supplies. This was a recognition by de Valera that the country was now prioritising survival over development. Lemass's department had been planning for another world war as far back as 1935. An emergencies supply branch had been set up in 1938 to stockpile essential commodities for six months in the event of war. He told Ryan:

SL: One of the things we had done before the war was to urge every factory to stock up with raw materials and a lot of them did this. At that time the Department of Finance interfered to some extent. Nevertheless, many factories throughout the country were in fact very well stocked with raw materials by the time the war started. We were able to keep up normal production. We did not have to introduce clothes rationing, for example, until '42 or '43. All the clothing factories and the mills were producing cloth.

At the beginning of the war de Valera warned that the success of the Department of Supplies 'will largely depend how far we shall be able to escape the larger evils which are consequent on the general disruption caused by this war'. His department controlled the supply and distribution of everything from trouser buttons to petrol. No Irish government had as much control over the lives of its citizens until the Covid-19 pandemic. In June 1940 the government assigned his department control of the price and of the export and import of all commodities as well as the 'regulation of the treatment, keeping, movement, distribution, sale, purchase, use and consumption of articles of all kinds'. Lemass's role in the wartime government gave him unprecedented power over the daily lives of Irish citizens, power that surpassed even the power he later had as taoiseach. He also remained part of de Valera's wartime kitchen cabinet on the critical issue of defence and security.

SL: As far as national policy was concerned, keeping out of the war and avoiding the multitudinous difficulties and threats which emerged in the international situation were the main problems. Now de Valera dealt with political problems himself. I was involved as a member of the government, but I would have been perhaps less intimately involved than some ministers as the problems arising in [the Department of] Justice handling the IRA situation. I gave my opinion when it was asked [for], and I gave it sometimes when it was not asked [for].

My time was concentrated on the work of the Department of Industry and Commerce and Supplies and I did not try to influence the course of events in any aspects of government policy to a greater degree than anyone else. Now at the outbreak of the war, of course, there was a very deep concern about the possibility of an IRA situation prejudicing our neutrality – the possibility of the IRA making some contact with the Germans or the German Secret Service and behaving in a manner which would justify the British taking action against us.[2]

A lot of the legislation at that period immediately before and after the war was designed to give us power to deal with that situation and of course we began the war, I think, by interning 800 of them, or something of that kind. This was not necessary merely to prevent their being able to do anything effective, but it was also necessary as a sort of indication of our intention not to allow them to do anything effective. We passed the Emergency Powers Act during the war,[3] and I think that came rather late. It was a very comprehensive act, and yet it wasn't comprehensive enough.

The government began to rapidly expand the defence forces. The numbers doubled from 20,000 at the start of the war and reached a high of 41,000 full-time soldiers in June 1941 while the reserve, the Local Defence Force, was built up to 106,000 men. At its height approximately 250,000 men were in the Irish defence forces. The prospect of invasion was most acute in 1940, but the German inability to control the skies over southern England saw the imminent danger of a similar invasion of Ireland pass.

SL: This type of [passive] resistance, of which I suppose Ghandi was the great exponent, can be very effective, but it would only work with certain classes of people. Most people try to avoid getting involved in a row but once involved they will fight back. The Danes, before the war, abolished their army on the grounds that they were incapable of effective defence against any neighbours who might invade them.[4] Denmark was occupied within 24 hours by the Germans. It possibly would have been occupied anyway, but there might have been considerable hesitation on the part of the German generals to commit the required number of men to occupy Denmark, with the possibility that the British would have sent reinforcements. This was our policy during the war. We did not feel that our quarter of a million men could effectively defend Ireland against a serious German or American invasion, but the existence of our army and the certainty that they would offer some defence, was a factor in the plans of any invasion.[5] The Germans would be slower to invade Ireland if they felt they had to fight as this would involve a continuous supply of arms. If they felt that by dropping a parachute regiment into Mullingar, they could take over the whole island without opposition they would almost certainly have done it, if only for the nuisance value. Ireland must have a sufficient force, not to defeat an attempted invasion, because in a small country this is inconceivable, but to deter the attempt.

After the fall of Poland in September 1939, the war settled into a period of quietude known as the Phoney War which lasted until April 1940, when Nazi Germany invaded Denmark and Norway.

SL: Enough was being produced, and if not produced, was supplemented by imports. No serious crisis on home production really emerged during 1940. 1940 was the Phoney War, and pre-war stocks in the factories, as well as in the government stores, managed to keep things going fairly normally. I was back into Industry and Commerce again before the crunch began to come.[6] We had no cotton and other factories would come along and say that they were missing some essential material to maintain their production.[7] Certainly, I had the responsibility of trying to work out a social policy for the situation.

There was a general necessity at that time, strangely enough, to control emigration. Workers with the requisite skills to maintain production in Great Britain could be induced to go there by offers of big wages, so naturally we tried to stop that.[8] The British government was also anxious to control immigration on a number of grounds – one was health grounds. They had a pathological fear of an outbreak of an epidemic in Great Britain, with the poor nutrition of the country and so on, and they had established many systems of control of public health and one of the things they were proposing to do was to apply all these controls to Irish immigrants at the port of entry. We did not want this. We felt it was derogatory to the dignity of Irish people, so we decided we would establish these controls here.

We also increased unemployment assistance to workers who were refused emigration facilities. We could not say to a man,

'You are not allowed to go to England; we cannot guarantee you a job here.' But what we could guarantee him here was higher unemployment pay. I was still talking about its being a period for opportunity. As I saw it, Britain was going to be short of all sorts of supplies which we could give them – we could do the industrial operations. This had happened in the First World War, mainly in the manufacture of munitions and clothing for uniforms and all that sort of thing, but it didn't happen in this war. At that time, I certainly thought of it as a policy that we could adopt, undertaking in this country to do many of the industrial activities which Britain would have to cease doing in order to turn over to the production of arms. We didn't offer at any time to produce munitions – there was an order for khaki cloth which we allowed the Limerick Clothing Company to accept and which kept them going all during the war.[9] There were arrangements under which damaged ships could be repaired and at that time the only dock we had was in Dublin – the Liffey Dock Yard Company – the British undertaking to supply the steel and all the rest of it. These were often British ships. But we never got what I thought at that time was possible, namely a British agreement to say that some particular type of machinery or equipment which was required by British industry or which British industry was supplying itself would be supplied from here, so that their capacity could be turned over to military operations.

Of course, circumstances were entirely different in the two world wars, because this reflected their reaction to our neutrality in this world war, this reluctance to allow us to be responsible for any part of their essential supplies and no doubt they had a certain desire to see us suffer economically in the consequences because of our neutrality, whereas in the First World War we were regarded as the one country and it didn't make any difference whether the work was done here or in Great Britain. But we never got anywhere with that at all.

At first, we had no real difficulty in getting arms supplied: the British, recognising that the main danger to them in 1940 was a German invasion of Ireland, were willing enough to supply a certain defensive type of equipment which enabled us to build up an army of about 250,000 men and arm them.

After a time, the British supplies began to dry up; when the danger of invasion passed them, they no longer felt any need to divert any part of their equipment to us and that was understandable enough – they wanted it for their aggressive war and we had to go hunting around various parts of the world for any material we got. But I'd say that by and large most of the military equipment we had for the whole war came in during that first twelve months.

The war left people in rural Ireland in a better place than those in urban centres. Those from farming communities continued to feed themselves, but the diet of the working poor in urban areas deteriorated significantly as shortages became more acute. A survey of Dublin children in 1942 found 23 per cent of children under the age of four and 45 per cent of children under the age of two exhibited signs of rickets, which is caused by a deficiency in vitamin D extracted from calcium. This was blamed on the 'black bread' common during the war; the type of flour used to make it contained a toxin, phytic acid, that immobilised the absorption of calcium. Black bread resulted from higher extraction rates of flour from wheat, growing from 70 per cent pre-war to 100 per cent during the war. Extraction rates in Ireland were not lowered until December 1943 and flour was not fortified with calcium until June 1946.[10]

SL: A story in that regard is that we had got down to 100 per cent extraction flour: this was brown flour with all the bran left in it. The doctors began to say that this flour was producing rickets in children. This was obviously capable of being true as the bran in the flour neutralises the calcium and there was this calcium deficiency generally in the diet of the people. There was certainly an uprise in the incident of rickets in children. The Technical Committee[11] said this could be countered by introducing finely ground limestone into the bread and I made suitable enquiries into the possibilities of this finely ground limestone produced in sufficient quantities and they said it could be done in the cement works at Drogheda where they had the equipment to do it.

But I saw at once the headlines about cement going into the bread! We never did it in the end. Some other device was adopted which helped to solve this problem but that was the type of ad hoc arrangement that was made. In 1942 I was talking about the possibility of bread rations. In fact, we never did ration bread during the war. This only came into operation after the war was ended in 1947, and that was due solely to the failure of our own harvest that year and the European harvest generally. Also, the greater demand on the available supply of wheat throughout the world by reason of the fact that the war was over. Many countries of Europe were more desperately in need of supplies than we were. These then were the problems I was dealing with and in some respects they were very narrow margins of safety.

In April 1940, a month before the pivotal Nazi invasions of the Low Countries and France and the commencement of the Battle of Britain, Lemass and the Minister for Agriculture Jim Ryan visited London. Lemass laid out his concerns to Minister for the

Dominions Anthony Eden and Minister for Foods Lord Woolton at meetings on 30 April and 3 May 1940. The Irish were anxious to secure markets for Irish agricultural products; the British, facing a potential blockade similar to the one that had come perilously close to starving the country during the First World War, were also anxious to secure food imports from Ireland, but there was an obvious power imbalance. Britain was the only realistic outlet for Irish goods during wartime and Ireland had no merchant navy for its own needs. Fortunately for Lemass and Ryan, the British government was still relatively well disposed to the country at this stage, but the appointment of Winston Churchill as prime minister in May 1940, the rapid fall of France and the Battle of Britain saw relations rapidly deteriorate.

SL: For this period of nine or twelve months after the commencement of the war there was all this extraordinary feeling of unreality. Jim Ryan and I paid a visit to London to discuss arrangements with the British government. My recollection is that it was the week in which there was some fighting in Norway, the week in which Chamberlain used the historic phrase, 'Hitler has missed the bus.'[12]

During these discussions there was evidence of tremendous hostility, personal, I think, as well as on matters of policy, between Eden and Woolton, in which many derogatory remarks about Woolton were made by Eden and vice versa. Eden was to a large extent on our side ... Naturally enough, there was a reluctance for ministers to go to London because you couldn't hope that you'd be able to confine yourself in London to the particular matters you wanted to discuss – the particular matters of administration – you expected to be cornered to deal with the political issue of our participation in the war, the attitude to the war, and so on. So, it was far safer to send officials to deal with these matters of details and to keep ministers out. Indeed, I'm not at all sure that there were further ministerial visits to London from that meeting in 1940 until after the war, or very close to the end of the war.

I don't think there was another visit from a British minister to Ireland during that period. There was no personal contact until after the war and by that time, of course, there was a Labour government in.[13] I went over very shortly after they became elected to explore the situation with them. I found them extremely nervous about the political popularity of agreeing on anything with us. They were very conscious of the fact that there was a sort of anti-Irish sentiment prevailing in England because of our neutrality in the war. They were reluctant to make agreements – they did make agreements, but didn't keep them any better than the Conservatives.

The Irish state's dependence on Britain for its shipping requirements was acutely exposed by the Second World War. From 1922 on the state did not invest in a mercantile marine navy, leaving it instead to British-owned vessels to deliver ocean-going cargo. A worldwide slump in trade in the early 1930s saw many ships broken up for scrap. It was one of many lost opportunities, he told Ryan.

SL: My recollection is that I went down to have a look at the Cork Dockyard, which is now the Verolme Dockyard, and which at that time was on the point of closing down. If we could have thought in terms of operating our own shipping service at that time with these six ships, we could have bought them extremely cheaply.

At the outbreak of the war, there were just 56 Irish-registered vessels, all on Irish Sea routes. Ireland was also totally dependent on foreign shipping to carry bulk cargoes for commodities such as cereal crops and petrol. Nearly all merchant shipping flew under the red ensign of the British merchant fleet. The fault for failing to see the importance of an Irish-owned mercantile fleet entirely independent of British ownership rested with Lemass. Lemass did not have the same consuming interest in shipping as he did in aviation. He understood the problem but was uncharacteristically hesitant to do anything about it. He declined to purchase for the state the British and Irish Steam Packet Company (B&I) when it was offered to the state in 1935 after its British parent company went into receivership.[14] When war arrived, B&I's ships were requisitioned by Britain; the biggest losses were its newly built sister ships *Leinster* and *Munster*. The situation deteriorated rapidly throughout that year as Nazi Germany tightened its grip on the continent of Europe. Within the space of 15 months wheat imports fell from 103,103 tonnes per quarter in March 1940 to just 2,586 tonnes by June 1941.[15] Belatedly, Lemass set up Irish Shipping Ltd in January 1941 with his chief civil servant John Leydon.

SL: Responsibility for shipping became mine in the early part of 1940, during the period of the Phoney War – you must remember now that there was a long period at the beginning of the war when the war was a very unreal business and it was possible to talk … about economic progress, building new industries, and all the rest of it – that was, in fact, while the war was on. During that period, we were meeting our shipping needs by chartering ships – mainly Greek ships – and the British government was also in the market chartering ships. They came to us and said: 'We are bidding against each other for the available ships and we are putting up the charter rates on ourselves.' They suggested that they should do all the chartering – that we keep out of the charter market and that they would allocate the ships to us to meet our requirements. We agreed to this and I remember some time about July 1940 John Leydon came to me and said: 'We have not got a ship out of the British for two or three months and it looks as if we are being double-crossed. They have time-chartered all the ships that are available for charter and there is nothing left for us at all.' Now it was at that time that I went to the government and got the decision from the government to buy second-hand ships wherever we could get them and establish Irish Shipping Ltd.

Towards the end of the year [the Department of Industry and Commerce] was transferred back to me and I suppose it was early in 1941 that we bought the first ship – a Greek ship that had been taken out to sea by its crew with its sea cocks open to sink it so that they could collect the insurance. But the sea cocks were so rusty that the ship could not sink and it was brought back into port, where we bought it. The Greek name of the ship will be in some book, but we called it the *Irish Poplar*.[16] By the end of the war that ship had earned £3 million in gross freight. There were other ships got by various devices. When the Russians invaded Latvia and Estonia, a number of Latvian and Estonian ships that had been in the Atlantic took shelter in Irish ports and we made a deal with the British covering about 12 or more of these ships, in the Irish ports, that we would order them out of the ports on a certain date.[17] They would pick them up outside the territorial waters and we, I think, got five and they got seven – we took five of the ships and we ordered the others out of the Irish ports and the British took them up.[18]

One of the consequences of that was that the first of these ships was converted to an Irish ship and it sailed to New York. Russia was now in the war as an ally of the Americans, the Russians took legal proceedings to arrest the ship in New York because they claimed that the Russians owned the ship; so the ship was tied up there with the warrant posted to its mast for years. None of these ships could ever again go to New York. This did not apply in Canada – they could not accept this Russian claim and the ships were able to ply back and forth to Canada, which provided the main source of wheat supplies during that period. There was an Italian ship which we purchased – a fairly big ship down at the North Wall – and that involved some connivance with the British government to an extent which I am not quite sure about because the money for the Italian ship was paid into an Italian account in Switzerland and I think the Italian embassy in Dublin was able to draw on that account during the war and that could not have been done without British connivance in some way.[19] But the British were very sticky during the war with regard to ships and certainly appeared to be trying to impede our getting in supplies, forcing us into a position where we were more or less dependent on them for supplies. It was a complete default on their part, on their undertaking.

The commodity that gave Lemass the biggest trouble during the Second World War was tea – hence the wartime sobriquet 'half-ounce Lemass'. At the outbreak of the war, Ireland ranked second in the world in the consumption of tea and all of it was imported via brokers based in London. Tea was not an essential staple, but its availability was critical to morale. The hardships of the war could be better borne if tea remained widely available. Tea was rationed in Britain from July 1940. Ireland was to follow shortly afterwards.

SL: There were a couple of matters in which they double-crossed us completely. One was the question of tea, and here again we fell for their confidence trick in the sense that they were arguing that our competition in the tea markets, first of all in Rotterdam, was pushing up the price on them as well as on ourselves and we agreed to a central tea purchase. This agreement implied that we were to have exactly the same ration of tea per head as the British government had drawn during the war. It was early in 1941, I think, when wholesalers began to report that no tea was coming.[20]

The British Ministry of Food was then in Llandudno, and I sent word to them and they gave me an assurance that there was no change in the policy and all the rest, but in fact no tea was coming. I remember that there was some public agitation about this inability of traders to provide tea and there was a special meeting of the Dáil, I think, in January 1941, about the failure of the government to maintain the tea ration and while that meeting was on a notice came from the British government saying that our supplies of tea were being reduced to 25 per cent or so of the agreed quantity and I had to tell the Dáil that. 'Not merely are you not getting your one ounce per head, at present, but you are only going to get a quarter ounce per head in future.'

That was a complete double-cross and what irritated me most was that the British wholesalers, who then controlled the Irish tea market, made no effort whatever to protect our interests. It was that which led to the determination, when the war was over, to make sure that the British wholesalers would never get back into the Irish market. We legislated for it; we set up Irish Tea Importers,[21] introduced taxation and other arrangements to ensure that Irish tea importers would henceforth deal directly with India and not through the British market.

The arrangement we had with Britain was that they would buy all the available tea and give us the same ration as they had per head. It was two ounces per head at one time. At the time that they made it known that they were not going to keep this agreement, there was just no tea to be got. The war had extended to the Indian Ocean and there was no possibility of buying tea for ourselves – well, we bought tea for ourselves and we ultimately imported tea directly, but it was a fairly expensive business as it had to come through the Panama Canal and across the Atlantic, as it could not come any other way. We took the tea by train from New York to St John's, Newfoundland, where it was collected by our own ships there. The first ship was, I think, the *Irish Poplar*. It loaded up the tea anyway, and set across the ocean, not in convoy. It was just a little ship of three or four thousand tonnes, but it made it and came down in the Irish Sea and entered into the port of Dublin. As it was coming into port, a lightning strike took place in the docks, and a radio message was sent to the master of the ship to keep it out of Dublin, which he did. He turned it around in the Liffey and set sail for Waterford, where he unloaded his cargo. The first cargo of tea ever imported direct from India to Ireland came into Dublin by canal; it was taken from Waterford to Dublin by canal. This was the type of thing you had to deal with. We were able to keep the one ounce of tea ration by and large during the whole war and people regarded this as quite an achievement [which it was] because they assumed there would be no tea. When the war was over and more tea became available, we found we had about 40 years' supply of coffee in the country on the basis of normal consumption.[22] We had stocked up with coffee, which we got from Brazil against the expected failure in the supply of tea. We had to sell this supply of coffee to other countries where coffee dealers were prepared to buy, with some loss no doubt, but we got the stocks down to reasonable amounts in no time.

Of course, everybody developed the technique of using the tea two and three times, and there was quite a successful effort made to produce a synthetic coffee from barley. It certainly tasted like coffee, smelled like coffee and looked like coffee.[23] During the war there was a lot of experimentation in the direction of substitutes for things that could not be obtained. There was a scientific committee of which Professor Thomas Wheeler[24] was the chairman, and they did quite a lot of good work in adapting the capacity of some existing factories to the production of what was needed, and in producing synthetic materials for things that could not be obtained. Wheeler and his colleagues had a glorious time trying all these experiments. Most of their work was, of course, directed towards military purposes, adaptation of arms or explosive materials.

Lemass's reputation during the war was based on his stern and unbending attitude to the rules he set. He was not popular with a lot of suppliers and many felt his attitude was punctilious in the extreme, but few regarded him as being less than fair. He communicated with clarity on radio broadcasts explaining the situation to the Irish public.

SL: I used to spend most of my time in Industry and Commerce during the last years of the war signing orders which had the force of law. You were forbidden to have a turn-up to your trousers, you were forbidden to have a breast pocket in your coat! They were all orders of that kind – quite trivial but all designed to economise supplies in some respect – to keep things going. Of course, by the middle of 1941 or 1942 we were dealing with everything by way of order. We had very comprehensive powers. My conclusion was that during a period of war the public will accept any limitation provided it's fairly applied. I said at one time in the Dáil that if the necessity arose for me to make an order prohibiting men wearing trousers, the public would accept this until the day they saw one man wearing trousers and a lot of my work during all these years was preventing the black market, putting black marketeers in jail, preventing evasion of the rationing regulations, which all sorts of people were trying to do and this I'd say had the very widespread public support. I wouldn't say there was any sense of unpopularity so long as the public were convinced that the scarcities were unavoidable and that there was a fair and reasonable effort made to secure fair distribution irrespective of wealth or means or political influence.

As long as I was able to keep the people convinced that I was trying hard to be fair and ruthlessly trying to suppress the black market, which we didn't altogether succeed in doing. Nevertheless we had a very widespread investigation organisation and a fairly ruthless punishment – we even sent these cases to the military court in the end and some of my own personal friends got involved in this, but they went to jail just the same as anyone else. There was, of course, the fact that the black market no doubt reflected the normal human desire to be one better than your neighbour –

there wouldn't be any black market if there weren't any customers for the black market and the desire of somebody to get a little bit more than the fellow next door and to show how clever he was by getting that bit more – this kept the black marketeers in business. I had to ignore any special pleading at all – the mere fact that a person was evading the rationing regulations, no matter what his situation, no matter how he pleaded those special circumstances applied, you just had to ignore that. He had to go to jail, and he had to be seen to go to jail because of it. And it was a great satisfaction to me to get some prominent person or some very prominent firm and put them out of business or send them to jail, because this emphasised the impartiality by which the regulations were administered.

One infamous incident, the original Golfgate, involved at least five doctors who were members of the Portmarnock Golf Club. A fellow doctor told the Department of Supplies that his colleagues had all applied separately for a petrol allowance which would allow them to drive to Portmarnock to play golf. Doctors were given an extra petrol ration for medical emergencies only and Lemass's department contacted them to tell them that their petrol ration was to be cut as a result of their subterfuge. This provoked a fit of indignation in the Dáil from Fine Gael TD (and future taoiseach) John A. Costello, a member of Portmarnock Golf Club, who denied the doctors in question had done anything wrong. He thundered that their reputation as professional gentlemen had been traduced. Having made his point Lemass restored their ration, but he warned others in receipt of emergency petrol rations that they would be pursued if they abused their privilege.

SL: Doctors used to get petrol ration which they were supposed to confine to use only for the purpose of attending their patients, but one day, an inspector went down to Portmarnock Golf Club and he found about ten cars parked outside a cottage at the entrance to the course, all belonging to doctors, all of whom said they were attending, in a medical capacity, the person who lived in the cottage – she had 10 or 12 specialists and general practitioners there! Of course, nobody believed this. They all had their petrol rations withdrawn and their licence to use a car was withdrawn too. John Costello kicked up a tremendous row in the Dáil about this – depriving these doctors of the opportunity of serving and all the rest of it, but of course everybody was laughing at him.[25]

All I had to do was to say that each of these doctors gave the excuse that he was attending this one woman who lived in this cottage at the corner of the road to Portmarnock Golf Club on the same day, the same fine afternoon in June, or whenever it was, but nobody believed it. A lot of these were some of the most prominent and well-known doctors in Dublin. Eventually they got their rations back, but it was the appearance of enforcing this impartially that mattered.

There were very big firms caught. Some of the most prominent firms in Dublin were caught out and it was always a source of satisfaction when you got a big fish in the net because this helped to build up public confidence in the efforts to enforce the rationing system. I must say, I got a personal satisfaction out of it too. A lot of the people get away with irregularities in a small way and one always had to be slightly suspicious that our inspectors weren't being bought off, which the small people couldn't do and the big people could do and there were one or two cases of that type.

I must tell you a story of 1941/1942 when nearly all petrol

supplies had been used up and there were no supplies at all. A 15,000-tonne tanker was due to arrive late on Christmas Eve.[26] I received word that the tanker had arrived in Dublin port and was coming so I went home with an easy mind. It was so heavy and big that it could not enter the port and had to be sent back to Liverpool to discharge a couple of thousand tonnes, so that it could clear the bar at Dublin. It was sunk that night in Liverpool, and I had to make an announcement that the petrol coupon which normally represented the right to buy gallons of petrol had been reduced to a quarter of a gallon – a very drastic step to take. The supplies were brought in later and the coupon increased again. As I said, however, we were always working a very narrow margin, and you never had any safety factor at all. There were many other incidents of that kind, some not very important, some very important. On the other side, there was the surprising easement of problems from some sections of the British government. They attached so much importance to ships that there was never any difficulty in getting steel for the Dublin dockyard, for repairs, no matter whose ships were being repaired.

You never knew what problems each day was going to bring. In many cases the problems came to me with the answers, either from John Leydon or the officer dealing with the matter. Nevertheless, there was always the possibility of having to deal with some sudden emergency in supplies. The main anxiety during that period was to break up the black market, which was fairly active. It was desired to ensure not merely that the available supplies were getting to distributors, but that nobody was getting away with any irregularity at all.

My recollection of the period '42/'43/'44 would be one of many possible crises that never developed, as well as ones that did, crises that had to be tackled as they developed but did not ultimately produce any catastrophe. At the same time, we had post-war development planning going – various committees, bills being drafted and presented in the Dáil and then put into cold storage for post-war operation. It was quite a busy period and there was no possibility at all of turning your mind to matters of purely academic or general interest. Day after day, hour after hour, no matter where you were, you had to leave your telephone number because somebody was bound to turn up with some problem or other. I remember the introduction of clothes rationing. Eddie Maguire[27] even made a protest, organising shop assistants to march through the city in protest against it. As a matter of fact, when we wanted to abolish the rationing in the end, they objected equally strongly because they were afraid that the free-for-all was going to harm them. The only people who organised any resistance to these ration schemes were vested interests, those who had the chance of making some quick money during the war. The general public during that period accepted all those restraints and restrictions almost without a murmur, and I think were satisfied that I was trying to distribute scarce supplies fairly without reference to social status, wealth, economic importance or political affiliation.

We were tremendously fortunate in the sense that there was one thing we were not short of and that was food. In so far as any scarcity emerged it was because we decided to export food after the war. We had large supplies of most foods. In 1947 the world was starving and we began to ship emergency supplies abroad. This involved restrictions on home consumption and there was a lot of agitation against this policy. Looking back now at that period I would say that I was not at any stage trying to do more in the sphere of national policy than urge on others the development of post-war plans – drainage, housing development – and all the things we were talking about then.

The Arterial Drainage Act [1945] was passed; the Rural Electrification scheme and legislation was passed [1946]; there was fairly comprehensive housing legislation – in fact, there were a whole lot of major acts designed to facilitate economic development after the war, which were passed during that period and just put on the shelf to be taken down and used when the war situation had ended and supplies made it possible to do things. A great deal of the time of the government during these war years was devoted to this problem of thinking out how we were going to handle a post-war situation. Mind you, a lot of the assumptions we made were wrong.

Lemass and the Roman Catholic Church

Seán Lemass's relationship with the Roman Catholic Church during his years in politics were characterised by ambivalence. He was the least religious and deferential of Irish taoisigh until Garret FitzGerald in the 1980s, who tried to change the sectarian nature of the Irish state through his constitutional crusade. Many of his contemporaries considered Lemass to be a non-believer. My late *Irish Times* colleague Michael O'Regan told me a story about Lemass, who after attending a funeral, turned to a friend and said: 'It's all a cod, once you are gone, you are gone.'

Lemass's irreligiousness did not extend to confronting the full power of the Catholic Church in Ireland. Irish independence had left a legacy of Church control over the school system and the hospitals. Irish people were steeped in religiosity and until the 1960s, with the advent of television and the reforms of the Second Vatican Council, were generally inclined to accept the Catholic Church's teaching on social matters.

Nevertheless, Lemass never deferred to the Catholic hierarchy in a way his contemporaries did. John A. Costello infamously stated after the 1951 Mother and Child debacle: 'I, as a Catholic, obey my Church authorities and will continue

to do so.' Such a comment would be anathema to Lemass. Lemass's attitude to the Catholic Church was coloured by the Civil War, when the Church hierarchy came out strongly against the anti-Treaty side. Many of those on the anti-Treaty side were denounced from the altar and ex-communicated. Éamon de Valera spent much of his career as taoiseach repairing relations with the clergy.

SL: One [thing] that happened during my time was the elimination of the influence of the clergy on politics. Way back in the early stages, the clergymen was a very potent political force in the rural parish. The first time I ever went from Dublin to address a public meeting in a country area was during the by-election in Laois/Offaly at a place called Castletown, I think it was. I stood up after mass, the whole congregation came up and stood around me. The parish priest came out and chased them all away, literally chased them away. He waved a stick at them and said: 'Go away, go away, and don't be listening to that nonsense' and left me with about three or four people. That would be 1924. I would not say that those who were chased away necessarily voted against us, but they were not prepared to stand their ground and tell the parish priest to go to hell, that it was no business of his to interfere in their political activity, which they would do nowadays to a very large extent. In those days it was a tremendous asset to have a parish priest on your side; there were not many of them, but there were a few on the republican side at that time, and where you had them you used them to the maximum extent because it did tend to take away the anti-clerical appearance that the movement had. Nevertheless, it was true to say at that time that all the young priests coming out of Maynooth were with us.

There was a tremendous influx of young priests, most of them on our side, which, in due course, helped to improve the situation. During the Civil War period the Church had been condemning us. There had been various ex-communication orders against us and we had emerged from that period with a sort of anti-clerical appearance. When looking for votes it was important enough and there were many well-known parish priests – Canon Maguire, Fr Burbage,[28] and others – and people like that were always brought to the fore on all such occasions just to identify them with the party and identifying the party with them, but the great majority of priests were very strong against us and were a political nuisance.

I can still remember another occasion going through the country. I attended mass at a church in Tipperary – I forget now where it was – where the parish priest stood up in public and said: 'Men and women, after this mass there is going to be a meeting outside the church and there are young men from Dublin here to talk to you; for the first time you are going to hear the truth, but those of you who took the Free State shilling need not wait; you are not wanted at this meeting.' This type of belligerent support was just as difficult in the political sense as the opposite; nevertheless, it was a good thing to hear in this church.

Today the parish priest has no dominating political influence at all; there is a complete change in the public attitude to them. Indeed, I said at one time, the best thing for anyone going for election was to have a row with his bishop provided it was a row on the subject of resentment of clerical domination in politics. The public would be with you on issues of that kind.

Lemass's refusal to be cowed by the proverbial 'belt of the crozier' was exemplified in 1945 as a result of his row with the Bishop of Galway, Dr Michael Browne. Browne was appointed Bishop of Galway at the age of 41 in 1937. He quickly made a notorious reputation for himself in seeking to interfere in every aspect of diocesan life, most notably his attempts to segregate the sexes bathing at Salthill.

The defining issue for Lemass, though, was not one of faith or morals, but rather the arcane issue of vocational organisations. In 1939 Bishop Browne was appointed chairman of the Vocational Organisation Commission. The purpose of the commission was how best to organise vocational bodies in Irish society. These included trade unions, trade guilds, employers organisations, the credit unions and representative bodies such as Muintir na Tiré and the Irish Countrywomen's Association. Vocationalism was a big subject internationally in the 1930s and 1940s as democracies tried to organise society in a way that did not lead to totalitarianism. The commission envisaged a vocational commission that would advise the government on policy. The politicians and civil servants saw it as a threat to their power base.

The report was eventually published in August 1944 and did not attract much attention until Lemass raised it in the Seanad in March 1945. The report criticised the stifling impact of Irish bureaucracy and the conservatism of the civil servant classes. Lemass took exception to the depiction of his own civil servants in the Department of Industry and Commerce as being slothful and conservative. Many had been co-opted into his Department of Supplies and had literally kept the lights on in the country during the Second World War. He condemned it as a 'querulous, nagging, propagandist and a slovenly document'.

Browne took this as a personal affront, as Lemass fully intended it to be, and the pair exchanged letters in the *Irish Press*. Browne said Lemass had found 27 errors in the document but provided no evidence for 15 of them, and seven others were based on a quibble or a technicality. There were in fact only three errors, he said, and they were minor ones. Browne believed Lemass's criticisms only served to underline the accuracy of the document. The principles of the document had been 'taught to us by Pope Pius XI,' he reminded Lemass. Browne concluded: 'When Mr Lemass uses the word "slovenly", he really means that he does not like our report and that he thinks himself entitled to abuse what he does not like.' Lemass was unfazed.

SL: I think there is a political advantage in having a certain anti-clerical tinge. The only time in my life that I ever got an enormous vote, the highest ever accorded to any candidate in a general election, was when I was having a full-scale row with the Bishop of Galway and this was dominating the political scene. And I found this on other occasions too – that having a good row with the bishop is quite a political asset and you do not suffer politically for it because [there] is an anti-clericalism in the Irish people. Of course, de Valera was a remarkable person. He never went around the country but he visited every convent and school and called on the bishop and, in a very short time, he had all the nuns in his hands and the monasteries were centres of support for Fianna Fáil and Fianna Fáil policy, but this was largely due to the personal attention he gave, and his own personal liking for contact with these people.

A lot of people would conform; people who did not like being out of conformity with their neighbours would run for cover when the Church attacked the state. After a while politicians came to realise that it was not giving them public disrepute at all; public disrepute went to the man who did not stand up to unreasonable interference. There is a strong streak of anti-clericalism in the Irish character. Dr Paddy Browne [Monsignor Pádraig de Brún][29] of University College Galway always used to proclaim his anti-clericalism. He made a very clear distinction between Catholicism and anti-clericalism. He was a Catholic priest, but he strongly resented clerical domination in politics and interference outside the clerical sphere. I think this is very common among Irish people. While they pay their tribute to their parish priest and respect him in every way, they do not like him to extend his influence beyond the Church or things that are naturally associated.

DR: Under the Fianna Fáil government, what was the relationship between Church and state?

SL: I must say in my time I never had any difficulty at all either with Dr McQuaid [30] or the cardinal[31] (John Francis D'Alton) or any of these people in respect of any matter. As minister I had not much to do with them. On one occasion I set up a commission on youth unemployment.[32] Dr (John Charles) McQuaid, Archbishop of Dublin, was chairman of that commission. Shortly after its formation, the committee made an interim proposal to raise the school-leaving age. I immediately pointed out the implications of this – building new schools, training new teachers, the physical needs which they had never fully considered. Dr McQuaid apologised for bothering me, withdrew his delegation and withdrew the report completely.

DR: During the period up to 1957, the government as such, of which you were a member, never had the feeling they had to look over their shoulders at Maynooth?

SL: No. Before 1957 I would not think so. In the drafting of the constitution of 1937 there must have been a great deal of discussion with theologians to get the various constitutional points which concerned the Church expressed in a proper way. Any attempts by bishops to criticise the constitution were slapped down from the Vatican.

The extent to which the Catholic Church's dominance of Irish society was accepted by the public was evident from a 1962 survey carried out by the Jesuit sociologist Fr Bruce Biever of attitudes to the Church in Dublin city and county. Ninety per cent of those surveyed thought the Catholic Church was a force for good in Ireland and 88 per cent believed that, in a clash between Church and state, the Church must prevail. Biever concluded that politicians were 'quite helpless in the face of such a cultural climate' – yet he also detected a glimmer of change. Among those who had completed their Leaving Certificate, a minority in the state in the early 1960s, attitudes to the Church were the reverse, with 83 per cent disagreeing with the proposition that the Church was a force for good.

DR: You would not accept then that the individual in Ireland is indoctrinated from the word go – he is free to make an independent choice?

SL: I would not say that pupils are conditioned in our schools in this matter. In some of the clerically run schools, there might be a tendency to emphasise the authority of a bishop. I do not remember having any difficulty, sense of strain or problems in dealing with the Church. My personal relationship with all the principal archbishops and the cardinal was always very good. Whenever I wanted advice about anything there was never the slightest suggestion that they felt it their duty to impose any point of view upon me. I could have been very lucky; nothing emerged in my time which would have caused a conflict. I can only testify on my own personal experience in that regard.

CHAPTER 7

POST-WAR MALAISE

'During the war we were a pariah and had little or no diplomatic contacts with any country except purely in practical matters.'

During the war there were two general elections in quick succession. The first, in 1943, saw Fianna Fáil lose its overall majority and operate as a minority government. De Valera was not satisfied with this outcome and called another snap election for May 1944. He sought vindication for the party's stewardship of the country and was rewarded with 76 seats – 70 were needed for a majority. Lemass's vote share in Dublin South increased to nearly a third of the poll.

De Valera's government began to turn to the post-war settlement beginning in 1942 when a new Cabinet Committee on Economic Planning was formed, comprising Lemass, de Valera and Seán T. O'Kelly. Lemass was influenced by the Beveridge Report published in Britain in 1942, which envisaged full employment and a welfare state based on contributions from workers. Its author, William Beveridge, spoke about battling the five giants: idleness, ignorance, disease, squalor and want.

Ireland emerged from the Second World War isolated but relatively unaffected. The country had been spared the horrors visited on so many other countries, though the hardships had been considerable. Heavy censorship had operated throughout the war, with the historian F.S. Lyons likening the Irish public to the inhabitants of Plato's Cave, whose only vista was the limited one in front of them. Outrage among the Allies about Irish neutrality was compounded by Taoiseach Éamon de Valera's decision to visit the German representative to Ireland, Eduard Hempel, in the immediate aftermath of Adolf Hitler's death. While Ireland did not share the privations of the Second World War, neither did it share in the post-war boom which saw western Europe recover quickly from the war and enter a period of peace and prosperity.

SL: We had an election in 1944 which gave us a majority, and we did not envisage another election until 1949 or so. We saw ourselves in complete control of the national situation during this post-war period, responsible for all the post-war planning and the commencement of the execution of these plans. There were quite a number of decisions taken then which were significant – the decision relating to the wider development of turf and the decision to base future power development solely on turf as long as that could be done and the decision to expand the capacity of the ESB.[1]

During the war we were a pariah and had little or no diplomatic contacts with any country except purely in practical matters. We were tremendously fortunate in the sense that there was one thing we were not short of and that was food.[2]

I remember around 1946 the *Sunday Independent* began to run a campaign against the shipment of food to Europe. It began to organise signatures for a campaign, and every Sunday it had a list of people who lent their names to this campaign. The first Dáil member to appear on this list was Oliver J. Flanagan.[3] He was unfortunate, because the day after his name appeared, we got a special message from the pope thanking us for this help and expressing appreciation of the spirit of Christianity in the Irish people.[4] From that day on, not a word appeared about the campaign. The following Sunday there was not a reference to it although, after Flanagan's name appeared, they promised that other politicians' names would appear. He was just a day too soon.

During the period after the war, when we were shipping some supplies to the continent, a conference was held in 1947 in London, to see what could be done about the world's food shortage, mainly wheat.[5] I remember being able at that conference to go up and say the Irish government was prepared to make available for the relief of Europe so many tonnes of bacon, sugar and meat. This had a tremendous effect; of course we were buying goodwill for ourselves.

Aviation was one of Lemass's enduring passions, which lasted throughout his time in politics. The Second World War saw the rapid development of combat jet aircraft, which had a knock-on effect on the commercial sector when hostilities ended. In the pre-war period Foynes was the airport for the flying boats that flew the Atlantic for a short but important period in aviation. On 9 July 1939, Pan Am's luxury flying boat the *Yankee Clipper* landed at Foynes to become the first commercial passenger flight on a direct route from USA to Europe. During the Second World War, Foynes continued to operate commercial flights, albeit with a much more limited capacity. Aviation developments during the war quickly made Foynes obsolete for transatlantic traffic. The development of Rineanna, which became Shannon Airport, began in 1936, its first commercial flight was in 1939 and by 1942 scheduled services had begun, albeit severely restricted by the war. At the end of the war Shannon Airport's runway was extended to allow for transatlantic flights. The first arrived in October 1945. Commercial aircraft still had not achieved the range to allow for non-stop travel between North America and Europe, making Shannon a first stop for transatlantic flights.

SL: 1945 was a year in which I became concerned with civil aviation development. In all the preparation for post-war development, the growth of civil aviation was expected to be very rapid and extensive. This was partly due to the improved performance and the increased load capacity of aeroplanes as a result of wartime research and development, and partly because all civil aviation development had been suspended during the war and, in any event, only limited operations had been possible. In that year we reached agreement with the United States of America for the operation of transatlantic air services, and also with Britain for the operation of the services between Britain and Ireland.

We also reached quite a number of other bilateral agreements with other countries, not all of which were immediately followed by the operation of services, but which constituted the legal framework within which these services were subsequently developed. The transatlantic agreement involved a compulsory stop at Shannon, but this was not really a problem at that time because the capacity of aeroplanes was such that they could not normally fly further than Newfoundland/Shannon, and no company was prepared to schedule services of greater length than that. About ten years later, larger, long-distance planes began to operate.

DR: What awareness was there nationally of aviation's future?

SL: There was certainly a failure in the country, and even more of a failure by the Fine Gael party, to recognise that this was going to be the air age, that we were entering a new era in which more and more traffic, passengers and freight were going to be moved internationally by air. In particular, there was a failure to appreciate its significance for Ireland.

Previously, as a result of being an island, we had suffered the disadvantages of high transport costs. However, there is no disadvantage in flying to Ireland or bringing freight to Ireland by air, and this fact put us into the mainstream of international travel. The important decision at that time was that in the new air age which we anticipated, Ireland should play an independent role.

We might have relied on the possibility of American and British companies providing us with some sort of a service, but this would have been a false and short-sighted economy. Just at that time the British could not have catered for our needs; they did not have the planes. They were developing their continental and other services very rapidly; Ireland had a very low priority with them, and the agreement which I made with Lord Winston, the British Minister of Civil Aviation, was for a fifty-fifty ownership of Aer Lingus, which would operate a monopoly service.[6] This was primarily accepted by them because they could not operate the service independently or could only operate it with planes which would be inferior to ours. In 1950 or 1951 the joint ownership of Aer Lingus was terminated.

Before the war we started to take an active interest in Atlantic aviation operations even before there were planes capable of flying that distance. We saw the very great developments in aircraft construction techniques made during the war and we knew there was going to be an enormous growth in civil aviation. We also recognised the strategic position Ireland occupied in relation to transatlantic operation. There were earlier discussions about plans for a four-power company – Canada, Newfoundland, Britain and ourselves operating a joint transatlantic service. We had these various discussions with experts regarding the location of airport facilities and the type of facilities to be provided.

But the big decisions that were taken in 1945 were, first of all, that the future was with the land-based plane, which meant the construction of the land airport at Shannon; that this airport had to be equipped with all the landing aids and navigational facilities of the highest international standard; and, of course, finally, that we were going to take an active part and we were not going to rely on other countries providing us with transatlantic services. This would never be to our benefit.

I mentioned that earlier in the war we had been giving a lot of thought to post-war development problems, and I had been enacting legislation like the Rural Electrification Act[7] and the Arterial Drainage Act[8] for implementation after the war. The Shannon Free Airport legislation[9] was of the same kind. And towards the end of the war period, we had laid most of the legislative basis for the plans that we could foresee as possible at the end of the war. But the post-war scarcities of material persisted much longer after the war than I had thought was likely, partly due to the very severe weather conditions of 1947. And just when normal conditions were now in sight the Korean War started.[10] In fact the handicaps and restrictions caused by war were with us until 1957 or 1958. Also, it was only about that time that the British government began to remove their controls and regulations and allow freedom of trade again. As a result of all this, many of our schemes came into operation slowly or haphazardly as an opportunity arose.

One of the biggest challenges facing the post-war de Valera government was inflation. Between 1939 and 1946 prices spiked by 70 per cent, caused by the worldwide commodity shortage and the cost of shipping. The end of the war created rising expectation among Irish workers, whose wages rose by only an average of 13 per cent in the same time period. In 1941 the government introduced the Standstill Order through emergency powers to control both wages and prices. In theory, wages would be kept low while the government kept price controls on vital goods. In reality, the cost of goods outstripped wages considerably and living standards fell. A mass exodus of workers to Great Britain where opportunities and wages were higher began during the Second World War and did not end until the 1970s. The demands for higher wages threatened an inflationary spiral and Lemass's big post-war task was to curb industrial unrest.

One of Lemass's chief post-war achievements was the Industrial Relations Act 1946, which established the Labour Court to adjudicate in trade disputes and provide a conciliation service. Labour historian Brian Sheehan described it as 'the most significant institutional development in Irish industrial relations post-World War

Two. The standing it enjoys today was never inevitable and remains contingent on the behaviours of its users.' The act also set up joint labour committees to set wages and conditions in certain sectors, with legally enforceable mechanisms. Many of the institutions set up by the Industrial Relations Act remain in place today. Lemass also brought forward the Prices and Promotion of Industrial Efficiency Bill of 1947, a far-reaching attempt to stimulate industrial development by rewarding those companies that manufactured for export while punishing those who had profited excessively from the protectionism of the past. The bill fell when the general election was called in 1948, but it was proof that Lemass was already moving away from the policies of protectionism which had been in place since the state was founded.

DR: I imagine that with the passing of the Industrial Relations Act[11] *in 1946 you hoped for a period of industrial peace?*

SL: 1946 stands out in my memory as the year of the Industrial Relations Act. This occupied most of my time during that year, both in its preparation and in getting it through the Dáil. By 1946 it looked as if we were in for a period of industrial peace. Regrettably, this was not to be the case. This was partly due to the fact that the extraordinary boost in prices which took place in 1947 came more violently and much sooner than anyone had thought likely. There were quite a number of trade union leaders who were against repealing the Standstill Order, and who told me privately that they wished to see it continued in force, though authority to increase wages should be given more liberally than had been done previously. The Standstill Order permitted an increase of wages on a uniform basis.[12] It provided for, say, an increase of ten shillings a week for everybody. This was proportionately a lot more to the lowest-paid worker than to the higher-paid worker.

The gap between the unskilled worker, at the bottom of the scale, and the skilled worker, at the top began to close. This was attractive to a lot of the unions which were catering for the lower-paid men. It also had the effect of ensuring that these increases in wages were shared by everybody, whether they were trade union members or not – and I suppose more than half the workers in the country were not trade union members. Many of the more tractable trade union leaders were able to see this. It did not produce industrial peace because 1947 was a bad year as far as strikes were concerned.[13] There were demands for higher wages, owing to higher prices. The employers feared that the world was facing a slump similar to that which followed the First World War, and, therefore, there was strong resistance to wage demands.

The Irish Commission on Emigration estimated that between 1945 and 1951, 100,000 Irish people had emigrated in search of the high wages being paid to those who were participating in the massive reconstruction of Britain and the security offered by the welfare state. The war saw the beginning of mass emigration to Great Britain, which persisted until the 1970s and resumed for a time in the 1980s.

SL: I presume after the First World War there must have been also this upsurge in shipbuilding and renewal of international trade. We had assumed that there would be a post-war economic slump in Great Britain and that up to 200,000 Irish workers would return to Ireland looking for employment. This did not happen, so many of the projects were never carried out.

Basically, we assumed that the experience after this world war would be the same as the last; that there would be an immediate economic slump with widespread unemployment such as occurred after the First World War; that all the Irish people who were working in England would be sent home to us because of economic depression in Great Britain and there were physical works planned like roadworks and that sort of thing, which would try to absorb a large number of returning Irish workers. We thought conditions there would be made unpleasant for them and that they would come home. This never happened at all. Indeed, for seven or eight years afterwards, emigration was higher than it was even during the war, so a lot of the plans of public works, mainly roads, which were being prepared, came into operation much more slowly. Things never work out exactly as you plan, but nevertheless, I suppose no harm was done, both in the exercise of planning and in the actual plans that were implemented in legislation – they've all been brought into operation, haven't they?

The immediate post-war years were dominated by something no government could control – the weather. The summer of 1946 was one of the wettest in memory. The rain started to fall in August and continued into early September. A huge national effort saw city dwellers co-opted into the 'battle for the harvest' campaign. The harvest was saved, but wheat yields were well down and the quality was poor. Compounding the problem was world grain shortages. At the beginning of January 1947, Lemass announced something the government had been able to avoid doing during the war – rationing bread. The weekly ration fell from 6lb to 4½lb of flour per person per week. Coal supplies, too, were still subject to severe post-war restrictions and were only at 40 per cent of pre-war levels as the British hoarded coal for their own ends. Bad weather and a strike led to a bad turf harvest too. There was little margin for error as the country entered 1947. No one could predict then how the most brutal and protracted winter weather in living memory would make a bad situation worse. Freezing weather began on 24 January 1947 with a snowstorm and plunging temperatures which took people by surprise. A month later the worst snowstorm seen in Ireland in 50 years hit the country and it was the middle of March before conditions started to improve.

DR: Why was it necessary to re-introduce rationing in 1947?

SL: If we had not got that economic crisis in 1947, things might have worked out a great deal better. 1947 was a real crisis year in which unexpectedly there was scarcity when everybody had been looking forward to plenty. For the first time we had to introduce bread rationing. There was snow and ice in England up to the end of April and during all that period the British could not even work the coal mines, so there was no fuel and the crops could not be sown. This situation prevailed not only here but in England and all over the north of Europe. It was quite an exceptional year. We had had no rationing of bread during the war, although we had a deterioration in quality. The rationing of bread in 1947 was due to a curtailment of supplies.[14] This was not entirely due to the harvest failure of that year.

It was also due to the fact that the international supplies which were available were being parcelled out to individual countries by international agreement. Each country had to maintain a rationing scheme in order to establish entitlement to international supplies. In 1947 we were party to the International

Wheat Agreement,[15] which enabled us to buy a certain quantity of wheat at a fixed price or within a certain price range. The main free source of supply was Argentina, which was ruled by [Juan] Perón and buying wheat from Argentina was a matter of giving various bribes here and there to be allowed to buy it. Perón's son-in-law was the collector of the bribes. You remember, of course, the enormous stacks of turf and timber along the main road to the Phoenix Park?[16] These were all built up as emergency supplies and it is probably true to say that we began to dissipate these supplies against the expectation of renewed production of coal too soon. The coal crisis of 1947 was the worst and there was a very frantic effort to try to build up these stocks again. We had a period in 1947 when the wartime stocks were gone and the turf was not coming, and I negotiated a small quantity of coal from Britain. There was some difficulty about coal for a long time.

The hardships of the Big Freeze had a knock-on effect leading to two budgets in 1947. The first, in May, put up taxes on tobacco, alcohol and entrance to dance halls. The second, a supplementary budget in October, was brought in to raise revenue that would be used to introduce food subsidies to mitigate the price increases that were hurting the poorest in Irish society. The Fianna Fáil government did not endear itself to the wider electorate with a rise in income tax, further rises in duty on beer and cigarettes, while also hiking the price of cinema tickets.

SL: In 1947, when Frank Aiken was Minister for Finance, there was a serious miscalculation as to the revenue yield. We had two budgets in that year, first the ordinary budget and then later on, another budget which was brought in on the occasion that we introduced the food subsidies which were intended to deal with the exceptionally high prices caused by the abnormal conditions of 1947. We had a considerable argument in the government about that. I had proposed that we should pay food subsidies to an extent that would cut the cost of living by 10 or 12 per cent, and I was quite prepared to defend additional taxation to be able to do this. Prices had begun to shoot up and this was certain to lead to demands for higher and higher wages, which would never be reduced again, while prices, as we thought, would start to come down in 1948 or 1949.

The idea of these subsidies was to take this peak off the rise in costs, so that the growth of wages would be more rational and more regular. But partly because there was not a sufficiently critical examination of the material given by Finance officials and the Revenue Commissioners, we ended the year with an enormous tax surplus, which the coalition government inherited.

The proposal to introduce the food subsidies came from me. I was responsible for labour relations at the time. The Labour Court had been set up; the Industrial Relations Act had been incorporated; the first round of wage increases which were anticipated at the end of the war had been concluded when quite suddenly there came this upshooting of prices and it was my feeling that this was going to distort our wages pattern, because of a temporary situation which would not last more than about 12 months. This led me to bring the subsidy plan to the government.

The government was reluctant to accept it, mainly because of what they assumed would be the very high cost in taxation and to some extent, the budget surplus of 1948 was due to the Department of Finance's effort to exaggerate the cost and make us impose taxation unnecessarily. In fact, we could have carried all these subsidies in 1947 on the budget surplus without increasing taxation at all. If we had done this the result of the 1948 election might have been different, but that was part of the price we paid for the uncritical acceptance of the Department of Finance's estimates.

Having accepted the principle of food subsidies and an autumn budget, I could not argue that no extra taxation was necessary. I began to have a suspicion that this was the case because the revenue returns were coming in. These were substantially higher than had been forecast, but I was not very perturbed about this because I expected we would still be dealing with the 1948 budget, and if this proved to be so we would have been able to implement some of my pet schemes or, alternatively, to reduce taxes. The government's efforts to try to hold down the cost of living by food subsidies came perhaps a little bit too late, because the taste of higher wages or the pressure for higher wages had built up so strongly that it proved impossible to reverse this trend.

In 1947 the United States introduced the Marshall Plan in response to the dreadful post-war conditions in Europe. The US agreed to lend $13 billion, the equivalent of approximately $187.4 billion in 2017, for the reconstruction of Europe. Though Ireland was regarded dimly in State Department circles because of Irish neutrality in the Second World War, nevertheless the Americans thought it prudent to include the state. It offered Ireland $128.2 million in loan aid (the equivalent of €1.8 billion) and $18 million (€223.7 million) in grant aid. Though the sums seem low by contemporary standards, the total Irish government budget in 1947 was £IR56 million (€2.55 billion today). Between 1949 and 1952 nearly half of all capital expenditure, including rural electrification, reforestation and land reclamation, came from Marshall Aid money.

SL: We had no problem in accepting the Marshall Plan or agreeing to participate in it, or agreeing to become a member of the organisation which was set up to administer the OEEC [Organisation for European Economic Co-operation]. The only conflict that arose, as far as we were concerned, related to the exclusion of Spain. The communist countries had been invited to participate; Czechoslovakia had agreed to come and then the Russians waved the big stick and the Czechoslovaks backed out. The same situation arose with Finland. I felt that it was wrong that the communist countries should be invited to participate, while Spain was excluded. However, I was deterred from making this a public issue at the conference on private assurances that this was a temporary situation only, and that after the conference was over Spain would be in.

DR: Of course, by 1948 all the post-war difficulties, both expected and unexpected, had arisen.

SL: Yes. The unexpected was the scarcity of supplies which, it was assumed, would, three years after the war, have disappeared altogether, and the upsurge of prices during 1947, due to the abnormal weather conditions of that year. The expected ones were the normal difficulties of getting economic life going again. In one respect, we were better off than we thought we would be. We expected a very large return of Irish workers from Britain –

something like what took place after the first war. Of course, after the war we misjudged the economic climate a great deal. First of all, the economic crisis we had expected did not emerge. On the contrary, the world had gone into a boom. In 1947 however, there was an unexpected supply crisis that was entirely due to a terribly severe winter which stopped coal production and prevented crops being sown.

The 1948 general election was called by Éamon de Valera for 4 February. Fianna Fáil had been in power for 16 years, navigating the state through the economic and political turmoil of the 1930s and the Second World War. The cumulative effect of being in power so long was beginning to tell. De Valera, now 65, and his cabinet, most of whom had been there for 16 years, looked tired. The Fianna Fáil government was implicated in the Locke's Distillery affair in which senior members were accused of selling valuable stocks of mature whiskey from the County Westmeath distillery to 'international chancers', according to the Fine Gael TD Oliver J. Flanagan. A short-lived tribunal exonerated all members of the party, but reputational damage was done.

The foundation of the short-lived party Clann na Poblachta in 1946 presented a significant threat to Fianna Fáil. Clann na Poblachta billed itself as the republican party that Fianna Fáil no longer was. It attracted those who had been anti-Treaty during the Civil War and were angered by the execution of IRA prisoners during the Second World War. Anger was compounded by the death on hunger strike in Portlaoise Prison of IRA prisoner Seán McCaughey in May 1946. McCaughey had been sentenced to death for the attempted murder of IRA chief of staff Stephen Hayes, who, he claimed, had been a government spy. McCaughey was the first Republican prisoner to undertake a blanket protest. De Valera refused to intervene to save his life.

The executive of the fledging Clann na Poblachta party was dominated by Old IRA members who had been involved in the War of Independence. Its leader was French-born Seán MacBride. He was the son of Major John MacBride, who had been executed after the Easter Rising, and Maud Gonne, an aristocratic Irish nationalist and the muse of the poet W.B. Yeats. Along with its republican streak, some in the new party, emboldened by the 1945 Labour landslide in the UK, wanted a more radical approach to social issues. The threat posed to Fianna Fáil by the new party was apparent by October 1947 when Clann na Poblachta won two by-elections from Fianna Fáil – MacBride in Dublin County and Patrick Kinane in Tipperary. There was a strong anti-incumbency feeling in the country, with the by-election returns showing that many voters did not transfer to Fianna Fáil.

SL: I was in London when the results of the 1948 by-elections came in. There were three by-elections. We won one and lost two to Clann na Poblachta. De Valera rang me up in London and said, 'What would you do?' I said: 'You are not the man I think you are if the Dáil has not been dissolved before I get back.' It was dissolved.[17]

I think that was bad advice at the time. It might have been wiser if he had waited a bit longer, having regard to the various things that were happening at the time and the effect it would have on public opinion. Anyway, it was the advice I gave him, and he took it and had the election in 1948 which led to the first coalition government. Whether that was the right decision or not, I am not so sure. If the result of the election was influenced to any extent by the autumn increase in taxation – the taxes on beer and cigarettes and on cinema seats and things of that kind, then we were wrong, because that was unnecessary and could have been relinquished again after the 1948 budget.

If it was affected by the rise in Clann na Poblachta it would have been wrong too, because that was a flash in the pan; it ceased shortly afterwards. During the election campaign, there was not any sign that we were going to be beaten – it did not look like it.[18] The Clann na Poblachta party was the headache. We assumed that anything they would get, they would take from us. They were purporting to be more republican than ourselves – a 'ginger' group which was anxious to urge Fianna Fáil to play that way. There was a considerable difference in views during the election campaign as to how well they would do in the election. I did not think they would do well at all, but there were others in the party who thought they would gain 20 or 30 seats, so uncertain was the situation. Even the ten they got was more than I was prepared to forecast for – I thought they would get eight or nine.

It was some time after the election that I analysed the results in depth to try and discover to what extent the Clann na Poblachta party had taken support from us and it was very hard to establish that they had done so at all. Personally, I hold a theory that there is between 5 per cent and 10 per cent of the total vote in any election which is available to any new party, no matter what its policy is, or what it stands for. There is always a percentage of the people who are disgusted with all the existing parties and so will vote for any new party, no matter what it represents if it makes any show at all. And this is, I think, what got them so far.

We have had these parties from time to time which make show at an election and then disappear.

A lot of the genuine and sincere people joined Clann na Poblachta in the belief that Fianna Fáil required a 'ginger group' on their left to spur them on and quit at once when they found Clann na Poblachta and Fine Gael in a coalition government and from then on the party could not get away with anything.

I think most people would agree that MacBride, at that time, could have become an important political influence in the country. He could have held a party together which would have been in a position of holding the balance of power in the Dáil if he had kept out of the coalition. He could have done that by keeping Fianna Fáil in office, if he had been prepared to vote for Fianna Fáil and then to act as the checking and stimulating part of the ginger group. He probably would have gained support for a time, but, of course, his own personality was such that he could not follow a consistent line and the weaknesses of his personality would, in time, have become more exposed and he would eventually have lost support. But that is only speculation.

The results of the February 1948 general election saw Fianna Fáil lose its majority. Its share of the vote fell from 48.9 per cent to 41.9 per cent, though it was still by far the biggest party. It won 68 seats, six short of a majority; Fine Gael, which had another poor election, won just 31 seats; Labour 13; Clann na Poblachta 10; Clann na Talmhan 7; the National Labour Party 5; and independents 11 seats. Lemass's share of the first preference vote declined slightly, but he still garnered almost 30 per cent of the first preference vote in Dublin South.

The result was disappointing for Fianna Fáil but it could have been a lot worse given the party's 16 years in office and the many problems that assailed it. Fianna Fáil expected to form a government with the support of the National Labour Party, which had split from the Labour Party in 1944 over alleged communist infiltration. The National Labour Party was dominated by officials from the Irish Transport and General Workers' Union (ITGWU) and the Congress of Irish Unions (CIU), both of whom preferred the devil you know to a Fine Gael-led coalition.

Talks with Fianna Fáil foundered on the National Labour Party's request for a formal coalition agreement, which de Valera refused. Instead, Fine Gael leader Richard Mulcahy put together a coalition consisting of itself, Labour, the National Labour Party, Clann na Pobhlachta, Clann na Talmhan and six independents. Together they managed to put together a coalition with 75 seats, enough for a one-seat majority. Mulcahy's record in the Civil War as part of a government that had executed 81 republican prisoners made him unacceptable to his coalition partners. Instead, John A. Costello, a barrister turned politician who had never been a minister, became taoiseach.

SL: When the result of the 1948 election came in, we thought we had won. James Everett[19] [National Labour Party leader] and his four or five National Labour deputies had fought the election on the grounds that they were going to support the re-election of Mr de Valera as taoiseach and the selection of a Fianna Fáil government. As far as our party was concerned, we had won the election. But they [Fine Gael] got at the National Labour Party; they made Everett a minister and this won the Dáil party in favour of the coalition. Our information was that the national executive of the party, including people outside Dáil members, were against this and in favour of supporting Fianna Fáil, by a majority, but that the Dáil members acted on their own – they ultimately merged with the Labour Party and disappeared, as such, altogether. The only other explanation, and probably the reason why we did not get an overall majority in 1948 was, first of all, our 16 years in office, which is always a factor. People get tired of the same people in the same post and vote for change often, just for the sake of it. Second, we had come through the war as a party responsible for all the restrictions, all the irritations during the war. This was the explanation given for Churchill's defeat in Great Britain. It was a sort of natural, human reaction of blaming individuals for being subjected to all the difficulties they had met. Of course, this was the line the opposition parties played to. They said, we could have managed these things better by having bigger rations, more supplies, more extensive preparations. All this was realised after the event.

CHAPTER 8

OUT OF OFFICE

'I met [Noël] Browne at that time and would say he was incapable of listening to reason, he was so filled with hatred. Now every effort is being made to restore Browne's reputation by the leftists in RTÉ and people like that but he does not really count and never will count.'

Seán Lemass found himself in 1948 at the age of 48 with a wife and four children and a 40 per cent cut in salary. Éamon de Valera's parsimonious attitude to politicians, pay saw ministerial salaries capped at £1,000 (€40,000 a year), but a TD's salary was only £600 a year. Lemass was famously incorruptible during the Second World War and would not allow a gift of tea from suppliers into his home. Neither did he allow his state car to be used for family occasions. To compound what for him was an anxious time, Lemass's three daughters all got tuberculosis at the same time, Maureen worst of all. They were nursed at the family home in 53 Palmerston Road by Kathleen Lemass. 'It was before they had discovered the drugs to cure TB easily and people were dying in their thousands from it in this country at the time. It was a real killer, and I was worried to death,' Kathleen Lemass recalled decades later.[1] Her husband took out a loan of £1,000, the equivalent of a year's ministerial salary, to tide him over his financial difficulties.

Lemass's only extravagance was suits. Given his family background in tailoring, this was understandable. There were persistent rumours around this time that Lemass was a problem gambler, but no evidence has ever been proffered to back those rumours up.

SL: In 1948 when we ceased to be [in] government, our world came to an end. In a sense this impression was emphasised because we did not expect to be beaten; we thought we had won the election. We thought the National Labour Party was committed to support us and we would have had quite a comfortable majority with their support. Then they switched and we lost. This was a bombshell. It was quite interesting to see how this affected people – I would find my drivers in tears; for them the world had come to an end too. One of the most embarrassing periods of my life was when I was driven home from the Dáil in 1948, and the next morning I had no means of transport at all; I wanted to get to the Dáil for a meeting and my son had a most decrepit-looking Ford car which I borrowed from him. When I started to drive it, I found that it had no brakes. I remember driving down the southern side of Merrion Square, wondering if I could get the car stopped before I reached the corner, and then stopping it by the simple process of rubbing off the kerbstone. There were no brakes of any sort. I then realised I had to acquire a car. There was even the problem of what to do for a living because the Dáil salary would be altogether insufficient.

Financial salvation for Lemass came from the *Irish Press*, the Fianna Fáil-supporting newspaper established by Éamon de Valera in 1931. Lemass was appointed managing director shortly after the formation of the inter-party government. He was also able to take up a number of directorships which he could not do while a minister. Paradoxically he soon became better off out of office than in it. Under Lemass's dynamic leadership, the *Irish Press* group launched the *Sunday Press* in 1949.

SL: We went out of office in 1948, but even then I regarded myself as a full-time politician. During one period I was managing director of the *Irish Press*, but I regarded this as just an extension of political activity, even though it gave me an opportunity of experiencing the handling of people and situations. This changed very quickly, and I found it dangerously easy to settle down into the routine of being an opposition deputy once my personal finances had been solved, giving me more money. I was aware of the danger of this. It was obvious the coalition government was only going to last for a couple of years and I didn't want to get into the position of getting much more money because I would be reluctant to go back as a minister. I deliberately tried to avoid letting my standard of living rise up to my new level of income because I didn't want any mental difficulty whatever. I asked myself what am I doing all this for? For the first time my personal feelings began to intrude upon what was, up to that [time], a purely party effort.

The government would depend upon four very erratic independent deputies. Dev sat back and the job of putting him back as taoiseach fell very largely on me. He would be quite happy to come to the Dáil and let [the independents'] conscience dictate and I knew that it was not solely conscience that would dictate. He would not let me buy any support, I couldn't offer any persuasion, therefore their duty to their country had to dictate. No one was going to persuade them. When the coalition came into power, they scrapped many of our projects. For those that were started, like the Rural Electrification Scheme, they tried to claim the credit. But I suppose the change of government – the emergence of a coalition government at that time made up of odds and bits of parties would have come at some time and probably it was just as well it came in 1948 and 1954. John A. Costello argued recently that this was good for the country, that it showed the possibility of alternative government and that it was good for the democratic idea in Ireland. This is a specious argument, something that they thought of long after the event. At the time they were merely thinking in terms of getting [into] office and they were prepared to make a deal with anybody on any terms that would get them into office. They were not thinking in terms of any long-term benefit to Irish democracy. Subsequently they developed the argument that it did do Irish democracy good. It certainly revived the Fine Gael party, which was practically defunct, and from their point of view it was justified. It killed Clann na Poblachta and Clann na Talmhan and the other small parties that were led into the trap.

One of the first acts of the inter-party government was to cancel the proposed transatlantic service to be operated by Aer Lingus. It did so on the basis that a deteriorating budgetary situation meant it was no longer feasible. Therefore, the state investment in seven aircraft capable of transatlantic travel was not justifiable. Lemass was furious.

SL: We took the decision that Ireland had to be actively involved as an independent operator in civil aviation both on the continent and across the Atlantic. I could never understand the reason for the coalition government's decision to scrap the transatlantic operation. This was to me completely incomprehensible. I am quite certain it was policy forced on the coalition government by [Patrick] McGilligan,[2] who just had this type of mentality. He said it was megalomania to try to equal any other country in modern techniques. Certainly, all the indications are that those members of that government who have survived in politics now regret that decision.

They realise that they were led up the garden by McGilligan and they have been trying to talk themselves out of it ever since, but they have never been able to do it very well. The Irish transatlantic air service began in 1947, with the decision to inaugurate transatlantic as well as cross-Channel air services. We bought Super Constellations to inaugurate the service. The coalition government called the whole thing off, sold the Constellations before they were delivered, and scrapped the whole enterprise. The question of whether we would have gained any advantage that we have not got now is very hard to answer. Transatlantic flying was in its infancy in 1948.

The Super Constellation was a good safe aircraft that inspired public confidence. I think if the transatlantic air service had got going then, we would have got a much earlier start to the tourist revival; hotels and facilities would have been established at a time when not many countries were devoting their attention to tourism. Of course, the industry would have run into economic difficulties during the 1950s and if it had failed because of its incapacity to earn money, it would have been quite a serious matter at that period. I don't think it would have failed as we purchased the planes well.

Perhaps the reason why the coalition did not go on with the

project was merely the peculiar mentality that it was maniacal for [the] Irish to operate an air service. The gutless attitude of the Labour Party in the coalition government was not to support anything of that kind. They fought this campaign on the basis that money was being spent on aeroplanes that should have been spent on housing. They maintained this attitude for quite a long time afterwards. There never was a question of any element of subsidisation or putting the taxpayers' money into aircraft instead of into housing, as was said in the 1940s. I must confess I was disturbed [that] these extraordinarily stupid arguments about wasting money on transatlantic aircraft[3] when we had other uses for the money were accepted by so many people. I mean not merely that presumably intelligent men should have made them, but that they were presumed to have some political influence as well.

DR: When Fianna Fáil went into opposition, you must have had plenty of time to consider new policy approaches?

SL: One of the big questions that arose for consideration when in opposition was whether we should start producing alternative policies to the government or not. Now this is a problem facing every party which has been in government, once it goes into opposition. At that time, the 1948 to 1951 period, the predominant sentiment was that this was a temporary interlude in the succession of Fianna Fáil governments, that this coalition would break down of its own accord and that we did not have to commit ourselves by any definite programme or policy for the next general election.

This was the attitude that prevailed at that time. On the second occasion in opposition this same attitude was urged by some members of the party. I disagreed with it strongly. I felt we would not get a majority in the '57 election unless we showed ourselves in opposition to be capable of doing things they could not do, that is, producing long-term detailed programmes and policies covering economic development and other fields. Very largely, I did this myself in the second period and sent it for publication, only subject to a qualifying condition that there was no firm commitment to do the things I was talking about.

Much of the earlier debates during that period in 1948 were occasioned by statements by the government attacking the former policies of Fianna Fáil, or the post-war plans of Fianna Fáil, so we were on the defensive to an extent that we should not have been. It was only when the coalition began to produce some characteristics of its own that we were able to go over to the attack. But during the earlier period, we were largely defending what we had done or were proposing to do, against misstatements, fairly often, by the coalition people. Perhaps I made a mistake in that period in the sense that I went out of office without taking any papers with me at all. Afterwards, from memory, I felt that many of the statements made in the Dáil were untrue or coloured in some way or another. My efforts to try to get the official papers published, by demanding that they should be tabled in the notes or some method of that kind, were not always successful. I could not say, 'That's not the plan I made.' I remember when I went back to office in 1951, the secretary of the department attacked me for this. He said: 'Why did you let them away with all these misstatements of fact?' I said: 'Because I had not got the full statement of the facts in my possession.' I had not taken any papers with me or any documentation at all and consequently could neither prove nor disprove these statements that were made, beyond saying: 'I do not remember that' or 'I do not believe that to be true.'

Of course, there had been a lot of talk about mismanagement and corruption. This was Clann na Poblachta's election campaign. While this was vague and unspecified in relation to the incidents they were talking about, the normal course of protection for us would have been to keep copies of the documents they were talking about – insofar as they related to Fianna Fáil.

Of course, all this died as soon as they went into the government. Several times you will find that I said after we had left office: 'Now you have been talking about this corruption, this mishandling of the country's affairs, you have all the papers now, why do you not repeat again what you said then, or produce the documents to prove it?' I think this was an important political matter in the sense that everybody began to realise that all this talk, which naturally humiliated the government, which had been in office for 16 years, was not being substantiated. None of the documentation which was supposed to substantiate it had been produced or could be produced.

The inter-party government of 1948–1951 is remembered for Taoiseach John A. Costello's decision in September 1948 to declare Ireland a republic. As far as de Valera was concerned, Ireland was a republic as a result of the 1937 constitution, the office of president having been created in 1938. De Valera had passed the External Relations Act following the abdication of King Edward VIII in 1936. He had removed all references to the British monarch in the Irish Free State Constitution and a year later inaugurated the constitution that survives to this day and contains no reference to the Crown.

Yet the External Relations Act did not break the connection with the Crown completely. The British monarch still appointed Irish ambassadors to foreign postings, a formality de Valera retained as it kept Ireland within the Commonwealth. By retaining a symbolic link with the Crown, de Valera hoped it kept the door open to unionists to end partition.

In September 1948 Taoiseach John A. Costello went to Canada. He was apparently offended by the presence of Roaring Meg, a replica cannon which symbolised the victory of King William III at the siege of Derry, and by the reneging on a promise at a diplomatic banquet to toast the President of Ireland. Costello repealed the External Relations Act and introduced the Republic of Ireland Act 1948, which ended all ambiguity about the nature of the state. Ireland became a de facto and *de jure* republic. The British retaliated by passing the Ireland Act, which deemed that Ireland had left the Commonwealth, but also formally stated that the status of Northern Ireland would not change while the majority wished to remain part of the United Kingdom. De Valera criticised the Republic of Ireland Act on the basis that it would be better to wait until Irish unity had been achieved to make such a formal declaration, but this was transparently an untenable position. This is the first time in Lemass's series of interviews with Ryan where he publicly airs his disagreements with de Valera.

SL: The External Relations Act came to the fore during that period. This was the act which established Ireland's republican status but maintained its link with the Commonwealth in the sense that our formal channel of communication with external powers was the British monarchy. De Valera thought of this as something which was essential to the ending of partition – he thought there was no prospect at all of ending partition except on terms which preserved our link with the monarchy.

I personally did not feel the same. First of all, I did not agree that this was of any benefit in relation to partition, especially in our understanding of the real basis of partition. I do not think it has anything to do with loyalty to the Crown. I consider it entirely a matter of religion – the reluctance to surrender a privileged position for one where they think they will be underprivileged. I suppose the test of this would be if the queen turned Catholic, would the Northern people turn Catholic with her? I would say they would not – that indeed would be the acid test – they would refuse to recognise a Catholic queen, with their own Orange outlook at all. Therefore, I did not believe that this External Relations Act was likely to be of importance in partition. I agreed to the link with the monarchy in 1937, because I believed this was a process of taking independence by stages, that the opposition of the British government to the final demolition of the Treaty and the enactment of a new constitution in 1938 would be minimised, and it was indeed prevented by this external relations device. If we had not got that then, they might have reacted differently. It is true that when India did the same thing ten years later, there was no question of British opposition to it.[4] But in 1937–1938, the circumstances were different and I felt that this was a move we would have to make later on as a further stage. I had been urging de Valera that we should take this further step. It was to some extent associated with our neutrality policy during the war. I felt this was compromised by the link with Britain and that the time had come when we could do something about it, but de Valera would not move – he still felt that this was going to be important towards the ending of partition – it was the sole argument he produced in favour of it. Of course, with de Valera, there could also have been a desire to justify the attitude he had taken in 1922, and this particular device, he may have thought, might have prevented the split in 1922. Then, when the coalition government did abolish it, we had different attitudes towards it. I said somewhere, afterwards: 'This step has been taken, and the only regret I have is that it was not done by a Fianna Fáil government.' This caused a lot of dissent and criticism of myself. We had arguments about it in the party, but I had said this because this was my feeling about it at the time. They felt we should have defended our action, defended the External Relations Act – but I felt this was going to put us in a completely wrong position, as we would have had to defend something that none of us really believed in at all. I was therefore of the opinion that it was far better not to get into the position of attacking the new act, much less suggesting that we were going to repeal it when we got back into power again. De Valera argued against this on the grounds that it was throwing away the last chance by which partition might be rectified. Of course, the attitude of the coalition members towards partition was ridiculous. John Costello announced that partition was going to be ended in three months. They had this all-party rally in O'Connell Street and set up a fund, all of which was just playacting and, if anything, was just making the situation worse than it had been, because the natural reaction of the unionists in the North was a consolidation of hostility.[5] That is why I always felt that anything of that kind would make partition more permanent, more secure than anything else – you could not break it down this way. It would have to be broken down from another direction altogether by creating the situation where it was increasingly in the interest of the North to establish a different type of relationship with the South, and ultimately to work together.

DR: Was it anticipated in any way, on the Fianna Fáil side, that our act might give rise to the British Act? [6]

SL: We did not know at that time that the British government had not been told about it. The British Act was intended to be a sort of rebuff to the coalition government, but, of course, that situation changed almost overnight, when the Indian republic was set up with this type of association. Ultimately, they changed this pattern; the president is now head of the state in India, but they are still within the Commonwealth.[7] There are a great many republics with no association with England at all except this declaration that they are members of the Commonwealth, but it does not commit them to anything. The Commonwealth means nothing now, except a historical memory – it is of no significance either in terms of trade, peace-keeping or anything else, This imperial preference, which started after the 1932 conference, has been eroded extensively. Countries only maintain it when it is in their interest – there is no sentiment behind it. I do not think it makes the slightest difference to us whether we are in it or not. There was a time in 1957–1958 when I was over in London, and Lord Longford began to play around with the idea of our coming back into the Commonwealth on the basis of ending partition. He went to [British Prime Minister Harold] Macmillan with this idea and he thought Macmillan was prepared to buy it. I told him, however, that the people in Belfast were not going to come into a united Ireland just because Macmillan told them to do so, or because Macmillan saw some advantage to himself in having the disintegration of the Commonwealth apparently halted by the return to it of the first country to quit. Anyhow, we got nowhere.

In April 1949 the North Atlantic Treaty Organization (NATO) was formed. In January 1949, the US representative in Ireland, George Garret, asked the Irish government if it would be interested in joining the fledging organisation. It was not an invitation to join, but an exploration of attitudes.

SL: In fact, the position is we were never invited to join NATO. The history is that when NATO was formed in 1948, during the period of the first coalition government, a letter was sent to the government here – to MacBride – asking did we want to be invited to become a member. MacBride sent the letter saying that as long as partition existed, Ireland could not join. This letter, which was typical of him, was based on a very shallow view of our situation but, because of it, no invitation was issued and no invitation has ever come since. It was never suggested since that we should seek membership.

The fragile inter-party coalition would eventually break apart over the Mother and Child Scheme. The war years had exposed the extent of ill-health among the poor, and the scourge of tuberculosis (TB). In 1947 Dr Jim Ryan, as Fianna Fáil Minister for Health, brought forward a bill that included a provision for free medical service for mothers and children up to the age of 16 without a means test. In September 1947 the Catholic hierarchy held that the bill was contrary to Catholic social teaching as it gave the state a greater say in health and health education for mothers. It was never implemented.

Clann na Poblachta TD and medical doctor Noël Browne became Minister for Health on his first day as a TD in 1948. Browne was an outsider in Irish politics. Though coming from a poor background, he trained to be a doctor with the help of a benevolent Irish family, the Chances. He was impatient and railed against the conservatism of Irish society. When he assumed office in 1948 Browne immediately began tackling the scourge of TB by building sanatoriums across the state and making the highly effective antibiotic streptomycin more widely available. TB was personal for Browne – he had lost both his parents and three siblings to the disease.

The Ryan bill was redrafted by Browne and reintroduced into the Dáil in 1950. It was immediately opposed by the Irish Medical Association (IMA), which feared that state payment for doctors would undermine their lucrative private fees. The Mother and Child Scheme is best remembered now for how it affected relations between Church and state. The Catholic Church hierarchy objected to the scheme on the basis that it would loosen the grip that the Church had on the Irish health system and that increased state control of health was against Catholic social teaching. Realising he did not have the support of his cabinet colleagues, Browne resigned and published all the correspondence with the bishops in the *Irish Times*. Costello, who had a very difficult relationship with Browne, responded: 'I am not the least bit afraid of the *Irish Times* or any other newspaper. I, as a Catholic, obey my Church authorities and will continue to do so, in spite of the *Irish Times* or anything else.'

Lemass, throughout his interviews with Ryan, showed a fierce antipathy to Browne. It was both personal and political. In 1957

Lemass had Browne removed from the Fianna Fáil ticket in Dublin South-East as there were fears that his constituency running mate Seán MacEntee would lose his seat. Browne was elected as an independent. He would later state, when Lemass became taoiseach, that he was the best of a bad lot. In his bestselling memoir, *Against the Tide*, Browne recounted that it was a personal assurance from Lemass in 1951 that made him join Fianna Fáil. Lemass told him Fianna Fáil was committed to delivering a good health service and would try to save as much as possible of Browne's doomed bill. Browne regretted his decision and called the 1951–1954 Fianna Fáil government 'one of the worst the republic has ever known', though he singled out Lemass as the one politician who was not 'playing puppet' to de Valera.

SL: Browne was the type of person who could never see anybody's opinion except his own … Browne is a queer fellow. He had ideas, but he bored everyone by talking far too much in the Dáil. He was not selected as a candidate for the 1957 election and this, I think, was partly an organised result. I met Browne at that time and would say he was incapable of listening to reason, he was so filled with hatred. Now every effort is being made to restore Browne's reputation by the leftists in RTÉ and people like that, but he does not really count and never will count. He regards himself as superior and would be completely intolerant of any opposition or disagreement within any party. He is a source of irritation and bound to be expelled from it in the end. Politics, for him, was an entirely personal matter. He made no attempt to judge the situation from a party point of view at all, from any point of view, in fact, except his own personal standpoint – it was purely a personal matter.

What happened here was not that there was a sharp disagreement between Fine Gael and Browne, but rather there was complete incompetence on Browne's part, in the way in which he handled the bill. It was quite obvious that any bill that dealt with a sensitive area where health and health education, etc., was involved, had to be discussed with all the Church authorities, and not merely the Catholic Church authorities, or controversy about it was bound to arise. So far as the public knew, there was no discussion like this at all; the bill was produced in the Dáil before any public discussion was even attempted. When it became obvious that the Catholic Church objected to some provisions of the bill and wanted them changed, Browne regarded this with resentment rather than trying to make a good bill of it.

He must have handled the bill badly, because, in a matter of a few years, almost similar legislation was passed by the Fianna Fáil government without any of these difficulties at all.[8] So therefore the problems were created, not by the terms of the bill but by the way in which it was handled. Even that may not have been the true reason for the disappearance of the coalition government. There was another group in the coalition – the Farmers' group – and some members of this group tabled a motion in the Dáil, urging an increase in the price of milk.

CHAPTER 9

LEMASS: THE MAN WITH THE PLAN

'While we were in opposition we recognised the need for discussion concerning a national development plan, which, at that time was regarded as a bit "pie in the sky" – rather vague and a little uncertain.'

The inter-party government fell on a relatively petty matter – a proposal to increase the price of milk by one penny a gallon – by which time Costello felt there was no point in lurching from one dispute to another. The 1951 general election was held on 30 May. Despite the apparent chaos of the coalition government, Fianna Fáil gained only one seat, while Fine Gael was rewarded for its time in government with a gain of nine seats (31 to 40). Lemass's share of the first preference vote in Dublin South-Central increased from 26 to 30 per cent of the first preference vote. The biggest losers were the smaller parties. Clann na Poblachta fell from 10 seats to 2; Labour (including the National Labour Party) from 19 to 16; Clann na Talmhan from 10 to 6; and there were 14 independents. At the end of the election the combined inter-party coalition thought they had the support of seven independents, which would have given them 72 votes, just enough to form a government, but Fianna Fáil recruited four independents, including Noël Browne, to vote for de Valera as taoiseach.

SL: That election in 1951 was, to me, a most surprising election in the sense that [the inter-party government] appeared to have disintegrated and therefore the prospect of their coming back as a coalition government was minimal, yet they very nearly did get back. Between them, they produced enough seats to continue as a government provided they swung some of the independents in their favour. Yet this time Noël Browne decided that his future lay in Fianna Fáil,[1] and I remember meeting him during this in-between period to discuss the situation as far as the independents were concerned. He told me that at this particular time, while we were meeting, the coalition had ffrench-O'Carroll and were working on him, offering to make him Minister for Health, offering all kind of inducements and promises. But, of course, ffrench-O'Carroll was quite a different type of person all round and did not submit to these offers. Ultimately, we came back into office by a one-vote majority, being supported by five independents, namely Patrick Cogan, Peadar Cowan, John Flynn, ffrench-O'Carroll and Browne. This was not a very stable combination, as you can see, but ffrench-O'Carroll and Browne joined Fianna Fáil and ffrench-O'Carroll is still a loyal member of the party.

The 1950s was a terrible decade in Ireland, with economic stagnation, mass emigration and political instability. The question was openly asked as to whether or not the independent Irish state had a future. The rest of Europe was recovering from six years of war more rapidly than anybody expected. West Germany's

Wirtschaftswunder was matched by France's Trente Glorieuses (1945–1975), while British prime minister Harold Macmillan would declare in 1957 that his compatriots 'never had it so good'.

Fianna Fáil returned to office in 1951 without a plan to pull the country out of its post-war malaise. De Valera, then 68, was almost blind and visibly ailing, yet he remained as taoiseach. He offered to step aside, but was persuaded by his party colleagues that he was the only man for the job, or so his supporters suggested at the time. Lemass was once again thrust into his role as Minister for Industry and Commerce on his return to power in 1951. He was also appointed tánaiste (deputy leader).

It would have been an opportune time for Lemass to take over as taoiseach. In effect, as he pointed out in these interviews with Ryan, he already had. De Valera was absent for long periods in Utrecht having a series of eye operations. The 1951–1954 Fianna Fáil government was not a success. 'The cabinet of 1951–1954 has strong claims to be considered the worst de Valera government. Opposition had not rejuvenated the party. Neither new men nor new ideas emerged,' J.J. Lee stated in his book *Ireland: Politics and Society 1912–1985*. Lemass took advantage of de Valera's increasing infirmity to seize control of Fianna Fáil's economic agenda during the 1950s. He told Ryan:

I had all the work I wanted to do, and all the power I wanted to exercise. In practice Dev had long since ceased to be a leader in the full sense of the term. If you got into difficulties with the Minister for Finance, you had to get him on your side to make sure a thing was done. I was certainly fully effective in the field of economic policy. In the preparation of the first programme, he didn't have any great part at all.

The basis of Irish industrial policy until the early 1950s was protectionism by way of tariffs and curbs on foreign investment in Ireland. The hope that tariffs would allow indigenous industry to supply the home market without facing the threat of foreign competition became obsolete in a post-war world increasingly dominated by the principles of free trade. The establishment of the European Coal and Steel Community in 1951 followed by the Common Market through the Treaty of Rome in 1957 made protectionism increasingly untenable for a small open economy like Ireland. Though Lemass gets much of the credit for turning the republic away from a protectionist model of industrial development to the export-driven, foreign direct investment (FDI) model that is the basis of the country's prosperity today, he was not the primary initiator. It was the inter-party government that established the Industrial Development Authority (IDA) in 1949 to promote Irish exports and attract foreign investment to Ireland. Lemass's response to the IDA Bill was to declare that 'at the earliest possible occasion we will terminate it'. He saw it as a typical Fine Gael ruse to control every aspect of the economy 'instead of urging it on'. It was also duplicating the role reserved for his precious Department of Industry and Commerce.

It was not his finest moment, and there may have been a kernel of truth in the observation of the Fine Gael TD Seán Collins that the 'semi-hysterical opposition' of Lemass was resentment that he had not come up with the idea first. Lemass did not abolish the IDA and quickly began to realise the importance of a stand-alone body charged with the implementation of an export-led industrial policy.

SL: It is true to say that by 1952 I was certainly beginning the process of coming to the conclusion that protectionism, as an instrument of industrial development, was no longer applicable and we would have to be thinking in terms of getting rid of protection. This was, I think, primarily due to the realisation that there were no further industries that could be set up under protection. I remember having a discussion with the Industrial Development Authority at that time and trying to prepare the list of industries for them to endeavour to get set up in the country and there were none left that you could hope to set up based entirely on the home market behind protection where the home market would be large enough to make economic production possible.

In any event, the emphasis was then shifting to development for exports and we realised a lot of industries were not thinking in terms of exports and one had to jolt them into the realisation that protection was not a permanent fact of life so by 1960 certainly I was beginning to talk in terms of this second phase of industrial development where protection would be of no importance, in which reductions in protection would have to be faced and exports and stimulation and encouragement of exports became the thing, but in fact nothing was done in this field until 1956–1957.

The inter-party government had used the Marshall Plan to pump money into a moribund Irish economy, but a number of factors conspired to create an alarming budgetary situation. The devaluation of the British pound, which was linked to the Irish punt, made imports more expensive, and the beginning of the Korean

War in 1951 caused a worldwide spike in prices. The Marshall Aid money was used up by March 1952 having been spent mostly on land reclamation and drainage. The Irish trade deficit ballooned to nearly a seventh of the country's GDP. Seán MacEntee was brought back as Minister for Finance in 1951 and prioritised balancing the books above all else. He introduced an infamous budget in 1952 which abolished subsidies on staples including bread, tea, butter and sugar. He coupled it with steep increases on the 'old reliables' – alcohol, tobacco and petrol. The budget contributed to a mood of pessimism in the country and its impact still lingered when the country went to the polls again in May 1954.

DR: To what degree was the removal of the food subsidies responsible for the defeat of the Fianna Fáil government in 1954?

SL: First of all, I don't think it is correct to say the food subsidies were all removed at that time. The final removal was in 1957. There was some reduction, but I don't think that made much difference. There was no question whatsoever that in the 1954 general election the issue that was being mainly raised by the opposition parties during the election campaign was the question of the rise in prices. This is what the opposition party campaigned on. They produced the famous leaflet showing the different household products, giving the prices at which they had been and the prices at which they were.

We were in a rather difficult position, shifting the emphasis away from these food prices to something more important and constructive because it had been a difficult period during which there had not been a great deal of economic progress. There had not been a consistent long-term development in that period.

It was a case of very largely carrying on the government in 1951 to 1954 with the support of these four independent members of the Dáil, and we were only in the process of beginning to recognise that pre-war policy conceptions and plans for economic development were no longer working. We had passed out of the phase for which these plans had been devised, and we had to get down to rethink, in a more comprehensive way, the whole business of economic development. You see, de Valera took the only possible course – I wish I had taken it subsequently – and we did go ahead to do the things we wanted to do and his attitude was 'If we fall by the wayside, OK, we will have another election and see what happens.' The only easy answer in this sense was that we knew the Dáil was not going to last its life. We knew it was going to fall with a general election before the lapse of the normal period. We did not care a rap whether the government went, so we did not trim our policy or try to adjust the course of events, certainly not for the purposes of staying in office.

At least on a couple of occasions de Valera announced the intention to have a general election, but he just kept in his own hands what the status quo was going to be and there was a motion in the Dáil to have it straight away, but we resisted this. The decision to have the general election in May of 1954, however, was entirely attributable to the weakening of the government position by the previous by-election results.[2] So far as my recollection is concerned, everybody knew it was coming. It was not a surprise election.

De Valera had hoped calling an election for May 1954 would strengthen his party's precarious position as a government propped up by independents. Instead, Fianna Fáil lost four seats and finished with 65 seats, its lowest number since 1927. Once unassailable in his own constituency, Lemass finished barely ahead of his nearest challenger, Maurice Dockrell of Fine Gael. Fine Gael gained eight seats and increased its share of the vote from 25.8 per cent to 32 per cent. Fine Gael then formed another inter-party coalition with the Labour Party and Clann na Talmhan. Clann na Poblachta won three seats and agreed to support the inter-party government, but not as a coalition partner.

DR: Were you surprised at the defeat of Fianna Fáil?

SL: I had no idea we were going to get a sweeping victory, but I thought we could repeat the 1951 situation. I must say the various indications and signs one noticed, going around the country during the election campaign, rather suggested this. There did not appear to be the likelihood of such a defeat. There was only a loss of four seats, but I would have laid money against losing four seats. I would have laid even money against gaining four seats. It just shows how unpredictable the final seat is in each constituency.[3] The final seat in each constituency was by a very small margin. I would say that rising prices were the main factor. The general discontent about rising prices would not have been as pronounced or as serious if we could show substantial economic progress. I think prices are still going up, but there is far less public discontent about it because, due to economic progress, people are better off. That wasn't so then.

MacEntee was the Minister for Finance at the time and he had an accountant's mind. His job was to balance the budget and keep it balanced and not to worry about the consequences, and there were many occasions when I thought it would have been in the national interest to have taken a chance on running a budget deficit in order to give some stimulation to the national economy, but this would be a chance.

You have got to think back to 1953. The economy was stagnant: the proportion of the total national income which the government was taking and spending had increased. I would have been doubtful at that time of the wisdom of maintaining the position that an increase in government expenditure should not outpace the increase in national income and that he should try to limit the increase in expenditure to whatever the increase in national income would be. Of course, this was not really feasible and it is true that over all these years the percentage of national income taken by the government and used for state purposes was much lower than in most European countries.[4]

This was partly attributed to the fact that we did not have the enormous defence expenditures that other countries had and no doubt there is a point at which, when the income per head is lower than it is in other countries, you must be prepared to accept a lower percentage of national income for government purposes in the sense that with a high income per head the government can afford to take more without affecting the standard of living of the people.

Of course, a large part of the government expenditure constitutes what our standard of living means. It is not merely the clothes you wear, the food you eat or the house you live in. It is also the educational facilities that you have for your children, the quality of the transport services, the roads, the electricity. They are part of our standard of living.

The second inter-party government took power in May 1954 and proved itself no better at dealing with the country's deep malaise than its Fianna Fáil predecessor. Once again John A. Costello became taoiseach with Labour Party leader William Norton in Lemass's old brief at Industry and Commerce. Norton refused to countenance an end to Lemass's Control of Manufactures Act, which was creating a serious impediment to investment in the Irish economy by not allowing foreign ownership. The 1950s was the darkest of economic decades for Ireland. Between 1951 and 1956 an average of 39,000 people a year emigrated, mostly to Britain, rising to 42,000 a year between 1956 and 1961. The population declined by 5 per cent between 1951 and 1961, despite a very high birth rate. Fianna Fáil once again found itself in opposition facing a weak inter-party coalition. Lemass would not waste his time in opposition this time around. He became Fianna Fáil's man with a plan.

DR: What would have happened had you been elected taoiseach some ten years earlier; how did the concept of a programme of economic development evolve; and did Fianna Fáil agree on its introduction?

SL: It was only gradually, after the restoration of normal conditions following the end of the war, that we began to recognise that the pre-war policies were no longer relevant to the post-war situation. Everybody assumed – as they did after the First World War – that normality meant getting back to pre-war conditions as quickly and as completely as possible. It was only slowly, from 1952 to 1957, that there came that acceptance of the need for change and the understanding that pre-war policies were no longer suitable, or else Ireland was no longer likely even to keep pace with the rest of the world in economic progress.

The conception of a national plan as distinct from a plan for individual sectors of activity was only beginning to find expression and at that period a lot of people did not consider it feasible. It is true to say, as far as the 1954 general election was concerned, that the considerable increases in prices which had taken place in that period and the promise of the opposition parties that they could reverse this upward price trend and reduce prices by 10 per cent did have an effect. There were strong advocates of the theory that the coalition government were doing so badly as a government – they had defaulted so obviously upon their promises, the economic results of their regime were disastrous – that we did not have to do anything of this kind. It was said that we should sit back and wait for them to collapse and go into office without a commitment of any sort.

With no national plan in place despite the state of the country, Lemass looked elsewhere for inspiration. The ten-year Vanoni Plan for Italy, named after the country's then Minister for Finance Ezio Vanoni, was announced in 1954. Italy had been defeated in the Second World War, but American aid, through the Marshall Plan, led to the Italian economic miracle, one common to many European countries after the Second World War, but not to Ireland. Italy's economic boom, though, highlighted the growing divide between the prosperous north and the Mezzogiorno (the south), where conditions of rural poverty and emigration were similar to those experienced in Ireland.

SL: The idea came to me from the Vanoni Plan. I got this through the Italian embassy here and began to relate it to Irish circumstances, trying to repeat the calculations they had made in the context of Irish circumstances and to adjust the aims of the plans to Irish circumstances. Actually, there was not a great dissimilarity between the conditions. Their main problem was insufficient growth; their problem area was the south and ours is the west, and they had emigration. They were not concerned with emigration in the same way as we were. They were trying to encourage emigration and entering into agreements with foreign governments to take so many Italian workers every year. This plan served as a very useful foundation for me working by myself on the preparation of these statements and for the first time I began to use the term 'full employment' as a statement of the economic objectives to be followed.

I said if we were to have full employment we would have to have some means of producing the number of new jobs that would represent the termination of unemployment. The one big error I made was to assume increased production would mean an increase in employment. I didn't appreciate that there was a great deal of slack in the industrial organisation of the country which would permit considerable increases in production without any increase in employment.

This second relationship was ultimately proved to be, if anything, even better than I assumed. I think I assumed that there would be one for one. For every worker who got a job in industry there would be another worker employed somewhere in distribution, entertainment or services. In fact, recent figures suggest that the increase in employment in services industries is greater than the direct increase in production employment.

In effect I was in control of industrial policy during the period the Fianna Fáil government was in office. But the government at that time had not developed a fully comprehensive economic and social development policy. Now it is very easy to say this without taking into account all the circumstances. The need for a comprehensive economic and social policy only became clear to me during our second period of opposition. Before that we had individual plans for power, industrial development, agriculture, housing, transport, etc. But no effort had been made to draw up a national development plan, estimating all the resources available for investment in development, and setting out priorities. While we were in opposition in 1954–1955, we recognised the need for discussion concerning a national development plan, which, at that time was regarded as a bit 'pie in the sky' – rather vague and a little uncertain, with its value not generally accepted, not even by the Fianna Fáil party.

We had a strong element in the party that argued, as we had all argued during the first coalition period, that there was no necessity on the part of Fianna Fáil, while in opposition, to commit themselves in any way to a particular development policy. The government was going to collapse anyway from its own internal weakness. Consequently, we would take over again and it was better to take over without any commitment on policy. When we were in opposition in 1954 and 1956, I prepared these economic plans. They were rather immature and incomplete, but two statements I made – one in 1956 – got very considerable publicity. They were printed as special supplements in the *Irish Press*. The party was not in complete agreement with the conception of committing ourselves to planning. Some of them felt it was unwise and unnecessary to commit ourselves to any policy because the coalition government were becoming so unpopular, that we could win the election without any commitments. At this time the whole basis of pre-war policy was being challenged; all the ideas we had been working before were now slightly obsolete.

On 11 October 1955, Lemass made his famous Clery's Ballroom speech in which he stated that full employment was achievable, but only if the government invested heavily in the economy. This would be best achieved by improving both agricultural and industrial efficiency and by training a workforce for both. He predicted that within five years 100,000 new jobs could be created, thereby eliminating unemployment, which in turn would lead to a large drop in emigration. Lemass believed the programme could be funded by government borrowing – a heresy among Ireland's conservative elite. The other plank of his industry strategy was to turn capital kept in Irish financial institutions away from investing abroad and towards investing at home. He declared it was not the government's role to spend as little as possible on public expenditure; it was the government's role to improve the living conditions of its people. This was a breakaway from the orthodoxy of successive ministers for finance who considered it their primary goal to balance the books. The speech came with a candid admission that Fianna Fáil's economic policies over the previous 25 years had not brought about sufficient economic and social progress. It was quite a startling admission, but no more than a statement of the truth.

SL: The main purpose they [the speeches] served was to bring home to others the idea that economic development was something that required to be thought out in a comprehensive way; that planned capital investment was necessary; the question of where the capital was to come from; what all this could mean in terms of jobs and where the areas for development lay. The first idea of a national plan of that kind came from these speeches of mine and even then [there] was a great deal of opposition in our own party to this commitment as they saw it.

One of the many problems facing the second inter-party government was the IRA's border campaign, also known as Operation Harvest, which began on 12 December 1956 with co-ordinated attacks on RUC barracks and infrastructure across the North. The first fatality was a Catholic RUC officer, John Scally. Seán South, a pious Catholic from Limerick, and 20-year-old Fergal O'Hanlon from Monaghan died following a calamitous IRA raid on an RUC barracks in Brookeborough, County Fermanagh on New Year's Day 1957. The two deceased were accorded martyrdom status, and their deaths prompted a wave of sympathy across the country, even among those not inclined to support the IRA. Their funerals were huge affairs.

DR: The IRA troubles must have posed a considerable problem for the government. Perhaps you could tell me about them.

SL: The violence on the border started during the period when we were in opposition, and there was no effort by the coalition government to do anything about it. In the first coalition government, John Costello said that they were going to take the gun out of politics. They were reluctant afterwards to admit that they had done nothing of the sort during either coalition government period. They were aware that the extremists were organising and yet there were no positive orders issued to the Gardaí to prevent them doing so. Seán Mac Eoin was Minister for Justice at the time.[5]

Mac Eoin wanted to avoid trouble. He did not want to admit that the problem existed, and this meant that the Gardaí were completely frustrated in their whole approach to it. By the time the second coalition came into being, the earlier mistakes were beginning to bear fruit. I was in Belfast when the first serious attacks took place, and I remember the newspapers rang me up to [ask] had I any comments to make.[6] Initially, it appeared that there was a general desire to avoid taking life and particularly the life of any civilian or Irishman. Attention was directed at military institutions and operations were carried out in a way which appeared to be designed to avoid bloodshed. There was an outlook there in the mid-'50s which made it possible for the ministers of the Belfast government to come to Dublin to negotiate agreements, but this was wrecked by the IRA campaign, which again raised the old Adam in the Orange people. We were only getting back to a situation we had been in before.

In late January 1957 Clann na Poblachta's three TDs announced that they were withdrawing their support for the coalition government. Ostensibly, their withdrawal was related to the government's economic policy, but, in reality, the party's executive, which was full of hardline republicans, instructed its three TDs to withdraw support because of the government's crackdown on the IRA.

SL: The Clann na Poblachta party was killed by the general belief which they generated that they could not be trusted to stay put anywhere. I suppose their initial mistake was to join the first coalition government. By 1954 there were only three of them in the second coalition and certainly Fine Gael or Labour might have expected MacBride to let them down on the first occasion the situation arose. We all expected it, but I don't think the announcement of their withdrawal from the coalition precipitated the general election in 1957. They made that announcement after they knew there was going to be a general election anyway. They were trying to restore their independence, but in fact they disappeared.

CHAPTER 10

DE PROFUNDIS: THE FIRST PROGRAMME FOR ECONOMIC EXPANSION

'Everybody had lost confidence in the country, in its capacity to make a go of it at all. If that could not have been reversed, then we would have been sunk, undoubtedly.'

In the 1957 general election Fianna Fáil won 72 seats, exactly half the seats in the Dáil. The IRA campaign saw a surge of support for violent republicanism on the back of its border campaign and Sinn Féin won four seats on an abstentionist platform. This left Fianna Fáil with an effective majority. Clann na Poblachta was reduced to a single seat after MacBride lost his seat. Lemass felt vindicated.

SL: I believed that as an opposition party we had no chance whatsoever of success, unless we could arouse public opinion and unless we could identify ourselves with some plan of action which would be regarded as exclusively ours. We did not, perhaps, feel that we might come back as a minority government, needing all the independents voting for us to give a majority of one, and it was this unsatisfactory situation that convinced me that the next time we would need a real swing of opinion to get the people behind us. Therefore, we had to appear as the only party in the Dáil with a clear policy, and that is what the publicity during the 1957 election was about. 'We have a plan. We know what to do. We can beat this crisis.' This is what I believe helped us to get the majority we required. It was not that we were merely asking that the people change one group of politicians for another, but that they were putting into power a party who had their minds made up as to what had to be done. We probably gave the appearance of having our minds made up to a greater extent than we had. We actually had not fully complete policies at the time, but nevertheless, this is what won the election for us. Did we expect to win? Yes, I think there was no question of our winning that election. We were obviously going to have a majority and if anything, I expected a larger majority. I thought we might have as many as 80 seats. We got 77, but one or two seats could easily have gone either way. There was no doubt in my mind about the outcome of that election. You could feel that the tide was with you and there was no real fight on the other side. We were confident we were going to win. If I had been asked to forecast the result I would have given us two or three seats more.

Everybody had lost confidence in the country, in its capacity to make a go of it at all. The whole movement for emigration during that period was attributable to a lack of confidence in the future of the country as there was inability to get employment here. If that could not have been reversed, then we would have been sunk, undoubtedly.

In March 1957, just after Fianna Fáil took power, Queen's University Belfast Professor of Economics Charles Carter estimated that Irish

Seán Lemass at a rally in the 1930s

© Ronan McGreevy

Left: The headstone on the Lemass family plot in Glasnevin Cemetery did not include the name of Seán Lemass's younger brother Herbert, who he accidentally shot dead, until a century later

Right: Memorial in the Dublin Mountains marking the spot where the body of Seán Lemass's older brother Noel was found in October 1923

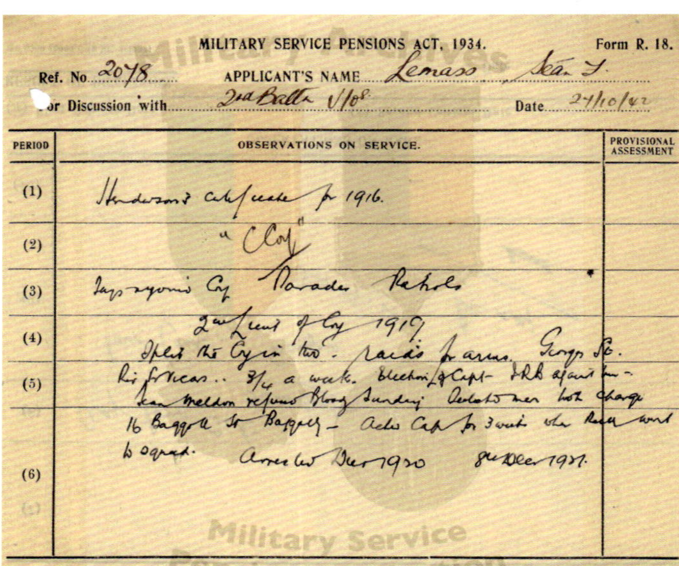

MILITARY SERVICE PENSIONS ACT, 1934. Form R. 18.

Ref. No. 2078 APPLICANT'S NAME Lemass Seán F.

For Discussion with 2nd Battn. I/Os. Date 24/10/42

PERIOD	OBSERVATIONS ON SERVICE.	PROVISIONAL ASSESSMENT
(1)	Henderson's certificate for 1916.	
(2)	"C Coy"	
(3)	Surrounding Coy Parades Patrols	
(4)	2nd Lieut of Coy 1919	
(5)	Split the Coy in two. raids for arms. Georges St. Rifles ... 3/4 a week. Election of Capt. IRB ... Sean Mellon ... Bloody Sunday ... 16 Baggot St Baggally – Acting Capt for 3 ... to squad.	
(6)	Arrested Dec 1920 8th Dec 1921.	

© Military Archives of Ireland

Seán Lemass's pension file application contains a confirmation that he was involved in the assassination of Captain Geoffrey Baggallay on Bloody Sunday, November 21st, 1916

Seán Lemass at the opening of the Erne Hydro-Electric scheme in Ballyshannon, Co Donegal in 1952. Lemass stressed practical cooperation between North and South as a precursor to ending partition

Dermot Ryan (extreme left) with Seán Lemass and future Taoiseach Jack Lynch and their wives at an event in the 1960s

Above: Seán Lemass went on an open top car ride through the streets of Washington in October 1963

Right: Seán Lemass gave a speech while in Washington to the National Press Club in which he spoke about the removal of partition

Above: Seán Lemass as Taoiseach met President John F Kennedy on two occasions. Once, during President Kennedy's historic visit to Ireland in June 1963 and then in October 1963. This photograph taken in the White House shows Kennedy in a custom-designed rocking chair that he used to ease his chronic back pain

Left: Seán Lemass with his wife Kathleen with President John F Kennedy and his sister Jean Kennedy-Smith, future US ambassador to Ireland, at a reception in Washington in October 1963

© Getty images /Independent News and Media

Left: Seán Lemass shares a joke with President Éamon de Valera. The two had the closest of political relationships, but Lemass was frustrated that de Valera clung on as Taoiseach for so long

Right: Jack Lynch was Seán Lemass's preferred successor as Taoiseach when he resigned in November 1966

Seán Lemass's visit to Belfast to meet the Northern premier Terence O'Neill in January 1965 was hailed as a breakthrough in North-South relations. Here the pair are with their wives, Kathleen (second from left) and Jean O'Neill

Princess Grace's visit to Dublin in 1961 brought a *frisson* of Hollywood glamour to Ireland. Born Grace Kelly, her grandfather John Peter Kelly was from Drimurla in Mayo. Here she is with her husband Prince Ranier of Monaco

Seán Lemass's hat beside a copy of the July 1963 *Time* magazine issue

Seán Lemass at his desk as Taoiseach in the 1960s. His pipe was his constant companion, but he would eventually succumb to a smoking-related illness in May 1971

income per head was only 55 per cent of that in the UK, and in Connacht it was just 45 per cent. In such circumstances the idea of Irish unification was a 'dreary fantasy', he concluded. He wondered why any Ulster unionist would want to live in a country he or she did not want to be part of and also be significantly worse off.

In 1956 Thomas Kenneth (T.K.) Whitaker was appointed secretary general of the Department of Finance. He was only 39, an independent and fearless thinker with a track record of speaking his mind on government policy. He challenged the Department of Finance's 'inverted Micawberism, its slowness to see the merits of a case, its maddening questions, its dilatoriness, its blind devotion to precedent, the dead hand with which it stifles every initiative'. Whitaker addressed the sense of despair in the country by assembling a team of civil servants in early 1957 to come up with an economic plan that would rescue the state from economic oblivion. He presented the paper, entitled *The Irish Economy*, to Minister for Finance James Ryan with a typically forthright observation that if nothing was done, it would be 'better to make an immediate move towards re-incorporation into the United Kingdom rather than wait until our economic decadence became ever more apparent'. Lemass, now in charge of government economic policy, embraced the tenets of Whitaker's plan. It was published in draft form in May 1958 and then as a White Paper entitled the *First Programme for Economic Expansion* in November 1958. Whitaker would later state that Lemass was the 'great moving dynamic spirit in all of this'. The programme was brutal in its exposition of the problems Ireland faced. Economic protectionism made no sense in a country haemorrhaging population. Irish industry would have to reorient itself towards free trade. The programme offered tax breaks for exporters and technical assistance to that end. The chief driver of the Irish economy was to be the private sector, but the government would help by investing in electricity, telecommunications, shipping and aviation. The programme set a modest growth forecast of 2 per cent, which it predicted would lead to a doubling in the Irish economy in 35 years. In reality the economy doubled in size by 1970.

SL: Dr James Ryan asked Whitaker to prepare his White Paper on economic expansion, which we decided to publish over his name. The publication of that White Paper was intended anyway but the novel aspect was to publish it over the name of the secretary of the Department of Finance. We had some doubts about the anonymity of the civil service, using the name of a particular officer. We made this decision because we thought the public would accept the re-thinking of our economic policies and the preparation of the programme based on what we saw more readily if it appeared as an economist's idea rather than a political one. That is why it was published in that form. The preparation of the first programme took a long time. It needed a lot of discussion, drafts had to be prepared and a cabinet committee was formed consisting of Jim Ryan, myself and the Minister for Agriculture at the time [Patrick Smith] to go through the draft. The main difficulty in preparing the draft was to resist the desire to smudge it a bit, to be specific in the commitments that it implied, to keep a few more options open.

The temptation to be less specific was there all the time. We had some doubts about the political decision to smudge it a bit. One of the basic decisions taken during its course of preparation was to talk in terms of a growth rate of 2 per cent per annum in economic production and although that was double the previous rate of growth it nevertheless looked rather small in relation to what we were talking about. The ultimate decision to specify a 2 per cent rate of growth was influenced by two considerations – first, to produce a programme that the public would see as reasonable, one that could be achieved; and secondly, if we did better than planned it would be an enormous boost to morale. There were some signs of restoring confidence in 1958, even before the first programme was published. This, no doubt, was very largely due to the propagandist efforts of the government and their efforts and their saying, 'We are going to pull this country out of the situation it is in. We may not know yet how we are going to do it, but we are going to do it.' Speeches like this and the anticipation of the publication of the first programme helped to produce a better atmosphere. The publication of the programme itself, and its acceptance by all organised bodies, the trade unions, the employers, the Federation of Irish Industries and the farmers, was a major achievement. They all said they were going to try to make it work. This had an immediate effect in 1959, even though the programme did not begin to take effect until 1960, when we already had a build-up of public confidence in the possibility of pulling out of this situation.

In July 1958 Lemass's own legislation, the Industrial Development (Encouragement of External Investment) Act, removed many of the remaining restrictions imposed by the Control of Manufactures Acts of 1932 and 1934. The former protectionist had dismantled his own policy and previous thinking on industrial development, self-sufficiency and autarky. There would be no turning back for Lemass or for the country. War of Independence veteran turned successful businessman Joe Griffin noted a new mood in the country as early as November 1958: 'We in Ireland are beginning – only beginning – to throw off the pall of gloom that has been darkening our days, confusing our minds and our policies, and distracting our intelligence and our energies. I sense it in many walks of life ... The doctrine of our poverty in material resources continues to plague.'

DR: The most significant thing was the programme itself, because it demonstrated the feasibility of doing better than we had done and caused people's attitudes to change.

SL: Yes, it forced people to think in terms of increased production and growth – we were not running away from the problems. Of course, one can never pinpoint all the factors that influenced the public mood, as it was influenced at that time. There is no question but that the air of deep despondency which existed in 1957 had disappeared completely by 1960 and 1961 and has not reappeared since. While there is a great deal of purely political criticism of different activities of the government, there is no change in the public mood at all. There was the initial stimulus of the publication of a programme which created a favourable economic climate and outlook, the influx of foreign capital and the fact that once the programme got under way it was almost certain to continue its own momentum.

Lemass's status during the preparation of the first economic plan underlined the absurdity of de Valera lingering in the office of taoiseach. De Valera was 74 when he was returned as taoiseach in 1957, yet he remained Fianna Fáil's greatest electoral asset, judging by his ability to secure an effective overall majority for the party. Lemass had been tánaiste in all the Fianna Fáil governments from 1948 on. He was clearly marked as de Valera's successor, but when was de Valera going to leave? Speculation on de Valera's succession began shortly after Fianna Fáil resumed government in 1957. There quickly emerged two realistic candidates, Lemass and James Ryan, but Ryan made it clear he did not want the position. De Valera's dallying copper-fastened Lemass's succession. 'Dev set it up for Lemass,' Charles Haughey revealed years later. 'He made him tánaiste, neutralised opposition. I'm sure he talked to the old guard as well.' On 8 January 1959 de Valera announced that he would be Fianna Fáil's candidate for the presidency. The presidential election had to be held by 25 June of that year, by which time Seán T. O'Kelly was due to complete his term of office. The announcement took many in the party by surprise; Lemass stayed silent at the time, but he was forced once again to wait.

DR: One of the questions I see here was – at some stage the question of whether the party would want you as taoiseach must have been raised. How far back was this before 1959, in other words the fact that it was clear that you were going to be taoiseach?

SL: I would say there was never any question in anybody's mind that when Dev went, I was going to step into his place. Dev might not have gone up for election as president in 1959. It did not necessarily have to be 1959. Seán T. O'Kelly had to retire, but there were other alternatives to Dev as candidate for the presidency. When he took the decision to stand for the presidency, I was surprised that he did not resign as taoiseach immediately. I think this was a bad tactic. I felt there was a suggestion he was going up for election as president and if he did not win, he was going to remain on as taoiseach. I felt that from the point of view of running the election campaign and exercising authority I should have been made taoiseach as soon as he announced his candidature. He should have given the public appearance of burning his boats so that people would say, 'If he is not president, he is nothing.' I felt a certain feeling of frustration that I was sitting around, designated as taoiseach, but not active or effective as such. It was only on the eve of the poll that he announced his resignation as taoiseach. It would have been wiser for him, both from the electioneering point of view and from the party point of view, to have resigned as taoiseach as soon as he went out campaigning.

The presidential election was held the same day as a referendum on proportional representation (PR) instigated by de Valera with the support of Lemass. Proportional representation on a multi-seat basis was enshrined in the 1937 constitution, but Fianna Fáil's narrow electoral defeats in 1948 and in 1951 convinced many in the party that it was not an electoral system designed to create stable governments. Instead, the party proposed a first-past-the-post system as operated in the UK.

SL: De Valera was in favour of the abolition of PR and we all shared his opinion. While there was a unanimous vote in favour of the PR legislation, there were degrees of enthusiasm in practice when we came to run the plebiscite in 1959. Much discussion took place as to the wisdom of linking the PR referendum with the presidential election. The general feeling was very strongly in favour of this course before the voting took place. Afterwards, there was some doubt partly because people could apparently work hard in the interests of the party while concentrating on one issue and forgetting to emphasise the importance of the other; partly because public sentiment could be in favour of giving the government one thing and not the other – not supporting them all along the line; and, I think, partly because there was some confusion in the public mind.

One of the problems which arose on that occasion, and will probably arise again, is how to present the issue in a form which does not imply voting for a negative. The people are asked to approve the bill by the question. 'Are you for it or against it?' That bill was presented to the public in the common parlance of politicians as 'the abolition of PR'. It was not put in the positive sense of voting for the straight vote system. It is contended that quite a substantial number of people voted 'no' because they were against PR, not realising that to get rid of PR they had to vote 'yes'. The extent of this is anyone's guess but it was said frequently at the time.

At the beginning, de Valera personally was disposed to favour the alternative vote rather than the straight vote. He certainly argued in favour of the single-member constituency with the alternative for a long time. During the discussion in the Dáil, Fine Gael said that if we changed to the alternative vote,[1] they would support the bill. MacEntee and Frank Aiken were strongly in favour of the straight vote. I had a more open mind, but by this time de Valera would not agree to the view he himself had been arguing beforehand. He had committed himself in various ways in the Dáil and had to stick to the new decision. I was in favour of accepting Fine Gael's terms, which would have implied a strong majority for the change, and the bill could have been amended accordingly. I personally would have attached more importance to the single seat aspect than the straight vote. I think de Valera made a mistake because we could have got the single-member constituency with the alternative vote through in 1959 with the co-operation from the Fine Gael party.

We were fighting the plebiscite for PR at the time. I felt this was a little bit unfair to me as I still didn't know whether I was going to be taoiseach or not. I would prefer if he hadn't been the candidate. This was despite the fact that, perhaps more than anyone else, I recognised he had passed the point of no return of being effective as a party leader. The whole management of the party was left to me; Dáil business was left to me, he didn't intervene at all. I was concerned with the formulation of economic policy. The preparation of the first programme was left to me. He was told what was happening, but he had not for many years attempted to initiate anything. At one time he was the initiator of policy, but this had ceased by 1948 or thereabouts. He then became the arbitrator, the man to whom you took your case when you had an argument or wanted something done and he decided whether to support you or not. He never asked why you did anything; new ideas did not come from him at all.

The presidential election and PR referendum took place on 17 June 1959. De Valera left it to the last minute to resign as taoiseach, tendering his resignation to the outgoing president, Seán T. O'Kelly, at 9.30 that night. The public were not enthused by either candidate and a turnout of 58.3 per cent was very low for the period. De Valera won with 56.3 per cent of the vote; Mac Eoin got 43.7 per cent.

The PR referendum was lost narrowly, by 51.8 per cent to 48.2 per cent. On 22 June 1959 the national executive of Fianna Fáil nominated Lemass to succeed de Valera as party leader and therefore taoiseach. The parliamentary party unanimously supported his nomination, the proposer being Seán MacEntee and the seconder Frank Aiken. Seán Lemass was finally taoiseach three weeks and a day shy of his 60th birthday. It was a job he accepted with great reluctance.

PART II

RELUCTANT TAOISEACH

"AN OLD MAN
IN A HURRY"
(1959–1966)

CHAPTER 11

PORTRAIT OF A TAOISEACH

'This is the life I had to lead and I have no sense of having suffered anything either in my relations with my family or myself personally.'

The man who became taoiseach on 26 June 1959 had spent his whole life from the age of 16 in the service of Ireland and his whole adult life from the age of 23 in politics. By the time he became taoiseach, his four children, Maureen (born 1925), Peggy (1926), Noel Jr (1929) and Sheila (1932) were grown up. He was never less than energetic, but in the 1950s he was frequently ill with phlebitis (inflammation of a vein usually in the legs) and had gall-bladder problems. He was laid up for a time after the 1951 general election, suffering from exhaustion, and again in late 1956 and early 1957. During his second bout of illness de Valera advised him to spend his time convalescing improving his Irish language skills. Lemass, who was as indifferent to the Irish language as de Valera was passionate about it, never took him up on his offer.

Lemass was not a big drinker, but he was a heavy smoker. He was rarely seen without his pipe and was happy to be photographed smoking it. It gave him an air of contemplation. He smoked nearly a pound of tobacco a week, a habit which many believe contributed to his death in 1971 at the age of 71. Politics had not made Lemass a wealthy man. A more corruptible politician could have used his status as Minister for Industry and Commerce to enrich himself, but Lemass was scrupulous both in being incorruptible and in appearing to be incorruptible. The Lemasses lived in rented accommodation until the late 1930s, when Seán Lemass bought his parents' home at 53 Palmerston Road in Rathmines. It would remain their home for the rest of his life.

Seán Lemass's marriage was a happy one, notwithstanding the demands of the job and his long absences from home. In a rare interview after he retired, Kathleen Lemass said her husband was 'serious-minded ... but I was fond of dancing and the gay life. But they say opposites attract, don't they?'

Maureen married Charles Haughey and the couple had four children. Peggy, who was christened Margaret, married an army officer, Jack O'Brien, and they had five children. Peggy later taught at the Institute of Education. Lemass's only son, Noel Jr, married Eileen Delaney and they had four children. Noel followed his father into politics, representing the Dublin South-West constituency from 1956 until his premature death at the age of 47 in 1976. He was also a parliamentary secretary in the Department of Finance from 1969 to 1973. His wife, Eileen, unsuccessfully contested the by-election following her husband's death but later won a seat in Dáil Éireann, which she held for ten years. She was also an MEP. Sheila married John O'Connor and they had four children.

Kathleen Lemass frequently accompanied her husband on official outings and 'enjoyed it all immensely. I always loved going out and meeting people, and my husband likes me to go everywhere with him.' Lemass, on the other hand, told Ryan he hated diplomatic dinners: 'most boring functions! This is the part I used to hate – white tie dinners in Dublin Castle. I loathed them. Literally, there would be a feeling of deep loathing inside me. This is not enjoyment.'

Though Lemass was among the most dynamic and hard-working of ministers, he also guarded his leisure time. He brought the same impatience to his working hours as he did to the business of politics. Stories abound of his irritation at being presented with businesses that detained him from leaving at the appointed hour of 5 p.m. Officials trod carefully when confronting him with some late business as he was putting on his hat and scarf to return home. He was far from idle when not in the office and spent much of his time at home reading government documents.

The family spent many holidays at the Hodson Bay Hotel in Athlone, owned at the time by P.J. Lenihan, who became a Fianna Fáil TD in 1965, four years after his son Brian Sr became a TD. Brian Sr had a long political career as a minister and was a presidential candidate in 1990. Brian's sons, Brian Jr and Conor, served in government. P.J.'s daughter, Mary O'Rourke, also had a long political career and served as a minister. When time allowed Lemass played golf, usually at Skerries golf course or a game of cards with trusted friends. He attended race meetings occasionally. He knew there would not be much opportunity for either after assuming the office of taoiseach.

DR: I've been trying to work out a profile of Seán Lemass, to know what he is like – what are his characteristics? What sort of person is he? In doing this I have decided that you like structure; you like a meeting at a specific time which ends at a specific time; and you like to have your breakfast at a specific time. In fact, you like things organised.

SL: That's right, I like everything in its right place and I suppose I'm a creature of habit too because when I go away for a holiday, I like to go to a hotel which I've been to before – I don't like going to new hotels. I like to do the things which I am accustomed to doing and to do them even regularly. From time to time I used to have groups which I played cards with – I liked to have that fixed night every week so that you could organise your life on the assumption that you were not available for other things on that night. On the fishing trips I go to the same hotel with the same people, and I would dislike having to go off to some strange place.

It's less trouble. To go fishing, it's more pleasant to go to the same hotel, meet the same staff, have the same boat with the same gillie in the boat than to be making contact with new people – I suppose it makes your recreation more enjoyable, it makes it less of an effort then establishing new acquaintances and getting to know new people and their peculiarities. I don't know, but I suppose this would be one of my characteristics. Whether it's a good characteristic or a bad one somebody else can decide.

DR: In a way you are against change, and yet you are a man who has brought about tremendous change.

SL: Before I became taoiseach, I used to go regularly to a race meeting on Saturday evenings. This was my Saturday recreation. I stopped work about one o'clock on a Saturday and went to a race meeting. I liked this very much; I liked meeting people; I liked the occasional flutter on a racehorse, although I was never a serious gambler in the sense that other people are, but I liked the occasion, and it became a habit of mine to go every Saturday to a race meeting. I'd be disgusted if there was no race meeting on because of bad weather or because it was too far out of Dublin. But when I became taoiseach, I decided that I couldn't do this as it wasn't in conformity with the dignity of my office and it took me a hell of a long time to adjust to the situation. I had nothing to do on a Saturday afternoon. Ultimately, I began to acquire a habit of bringing home the longer type of governmental reports which you'd want to study at leisure – copies of *The Economist* and *The Statist* and other papers of that kind, which were serious reading – and reading those on a Saturday afternoon. When the time came that this was no longer necessary, it was quite an effort again to adjust to a new way of life. This was to do with this serious type of reading on a Saturday afternoon when you'd no other time during the week.

DR: In other words, you found that structure, as I said earlier ...

SL: That's right; a tremendous satisfaction in everything being in its same place as it always is, and everything happening at the same time as it should happen.

DR: The interesting thing, as a man, is that you have been the cause of far greater change.

SL: Yes, I suppose that would be right.

DR: You want to give your time to a thing.

SL: Insofar as change was an objective of life, this was concentrated in the one area of public activity and you didn't want to give any time to the business of organising or thinking about changes anywhere else. Even though I've more time for things now, this is still true. A habit. It's a habit. This has become a habit now, even to the extent of being mildly irritated if, at home, something has been moved from the place to which it has been accustomed into some other place and I have to look for it. My wife now understands this, and, as far as she is concerned, everything is left where it should be. Although when she gets into my study and tidies up – she doesn't get in very often – but when she does, there's at least half an hour during which I'm intensely irritated because things have been touched! She doesn't tell me she's been working in the study, she lets me find that out for myself.

The grandchildren come to the house periodically and for various reasons my study is the light of their life; they love to get in there and explore and investigate as there are all sorts of odd things in it, so I've now got into the habit of locking the door when they are coming so that they can't get in, because otherwise everything would be in a different place afterwards!

DR: To what extent did the pressures that inevitably must arise affect your time at home?

SL: Well, I don't know. As far as I am concerned, I had a normal family life. It was the only one I ever knew. I tell the story about my daughter [Sheila] and the Reverend Mother in Muckross College.[1] The Reverend Mother said, 'Tell your father to do this' and she replied, 'I can't. I don't know him well enough.' Literally, that happened, but I was never conscious of a lack of communication in my family. They probably would think this a natural, normal thing too.

DR: What was the literal amount of time you were out? Were you out, say, six nights out of seven and Saturday afternoon and Sunday afternoon, or was it as bad as that?

SL: It could be at times. You could be out every night, but you would probably have a couple of nights a week at home, anyway. Weekends would vary, depending on electioneering or by-elections or things of that kind. The job of bringing up my family was done by my wife; the family are closer to her than they are to me, but I suppose this is normal in most houses. The mother is the linchpin of the family.

How long you would be out varied. You could be out at half past seven and return at half past eight; you would count that as at home. I did a lot of work at home, but this would not necessarily mean a break in family life. I used to bring home a great deal of reading and that kind of thing so the family were accustomed to me sitting in my armchair reading, but the children could come and ask me to do their sums for them. There would be no reluctance to interrupt my work. I should say my relationships with my children were quite normal and on the whole we had a happy family life in the fullest sense of the term. I may not have been as fully informed of everything they were doing as my wife was, but I would discuss everything with her.

This is the life I had to lead and I have no sense of having suffered anything either in my relations with my family or myself personally. I should think this is probably true of most ministers. As a minister you often feel that everybody is looking for something from you. This is the great characteristic, everyone wants something, a decision, award or encouragement or help in some respect. Every contact you make is somebody who wants something from you and this often gets you down. Nobody wants to do anything for you, the impression you get all the time is that everybody who calls to see you, rings you, or writes you a letter wants something from you. It might be just a decision, but it would often be something more personal or help in some form.

This is what you have to escape from, but escape is not easy either. I found if I went down the country that three nights was the maximum I could stay in any hotel; on the fourth day the fellows were coming who wanted something from me. Going abroad was a different matter because there were official functions to be attended. You could never disappear off the face of the earth and have a really relaxed holiday anywhere.

DR: I put down here, 'Does a man ever wonder is it all worthwhile?'

SL: I would not say so. Nobody comes into this business except someone who thinks it is worthwhile and who is deeply interested in politics and in the work of the government. I would say it would be foolish to undertake it for any other reason. Nobody does it for money because anybody who works as hard as a man has to, to win a ministry, could probably earn a great deal more somewhere else. Indeed, I think it would be true to say that most ministers would continue if their salaries were cut in half. They do it because they want to. Although I think they are underpaid it does not affect the attitude of the individual to the job.

DR: You liked to go home every night even if meant starting out at one o'clock.

SL: I would rather motor all night, then go to bed to have a few hours' rest than stay in a hotel and get up to return the next morning. I used to feel I could sleep better at home. I had to go to bed when people still wanted to talk to me. When I drove out of a town I had escaped; I would sleep much better in my own bed than in a hotel bed and I could sleep late in the morning rather than having to get up at an unearthly hour still tired. I rarely stayed overnight in any hotel. My wife used to encourage me to stay away; she said it was too strenuous. As long as I was in government, I used to try and get home at night. The outstanding example was in the 1957 general election, when I drove from Dublin to Tralee, addressed a meeting in Tralee, got into the car and came back to Dublin eating chocolate to sustain myself and to keep awake.

Having power is no good, it is the exercise of power. It is perfectly true that a lot of these social functions had to be attended as part of the job – you could not opt out of them. Nevertheless, they were an interruption. The part of government that I used to like most was sitting in the office with the problems set out in front of me, working on a solution, discussing it with other people, getting their views and ultimately seeing daylight. I used to enjoy this far more than public appearances or electioneering or the functions and the cups of tea.

These are chores; the really satisfying job was the analysis of problems and their solution in the silence of my own office. I think this must be true of most ministers, though I suppose some of them like the public aspect of it more than others. Nobody ever asked to become a minister. Some prefer not to be asked but will accept a post because of a sense of loyalty to the party. A man is no good as a minister unless he is completely dedicated to his job and his government and really concerned to do something worthwhile for his government and his own reputation.

Certainly, for a large part of my life I would not have swapped my job, nor did I ever want to become taoiseach. When I became taoiseach, I was very concerned because I felt it was going to change my way of life. Things which I would have done as a private citizen or as an ordinary member of the government I couldn't do as taoiseach. I was fairly worried as to how the public would look upon me as taoiseach after de Valera and how I was going to work out. I wondered whether I would succeed in holding the government together, getting it working the way he did and naturally what the verdict upon my job was going to be. The public felt my work as Minister for Industry and Commerce had been fairly good. I would have been happy to stay there all my life. I would have preferred if time stood still, and de Valera did not get too old to do the job. When the time came, they urged him to go forward for election as president. I argued against it suggesting somebody else for president and pointing out that although he could not be as active as taoiseach as he normally should, it was not essential in the circumstances. He would just have to sit in his office and continue to exercise an adjudicator attitude, and I would be the deputy and see that the work was done. I admit this was selfish; I didn't want to upset my own position.

CHAPTER 12

INTO THE SIXTIES

'I think what the public are really looking for is an honest man and this is far more true now when television is the medium of communication. They may not get him, they may get a crook, but whatever he is, he must be able to present himself to them as a man who is to be trusted, a man who is seriously concerned to tell them the facts, and who can be relied on to do what he intends to do, as quickly as possible.'

Seán Lemass's election in the Dáil as taoiseach was a formality, but he first had to face political and personal attacks similar to those that would be faced by his son-in-law Charles Haughey 20 years later. Lemass's elevation to the role came just days after Éamon de Valera was unconvincingly elected president and Fianna Fáil's plans to change the electoral system were defeated.

Much of the commentary was informed by the view in the opposition that Fianna Fáil had tried to pull a political stroke by putting forward a new electoral system that was to the party's advantage. Former Fine Gael leader Richard Mulcahy said it had been nothing less than an attempt by Fianna Fáil to turn Ireland into a 'one-party state'.

The most personal criticism came from Fine Gael TD Oliver J. Flanagan, who claimed he could only associate Lemass with 'failure, graft and dishonesty', but, as ever, could provide no evidence to back up his assertions.

Lemass refused to rise to the taunts of his opponents. 'During the course of the debate, many things were said to which I would ordinarily like to reply, but I do not think this is the occasion on which to do so. All I will say now is that I shall endeavour to fulfil my duties as taoiseach to the best of my ability.' Lemass's nomination as taoiseach was passed by 75 votes to 51. He accepted the vote with humility, acknowledging that self-doubt was a necessary part of the job. 'I do not think it is possible for any man to face the prospect of becoming head of the Irish government without having doubts as to his personal ability to discharge properly the responsibilities of the office and anxiety as to how the country may fare during his term. I have these doubts and that anxiety.'

He then went on to set out a theme which he would return to throughout his seven years as taoiseach – the notion of patriotism.

> Personally, I believe that national progress of any kind depends largely upon an upsurge of patriotism – a revival of patriotism, if you will – directed towards constructive purposes. Patriotism, as I understand it, is a combination of love of country, pride in its history, traditions and culture, and a determination to add to its prestige and its achievements.

The first item on the agenda as taoiseach was to pick his cabinet. Lemass showed an uncharacteristic caution in reappointing almost all the old guard who had featured in Fianna Fáil cabinets since 1932. MacEntee was made Minister for Social Welfare and created tánaiste on account of his seniority. Having been tánaiste himself, Lemass had little regard for the role. 'The tanáiste's only function is to take the chair at cabinet meetings when the taoiseach is absent.' He moved Jack Lynch from Education to Industry and Commerce. Future president Paddy Hillery entered the cabinet as Minister for Education. He also created a fifteenth cabinet position, the Department of Transport, Fuel and Power, which was eventually filled by Erskine Childers. The critical role of Minister for Finance was retained by his friend Dr James Ryan.

SL: MacEntee was the senior minister. It would have seemed a rebuke to him if I did not appoint him as tánaiste, so I did appoint him. This raises the question of the age at which a minister should retire. One of the weaknesses in the cabinet here is that most of its members depend upon their jobs for their livelihood. It is serious for them if they find themselves out of a job. In other countries this problem does not arise. My view as to the capabilities of individual members of the government would be a personal view but I would certainly have no difficulty in putting them in order of merit from the point of view of efficiency if I had to do it.

The personal difficulty was getting A. [or] B. into the office and saying, 'I don't think you are good enough to be minister and I am removing you from the government' and if it came to a crucial point I tried to find a way of doing it which would take the bare look off it. I could never do what Macmillan did with his Chancellor of the Exchequer.[1] In our case there was also the realisation of a narrow working majority. One could not create a personal antagonism which would cause discontent in the party and could be used to destroy our majority. Macmillan had a majority of a couple of hundred, where withdrawal from the party usually means political death.

I would have preferred to make more changes than I actually made. I decided not to make changes except those consequential upon my own transfer from the Department of Industry and Commerce and the enlargement of the cabinet by an additional member. The creation of Transport and Power involved some changes, but I wanted to go even further. I considered the foundation of a fifteenth department and the identity of the minister.

There were good reasons for splitting up the Department of Industry and Commerce and setting up the Ministry of Transport, Fuel and Power. One was the understanding that the Department of Industry and Commerce was a very big department whose activities I could manage only because of my intimate knowledge of the department. I had been there all the time. But I felt a new minister coming in would have an undue load to carry as he could not possibly have the same integral knowledge that I had and therefore could not manage it successfully. That was the basic consideration.[2]

I had not decided on the implementation of any new policies. All the policy decisions appropriate to that period had been taken, but I did feel I could get these moving quicker than I could have done as Minister for Industry and Commerce. Dev, at this time, had ceased to be a driving force. Now I felt able to do what I had been unable to do before, namely put my foot down on the accelerator and get things moving more rapidly. There was no question of any change in policy. Policy is something that is always developing. You could never say that policies decided in 1959 would be applicable in 1960. Certainly, when I came into office as taoiseach there was no question in my mind of a change of policy. There were wide areas in which I wanted to explore the possibility of a change of policy but to my mind it was only developing from where we were, applying the same principles as before in a more effective way.

DR: You could fairly say, in other words, your personal philosophy and outlook had been pretty well absolutely in line with the party and country during the previous seven or eight years. There was nothing which you tried to do, and you decided, 'I won't do this because it would not be accepted.' Pretty well the general outlook and philosophy, you found it was yours?

SL: Yes, that is so. In some areas I did not attempt to influence the course of policy at all. For example, I would say Dev would have been hesitant about EEC [European Economic Community] membership. He would have been hesitant about taking too specific a stand in the United Nations. He felt very strongly that the small independent state had to keep clear of foreign external commitments; they were bound to lose out in any dealing with the bigger powers. I would not have had this feeling at all. I said at a conference which preceded the establishment of Marshall Aid in 1947, in Paris, that small countries must always be on the side of international co-operation and institutions to make this co-operation effective. Dev argued with me when I came back. His instinct would have been the reverse – to avoid commitment to international organisations, to try and maintain an independence of foreign obligations while it would not have been thought possible in this age.

DR: Now, what were the factors under your leadership which were basically responsible for the industrial production achievement of the first programme?

SL: I think it is fair to say that circumstances became favourable to us around 1959–60 for an increase in industrial production. Now, that alone would not have produced the high increase, but the factors which contributed were the publication of the Programme for Economic Expansion and the demonstration, through that programme, of the feasibility of achieving these results. More specifically, the withdrawal of the Control of Manufactures Act; encouraging foreign capital to come in and participate in Irish industrial development; and the general air of optimism which began to develop in the country.

Lemass's biggest challenge was twofold: to grow the economy; and so bring an end to forced emigration. This, he believed, could only be achieved by a change of mentality and an end to the stereotype of the Irish as a 'grievance-loving, lachrymose people, not very efficient or interested in modern technology'. He identified emigration as the principal threat to the state. In his 1953 book *The Vanishing Irish*, the Irish-American priest Fr John O'Brien pondered why it was that so many Irish people emigrated. Some, he recognised, did so for economic reasons, but for others it was an ingrained response to their circumstances. The civil servant T.K. Whitaker described emigration as a 'vicious circle' that would lead only to more emigration 'resulting in a smaller domestic market depleted of initiative and skill, and a reduced incentive, whether for Irishmen or foreigners to undertake and organise the productive enterprises which alone can provide increased employment opportunities and higher living standards'. Lemass believed that emigration was not just a response to the economic circumstances of the time, but a mindset to be challenged.

DR: Off-hand, I am not aware to what extent emigration has been analysed in those who leave because there is no employment and those who are leaving in order to get a better opportunity.

SL: I am not so sure it would. What is the cause of emigration? The lack of employment opportunities here or the comparison between standards of living here and elsewhere? The theory up to the present moment is the lack of employment opportunities. We attempted – the Fianna Fáil organisation, one time – to carry out an experiment of this kind. We got a 50:50 split: half the emigrants because they could not get jobs and half had a job when they left.

They wanted different jobs; they wanted to leave home; and nobody has really analysed the force of the desire of the young people, of the young men, to break away from the discipline of the family and the parish priest into an area where they can sin at last. And where all the money you earn is your own; this is so in every community.

DR: In our case, due to size, they tend to go abroad.

SL: They go to Dublin; that is why the population of Dublin is growing much more rapidly than the rest of the country. I remember asking Noel Huggard,[3] in Ashford Castle, if he had much trouble keeping the staff after he trained them. 'Coming to work for me is as good as emigrating.' 'What do you mean by that?' I asked. 'It means that they are here on their own; they can spend their money on their clothes; they don't have to hand it up to their father on a Friday night. They live in a glamorous atmosphere; they can get nothing abroad that they can't get here.'

DR: So, you see emigration as a somewhat inevitable progress towards urban living and metropolitan areas.

SL: The attraction of the city is enormous, away from home, away from the constraints of home. This is a very natural instinct. It is like the bird coming out of the nest to get away from it, trying to learn to fly on its own. I suppose there is even built in, in your men particularly, a certain antagonism to the parental control, which is part of nature's way of forcing them out to work on their own and set up their own families independently. This is human nature and I don't think you can change it, but it would be desirable from the point of view of the community if this natural desire to get away from home should find its expression within the bounds of the home country. I am not disturbed by the fact that there is some emigration. I do think a small country like this could never be completely without some emigration.

DR: Are you not afraid that what we are losing is the fellow who has that little more courage to go out, the fellow who had a little more gumption?

SL: This is an assumption that may or may not be true. I am not so sure it does not require more courage for a fellow to open a garage in his own town than to go and work in a garage over in England. What I am trying to say is that it requires more courage to stand up to the jealousy of your neighbours than to go away and work among strangers. We are talking about the enterprising man.

The fellow who sees an opportunity in his own home town that someone else has missed is the enterprising man. You are saying that the fellow who goes off to London is the enterprising type of man. I don't think this is true. I think there is now a fashion of escaping to London. People are not going to London because there is opportunity there, but because there is easier picking in it than at home. I would say the reverse is true; that the enterprising and courageous fellow is the man who stays at home and fights all the obstacles impeding his success.

What I am saying is that a community like ours, a small country like ours, expects some portion of the young people born here to feel that the world gives them greater opportunity than at home. This is not merely true of Ireland; it is true of young people everywhere. There is far more emigration from England around the world than from Ireland and it does not have anything to do, I think, with working conditions. There will always be people who feel there are very green fields over the other side of the hill, and go off looking for them, but I would not be very worried if this produced an outflow of population provided the outflow were not too serious, not sufficient to impede the natural increase in the population.

Lemass's government presided over the launching of television in Ireland. Ireland was one of the last countries in western Europe to get a television service. Britain had one from 1932, though it was suspended during the war. Lemass was involved from 1957 in bringing forward proposals for an Irish television service. He and other members of the cabinet were in favour of a privately funded but publicly supervised television station. Lemass, though, changed his mind when he became taoiseach and decided to set up a public broadcaster instead. On New Year's Eve 1961, Telefís Éireann was opened by President de Valera. Lemass was, in many ways, born too late for television. He never fully trusted the medium and was known to complain about programmes that did not reflect well on his government or the country. He conceded early, though, that a television station should not be a political organ of the government of the day. Television brought British and American culture into the living rooms of the Irish public.

DR: Would you say a particular pressure on us is the comparison, as a result of television and other forms of communication, with countries that have a stronger economic model?

SL: I don't know. I am not worried about it. We are one of the rich countries of the world, one of the top 20 as far as standards of living are concerned. The difference between our standards and the British or the Americans or the Swedes is quite small. The gap between our standards and the Africans is enormously wide and television is doing much more to show appalling low standards that prevail over most of the world than to show the higher standards in a few countries. The lesson, that we are one of the fortunate people in the world, is not always brought home through television and other means of communication; the problems we have are of no significance at all in relation to those of a great majority of mankind.

Despite his wariness of television, Lemass was a fluent performer on the medium and a keen student of the impact that it was having and would have on politics.

DR: Does television influence voting patterns, and, if so, how?

SL: I remember that after the British government election of 1964, I was very interested in the effect of television on public voting. I succeeded in getting two reports which had been prepared, one by the BBC and the other by ITV, regarding the impact of television on the voting pattern in the British election. Both came to the same conclusion that, fundamentally, television had no influence on the voting pattern, and much that had appeared on the television programmes passed over the heads of the people and was not even remembered by them.

The only things they were able to recall, after the elections, were specific things about the amount of the old age pensions, about things that were immediate and practical and had no wider political implications other than the immediate benefit to the individual. But all the discussions on British television about Britain's role in the world, Britain's economic policy and Britain's part in Europe were not even remembered by the public after the elections. One thing that television has done and will continue to do now, is to emphasise the importance of the personality of the party leader. He becomes very much more a person in the minds of the public than he was previously.

The public reaction to him, their trust in him, their acceptance of his reasonableness and intelligence is, and will continue to be, increasingly important in forthcoming elections. More than the personality itself, it is the impression of his personality which is given when he is seen that is important. What is said on television is very rarely remembered. In party politics the individual leader and top personalities are more important than formerly. In Britain, the only thing certain was that television had enhanced the acceptance and understanding of the personality of the leader alone of [Harold] Wilson on the one hand, or [Alec Douglas-] Home or [Edward] Heath on the other. It was not claimed for television to have done more than that. However, it probably had an impact where specific, hard, practical things were concerned.

I think what the public are really looking for is an honest man and this is far more true now when television is the medium of communication. They may not get him, they may get a crook, but whatever he is, he must be able to present himself to them as a man who is to be trusted, a man who is seriously concerned to tell them the facts, and who can be relied on to do what he intends to do, as quickly as possible.

Lemass's government prioritised the development of the Irish economy as its primary goal, but Lemass also brought about an expansion of Irish influence in foreign affairs. The Republic of Ireland Act of 1949 had settled Ireland's status vis-à-vis Britain and it was time to concentrate on other foreign policy goals. Ireland was admitted into the United Nations along with 16 other countries in December 1955. Its entry into the UN had been blocked by the Soviet Union, ostensibly because of Irish neutrality during the Second World War, but more likely because Ireland was regarded as being a country in the Western sphere of influence. De Valera appointed Frank Aiken Minister for External Affairs in September 1957. Aiken spent a lot of time at the General Assembly in the late 1950s and

1960s, gaining a reputation for advocating on behalf of former colonial states seeking statehood. This brought him into frequent conflict with the large powers. To the consternation of both the US and the UK, Aiken said there should be a 'full and open discussion' about whether or not Communist China should be allowed join the UN. At that time the nationalist Chinese government in Taiwan had the Chinese seat in the UN. The motion to admit Communist China in 1957 was defeated. China did not join the UN until 1971.

SL: Very shortly after I became taoiseach our attitude towards the Chinese membership of the United Nations was questioned. I had no hesitation in supporting Frank Aiken in his decision to vote in favour of a discussion of the admission of China. This caused phoney queries in the Dáil and one or two foreign representations. Cardinal Francis Spellman[4] was one man who attacked us. I was quite certain we were right; I felt the role we had to play in the United Nations and similar organisations was to get rid of all the false conceptions prevalent at that time which meant that a small country could attend the United Nations while a quarter of the world's population was not allowed representation. In that area, perhaps, I was responsible for a change in the direction of our policy as compared with Dev, but there was not any conflict with Frank Aiken.

In the late 1950s the UN Secretary-General Dag Hammarskjöld pioneered the concept of UN peacekeeping as a way in which the organisation could assert the will of the international community. Ireland's active part in the United Nations and its status as a post-colonial, non-aligned small country, albeit one anchored in Western values, was particularly attractive to Hammarskjöld.

Congo won its independence from Belgium in June 1960, but the country descended into chaos and its government requested the support of the UN. The resource-rich southern region of Katanga immediately declared its independence and Congolese president Patrice Lumumba was assassinated. Ireland was invited to join the UN operation in the Congo (Opération des Nations Unies au Congo, ONUC) on 16 July 1960 in response to the Congo crisis. Lemass immediately concurred. Within five days the necessary legislation had been passed through the Oireachtas. All those who participated in the first mission to the Congo were volunteers. Operation Sarsfield began on 27 July 1960 with the airlift of the 32nd Infantry Battalion to the Congo. Thousands turned up to Baldonnel aerodrome to see them off.

DR: What are your recollections of the decision to send Irish troops to the Congo?

SL: When the question of sending a contingent to the Congo arose, I felt that this was our first chance to get on to a stage where we could play an independent role and demonstrate the value of our independence because there was only a very short list of countries that would be accepted to supply a contingent for international forces. We were on this list, and I felt we would have been failing in our obligation to the United Nations and [would] default on our world obligations if we had refused. I was completely in favour and discussed the matter with the cabinet committee, determined to push it through even if it meant accepting the resignation of any minister who felt strongly against it. I had no doubts whatever.

The decision to send Irish troops to the Congo was one of my major decisions in public life. We were requested by the United Nations to send out a battalion of troops when the civil war started there. I had no doubt it was important that we should grant this request. We had previously sent officers to the Middle East, but this was to be the first occasion when an army would be directly under the control of the United Nations.[5] However, there was some disagreement in the government. MacEntee argued that [Patrice] Lumumba,[6] who was then the head of the Congolese government, was a communist and that we would be coming in on the wrong side. Frank Aiken was hesitant, but the majority was in favour of dispatching the troops. Finance opposed it because of the likely increase in defence costs. Defence favoured it because they believed that overseas service would be a boost to morale in the army. I made up my mind that we should comply with the United Nations request.

Of course, there were quite a few problems. I spoke to a priest who had come home from Nigeria after the first plane carrying Irish troops had landed in Kano in northern Nigeria, en route to the Congo. He said he was very anxious about their going to Africa in heavy tweed uniforms because of appalling heat. At one time I was in Kano myself, and when I stepped off the plane it was as if I were being hit with a hot, wet blanket. The troops must have suffered when they got there. We immediately arranged to provide them with tropical uniforms. These operations were an unknown venture in that we did not know what exactly was going on or how deeply we would be involved. Nevertheless, we felt we were doing the right thing.

I regarded the Congo operation as a great opportunity. I felt that our role in world affairs would be defined in a very positive way. Eleven ministers accepted the decision in the end. With regard to the Congo operation I consulted a cabinet group: MacEntee, who was tánaiste, Frank Aiken, who was Minister for External Affairs, and Jim Ryan, who was Minister for Finance. These were the people mainly involved, and we discussed this at length. Ultimately, I said, 'This is going to be done.' We then obtained approval from the government.

I felt one or two members of the government would be against it, and for them it was an 'in' or 'out' issue. This is the underlying situation as taoiseach. There were no drop-outs. On other issues a minister might not feel so strongly that his point of view was right, and fight it to the last ditch, but this was a highly charged emotive issue.

The Niemba ambush, which occurred on 8 November 1960, was the first incident in which Irish soldiers serving with the UN lost their lives in combat. A platoon of 11 men from A Company of the 33rd battalion were ambushed by Luba tribesmen, known as Balubas, at a bridge near the village of Niemba in the Congo. The men, led by Lieutenant Kevin Gleeson, went to repair a bridge that had been destroyed by Luba tribesmen who were trying to stop incursions into their territory by Katangese troops supported by Belgian mercenaries. The funerals of the eight men and another soldier, Trooper Anthony Browne, who was killed trying to escape, were among the biggest that Ireland had ever seen.

SL: There were anxious phases during the operations, the Niemba ambush and the raid at Katanga, and we were concerned as to whether Irish public opinion would support the continuation of Irish participation in the operation. We need not have worried; nobody in Ireland opposed our involvement except [Jack]

McQuillan[7] and one or two other politicians who tried to make political capital by urging the pulling of the Irish troops out when things got difficult. However, when they realised that they were getting no response to this suggestion from the public, they desisted. From our point of view, we made the right decision, and this also applied to Cyprus.[8] I really felt very proud when I reviewed the first battalion to go out on a public parade in O'Connell Street. I suppose we will always be on the shortlist of countries from which contingents will be sought for United Nations forces because of the fact that we are not part of any military alliance and also because of the fact that our troops proved so successful in the operations in which they were engaged.

DR: On 13 December 1960, you told the Dáil that just because other countries were contemplating the withdrawal of troops from the Congo, Ireland should not fail to afford modest help.

SL: Yes, of course, the Congo operation was not without difficulties. There were stupid allegations by [Noël] Browne and McQuillan, who were in favour of Tshombe[9] or putting him on trial for the murder of Lumumba. They were trying to involve us in the internal politics of the Congo. This was one thing we were determined to avoid. The job of a United Nations force is to keep the peace. We were not concerned with the internal politics of the Congo. We were concerned solely with keeping peace and preventing civil war and particularly with avoiding the creation of a vacuum which either the Russians, the Americans or Chinese might try to fill. This was the United Nations' major concern, to keep the peace.

The situation in the Congo was one in which the Great Powers could come into conflict. The United Nations efforts, which were directed towards avoiding this, were on a huge scale, and involved personnel from more than 20 countries. After a while some countries began to withdraw their people. For example, there was a change of attitude of the Indian government, when sporadic fighting broke out between Chinese and Indians on the Sino-Indian border and they wanted their troops home. But the Irish remained on to the end and we never considered dropping out.[10] The operation went on longer than we expected, and if it had continued indefinitely, we might have changed our attitude.

DR: Is it not possible, since it is continuing (Irish troops in Cyprus) and not costing us anything, to use it for training purposes?

SL: Yes, it is. But the position in Cyprus is entirely different from that of the Congo, in the sense that in the Congo the United Nations were dealing with a people who had no political sophistication and who had to be looked after to prevent them from harming each other. In Cyprus, which was a centre of civilisation for thousands of years, there were most astute politicians to be dealt with. Also, there are the two powers on the sideline, Turkey and Greece, who are liable to get into the conflict should the situation ever get out of control. Should this happen, the United Nations soldiers would find themselves in an impossible position. The local population in the Congo appreciated the United Nations forces, but this would not be true in Cyprus where the situation is different and the 'white man's burden' would not be acceptable. I was very apprehensive and still am about the position of Irish troops in Cyprus. However, I suppose that the danger of Turkish invasion has been reduced, although last year it was very much a possibility. If either Greece or Turkey were to invade the island, the UN troops would be completely powerless.

DR: On 29 September 1960, F.H. [Freddie] Boland[11] was elected president of the United Nations General Assembly. How important to Ireland was that honour?

SL: It was important because the support he received gave us an international role which was bound to be to the credit of the country, and it could indirectly help to further our economic development. But the main advantage of Boland's election was that we were reappearing on the international scene in a role which found general approval. It undoubtedly raised morale at home also.

His election was due to his own personal qualities and his suitability for the post, and also to the fact that Ireland had adopted an independent role in the UN. He had on occasion stood out against the United States and others, on specific points, and had shown a capacity to take an individual line. All these factors combined to make Boland an exceptionally well-qualified candidate. There was no opposition to his election, and this was a tremendous tribute to him.

A company of the 35th Battalion went to the Congo in June 1961. The company was sent to Jadotville, a mining town 90km north of the provincial capital, Elizabethville (now Lubumbashi), in early September 1961, ostensibly to protect the white, mostly Belgian, population. But when they got there they realised they were not wanted. Many white residents had a vested interest in the breakaway province. When UN troops broke their peacekeeping mandate and attacked Katanga installations in Elizabethville on the morning of 13 September 1961, during Operation Morthor, the Irish, isolated and exposed, were regarded as a legitimate target and were attacked four hours later by way of reprisal.

Attempts by UN reinforcements to relieve the company were met by heavy resistance at the Lufira Bridge, 27km away and the only bridge crossing between Elizabethville and Jadotville. Two days later, with the facts not yet known, Lemass dissolved the Dáil and called a general election for 4 October. Wild rumours immediately began circulating. The Irish media reported two days after the siege began that five Irish soldiers have been killed. A day later Radio Free Katanga reported 57 Irish fatalities. Lemass issued a statement expressing 'profound shock and sorrow' on behalf of the Irish nation, but added the wise caveat that the casualties were 'not yet ascertained'.

After five days the enemy requested a ceasefire, which the Irish accepted. However, due to a lack of support from the UN higher authority, this ceasefire in effect became a surrender. A Company, led by Colonel Pat Quinlan, was at this stage out of ammunition, food and water and surrounded by an overwhelming force. Quinlan and the 153 men under his command were taken as hostages for a month before being released. Remarkably, no Irish soldier was killed at Jadotville and just five were wounded.

SL: The worst experience was the report just after I had gone up to the Áras and dissolved the Dáil in 1961, that a company of Irish troops had been wiped out in ambush in the Congo. I had decided to open my election campaign in Athlone and these troops were almost entirely from Athlone. I didn't sleep a wink that night, partly because I was concerned about the idea of 150 being killed by savages in the Congo and partly because I realised that once the Dáil is dissolved that decision cannot be cancelled. There is no Dáil. I did not want to face the wives and children of these men and start talking about politics, so I cancelled the meeting in Athlone straight away. I can still remember that at six o'clock the next morning, Kevin Boland, then Minister for Defence, rang and said that report was untrue; these men hadn't been wiped out.

CHAPTER 13

THE EUROPEAN DREAM

'De Gaulle is very much entitled to be suspicious of the motivations of the British, which, I think, were very dubious. I do not think they had any other idea initially in relation to the Common Market except to destroy it.'

Six countries formed the European Economic Community in 1957 – West Germany, France, Italy, Belgium, Luxembourg and the Netherlands. The UK was invited to join but declined. The 'Six', as they became known, began to reduce tariffs with a view to moving towards complete free trade and agreed to pool sovereignty by creating political institutions in common. The Treaty of Rome (1957), which established the European Economic Community (EEC), was enthusiastically embraced by Lemass. As we have seen, he differed from de Valera in believing that multilateral organisations such as the UN or the EEC could be good for smaller countries. In January 1962 Mr Lemass outlined his case to the Six in Brussels. He told an impressive tale. In just four years Irish manufacturing exports had doubled, and the economy had grown by 5 per cent in 1961 alone. The Irish economy was now being prepared for entry into the Common Market. Ireland 'belongs to Europe by history, tradition and sentiment no less than by geography'. The problem

for Ireland was that the Six saw the country as effectively a single market with the UK and there could be no entry for Ireland unless the UK was admitted first.

SL: More than any other member of the government I had to go out and sell the idea of applying for membership of the Common Market, and I suppose I made 20 major speeches in a year [1961] on this topic. I went to chambers of commerce, major gatherings, management meetings, etc. You really felt the job was worthwhile on these occasions; you were not going to stand up and say a lot of nice trite things; you went to argue a case. You had to argue for it; you had to measure the problems that were going to arise for the country; you certainly could not appear to be trying to cover up and run away from these problems; you had to define the method by which the problems would be solved. That whole series of speeches I liked making.

I have always held strongly that when Europe is integrated economically, we cannot stay out, and that once it develops political institutions it will be impossible to have common commercial policies without common political policies. I argued this in connection with the original proposal to join the Common Market. On two or three occasions, at the ard fheis I argued that a country like Ireland is more likely to be better situated when its international trade is conducted in accordance with the rules of international organisations, rather than depending upon bilateral agreements which it might reach with more powerful neighbours.

My opinion was based largely on my own experience of never being able to make trade bargains with Britain on terms of equality. In many cases we were almost reduced to pleading for conditions which we thought were fair, but which they could arbitrarily agree to or not. The only occasions when that situation did not exist were in 1938 and, to some extent, when we were negotiating the [1965] Free Trade Agreement.[1] In the latter instance, the position of Harold Wilson's government was that, having announced they were going to make this agreement, they could not risk failure in the negotiations, except for some very justifiable cause.

We were as tough as hell and got our point of view on details, because we knew they could never defend the failure to make this agreement because of some pettifogging point of view or some comparatively minor aspect of trade. Also, we were dealing with the individual departments of the British government, the Board of Trade and the Ministry of Agriculture, on terms of equality. The pressures on them to make an agreement were as strong as those on us, perhaps even stronger in some respects, which would put no limitation on the country.

In 1960 a rival organisation to the EEC was founded, the European Free Trade Association (EFTA), led by the UK, with Austria, Denmark, Norway, Portugal, Sweden and Switzerland. These countries agreed the principle of free trade with each other, but were free to organise their own trading arrangements with outside countries. Free trade did not include agricultural products. This was crucial for the UK, which gave preferential status to goods from Commonwealth countries and Ireland. EFTA did not have nearly as significant an impact as the EEC did and British prime minister Harold Macmillan became a convert to the cause of European integration. In July 1961 it was apparent that his Conservative government was considering applying for EEC membership. If the UK joined the Common Market, Ireland would have no alternative but to apply for membership too. Fortunately for Lemass, the Irish public was overwhelmingly in favour. The first opinion poll on the matter was conducted in July 1961. Some 76 per cent of the Irish public was in favour, with only 17 per cent against.

DR: Were you influenced in any way by the Gallup poll in July 1961 on the Common Market?

SL: I did not feel influenced in any way by the first Gallup poll. All through the years, I have given deep thought to the Common Market. I was convinced of the importance and the advantages of selling the idea of membership of the Common Market. We conducted a very active campaign to create public support for our decision to join the EEC, so I would say there was no real surprise, no alarm or shock, when it was announced we intended to apply for membership. On the contrary, it was something the public had been expecting for some time. Remember that the National Farmers' Association was pressing us to make an application, even if the British did not do so. This was perhaps a bit unrealistic, but it helped to create a climate of opinion favourable to making an application.

DR: On 18 July 1961, you met Mr Macmillan in London to exchange views on the Common Market. What were the results?

SL: A general reassessment of policy by the British government was in process following the breakdown of free trade negotiations.[2] This led us eventually to apply for membership of the EEC. The purpose of my visit in 1961 was to find out whether they were contemplating any decisions which would affect us. I found them at the same time very hostile to the Common Market. I remember after a lunch with Mr Maudling,[3] then President of the Board of Trade, casually mentioning to him that our farmers' organisations were urging us to apply for membership of the Common Market, regardless of Britain's attitude to it. He reacted by saying that if we did so, we could expect maximum retaliation by the British government by way of tariffs against our goods. They did not, for some reason, urge us to become members of the European Free Trade Association. I was a little surprised and somewhat relieved that we were not invited to join it. Later on, they did invite us; in fact, they pressed us to join. They said at first that there could be no exception to the general conditions for any member country, such as we had been seeing, in the free trade area negotiations. The purpose of my visit was to find out what was happening and what the British government intended to do, what the British government thought was likely to be the long-term result of the collapse of the free trade negotiations. At that time, we had not considered the feasibility of a bilateral free trade area between the two countries. We wanted improvements in existing trade agreements and had put forward some fairly comprehensive proposals for an extension of the preferences already given mutually under these grants. The conditions we wanted were mainly trade concessions such as guaranteed prices for agricultural products and free entry for anything we could expect. The British expected then that the free trade association which they had formed would, ultimately, restart their negotiations with the Common Market. We had to keep watch on this development because it could result in our being left out of both bodies and have placed us in a difficult situation. However, the European Free Trade Association never really got off the ground as far as we were concerned, so it never became a problem.

DR: From this hostility to the Common Market did you feel that Britain's attitude to the Common Market was originally that they did not want it and therefore they stayed out to try and kill it?

SL: They quite definitely did not want it. They did not believe it would work when it started in 1957. The negotiations for the Free Trade Area concept were prejudiced from the very beginning by the suspicion in the minds of Common Market countries that Britain's aim was really to break up the Common Market by the device of the Free Trade Area. They handled these negotiations very badly. They went into arguments about microscopic details instead of trying to forge ahead once they had got, as they had in 1956, the decision of everybody to negotiate the free trade area. They wanted to hold on to their Commonwealth preferences and to maintain free entry to Great Britain for Commonwealth products, which was an unrealistic attitude. Their over-concern for detail created the impression that they had an ulterior motive which has nothing to do with the Free Trade Area agreement at all, namely, the breaking up of the Common Market. By 1960 they were still vehemently against the idea of Common Market membership. The following year they applied for membership, which was a considerable reversal of policy, and which presumably must have been largely the product of Mr Macmillan's reassessment of the situation.

DR: When you met Mr Macmillan on 18 July, had you any change of views following this meeting?

SL: No. I returned home and convinced the government that the British would follow with the news they were applying for membership, even though Macmillan did not say so in so many words. During the first half of 1961, we knew we were reaching the moment of decision on seeking membership of the Common Market. One of our major problems in this regard was when the British would make a final decision to apply for membership. We did not know when their decision would be finalised, although we were informed it was coming. By July they had arrived at a decision. They had sent some envoys to Australia and other Commonwealth countries to get their views. They had sounded out officials in the EEC. They spent some time making up their minds. I believed that they had in fact decided to apply, but they were not prepared to say so until the end of July.

Faced with the imminent application from the British, Lemass's government decided to act first. On 31 July 1961 Ireland applied for membership of the EEC. On the same day, coincidentally, Harold Macmillan announced that the UK too would be applying for membership. The British membership went in three days later.

SL: I told the government that the British were going to apply for membership of the Common Market and that I wanted everything ready so that our application could be sent in before theirs. This might be regarded as portraying a childish attitude, but I wanted to prevent it being said that we were merely following their example. Subsequently, Macmillan announced in the House of Commons that Britain was going to apply for entry to the EEC. Our application was in before theirs and we did not make our application conditional on British membership as the Danes[4] and Norwegians did. The whole idea of membership had to be sold. There was no alternative except full membership and an awareness of the need for membership that has to be built up. The Labour Party talked about associate membership in the usual way – to get the gains without paying the price. They tried to suggest that there was some alternative the government could consider which would put no limitation on the country.

In the Dáil Lemass was characteristically frank about the importance of Irish membership. It would be 'suicidal for us to remain isolated outside it. That decision, I think was taken with the agreement of the vast majority of our people, certainly with the agreement of all the articulate elements among them' – a clear reference to the Gallup poll that had shown overwhelming support for membership.

SL: While I did not think the British negotiations would last as long as they did, I could see no reason why there should be any delay in our case. If I had been asked in July 1962 when we would be in, I would have said within 12 months, without any hesitation. We did not anticipate failing to gain admission. Thus, while 1970 was the deadline for dismantling all tariffs, the process would begin long before that. So firm was my conviction in this regard that when, in 1963, de Gaulle indicated his feelings about British entry, we decided to go ahead exactly as if we had acquired membership.

I was very keen, personally, that our application for European Common Market membership should not appear to be associated with the British application. That's why we got it in a day or two before the British application was received. We rushed it in so that it would not be taken that we were making it conditional upon Britain's application being granted, as the Danes and

Norwegians did. Never at any time did I say we would not go it alone. I must confess I did not see the circumstances in which it would be possible for us to do this, but it was vaguely in the back of my mind that circumstances might arise in which the British government might say: 'You go ahead yourselves. We will not impose any penalty on you for doing this.'

I thought it just possible that the British might say: 'We will not interfere with existing trade arrangements, despite your action.' This could arise by reason of some desire on the part of the British to test the genuineness of the community. This was a very vague idea. But, no matter how vague it was, there was no sense in shutting it out, and there was no sense in saying to ourselves: 'We will not go alone.' At this time, of course, it is quite obvious that the community will not accept any members except in the context in which they are prepared to accept all applicants, but it was not quite so clear then.

But even so, I would still keep open the option of going it alone. It may never be exercised but I see no reason why we should close it out even from a psychological point of view. And by reason of Irish public opinion, I felt, as I have said, that we had to make our application independently of the British. I never said we would not go it alone if the circumstances justified that step. I felt that we should get away from the suggestion that we were just following the British.

Probably it would be true to say if we went it alone in the Common Market, we would have ten years of real hardship in which the adjustment of production here to meet the needs of the Common Market would be taking place, but by the end of ten years, we would be a great deal better off. The difficult part would be surviving for ten years. If we did succeed in doing that, we would be, perhaps, in a much better or stronger situation than we would be by following the other line. However, no government could hope to sell this policy and survive during the ten years when all the hardship would have to be experienced.

After the UK and Ireland submitted their bids for EEC membership, the process of negotiation began with both countries. It was not until October 1962 that the European Council agreed to the opening of negotiations proper on Ireland's application. Effectively, the EEC saw the UK and Ireland as one country for the purpose of trade as most of Ireland's trade went to the UK and the UK was by far the bigger of the two markets. This was brutally illustrated by the then London editor of the *Irish Press*, Desmond Fisher, who travelled to Brussels to interview Dr Walter Hallstein, the EEC president. Dr Hallstein pointed to a drawer and said that inside it was the Irish application, which he had not read and would not read. If the UK joined the EEC, Ireland could too; if not, Ireland was out.

The process was still ongoing when on 14 January 1963, French president General Charles de Gaulle unilaterally announced that he would be vetoing UK membership. He didn't even mention Ireland, but the inference was clear. UK membership was incompatible with the Common Agricultural Policy (CAP) founded in 1962, de Gaulle said, because the British insisted on allowing the importation of cheap food from Commonwealth countries. The UK was also giving large subsidies to its farmers. It was a maritime country with different markets. It was not a European country in the way continental countries were European, de Gaulle believed. Another consideration for the French president was the Nassau Agreement signed in 1962 between the US and the UK, under which the US guaranteed the British nuclear deterrent by providing Polaris-type missiles capable of carrying a nuclear payload, an arrangement that survives to this day. De Gaulle, who was in favour of an independent European defence, concluded the UK had tethered its long-term fortunes to the US rather than Europe.

SL: I do not think that either Macmillan or any member of the British government ever fully understood that they could not be half in and half out of the EEC. They had to make up their minds whether Britain was to be a part of a united Europe, and if so, they would have to resign themselves to the fact that they could not have a special relationship with the US which would give them rights and privileges against their Common Market partners or try to maintain their Commonwealth preferences. Macmillan did not realise that any indication of vacillation on Britain's part would discredit its application in the eyes of de Gaulle. As a result, I think he was surprised by the French veto.

I am certain of that. De Gaulle is supported by French public opinion because he moulded the opinion which was responsible for the French attitude. De Gaulle is very much entitled to be suspicious of the motivations of the British, which, I think, were very dubious. I do not think they had any other idea initially in relation to the Common Market except to destroy it. Even when they recognised they were not going to succeed in breaking it up, their application for membership was probably inspired by the idea that they could slow down its development in some way and perhaps change its character. It is only in the last few years that the British have realised that they are not going to succeed in their policies. They have come around – if their public declarations are indicative of their attitude – to accepting fully the whole idea of European economic integration. Yet they still have the imperial frame of mind as shown by their Commonwealth prime ministers' conference. Of what real importance is the Commonwealth? Nobody answers that question, but the British think it is important to their status in the world that they should have this collection of Africans and others, abusing them periodically at an imperial conference. I do not think it has any significance whatsoever, but it certainly has prevented the British from thinking of themselves as a completely European country. De Gaulle was quite right in questioning their motives. They are not saying the things he wanted them to say initially, and de Gaulle has modified his attitude on that account. But, as I said many times before, if the British had been talking in 1962 or 1963 as they are talking now, there would have been no difficulty with regard to their admission into the EEC.

DR: Did you expect that it would take some time for Ireland to gain entry?

SL: We began preparations so that all tariffs would be removed by the 1970s, being confident of having attained full membership of the Common Market by that date. Far from anticipating indefinite delays, we felt a certain excitement at the fact that things were moving too quickly. There was no indication of French opposition when, in 1962, I did the rounds of European governments and talked to the French government.

DR: Defence: do you see any implications with regard to NATO in EEC membership?

SL: Defence was never raised in any context at all in the course of our discussions except indirectly by de Gaulle, who emphasised his own personal view that Europe has to be capable of independent defence. De Gaulle consistently emphasised the importance of defence in Europe and the necessity for every participant country to recognise its obligations. However, defence set no problems for me. While we are not members of NATO, we had always recognised that European economic integration was going to involve us in discussions about European political integration; a European state would have to have some policy with regard to a common defence. Once or twice in prior conversations the Dutch or Belgian people suggested that there might be some question about our membership of the EEC because of our non-membership of NATO, but this disappeared.

The fact that we were not a member of NATO was not a handicap as far as de Gaulle was concerned. In fact, he wanted to see that we were members of the European community, but this had nothing to do with European defences. The NATO treaty is greatly misunderstood. I remember when the question arose on Telefís Éireann the people interviewed talked about foreign bases, which are not involved in it at all.

De Gaulle's veto of UK entry, which also applied to Ireland, was a major disappointment for Lemass, but he was not deterred from pursuing EEC membership, having already concluded that Irish business needed to be prepared to face the challenges of free trade in or out of the EEC. In February 1963 a UN report listed Ireland, along with Greece, Iceland, Portugal and Spain, as 'under-developed' countries in Europe. The UN report was commissioned for the International Commodity Trade Commission. It drew an immediate rebuke from Lemass in the Dáil, who described it as 'nonsense'.

DR: Were you surprised at this classification? Do you feel that this report would in any way impede our entry into the EEC?

SL: We accepted this because there were material advantages in accepting this classification, both in terms under which we were regarded in the free trade area association and in the other practical benefits which were designed for countries in this category. Indeed, I remember telling J.C.B. McCarthy,[5] when he went to one of the committees in the 1950s, to identify us with the Turks and the Greeks so as to get all the concessions which they were looking for. I did not want Ireland to become just a residual beneficiary of these concessions. But of course things changed. First, our economic situation here was improving. Second, from the point of view of our seeking membership of the European Economic Community, this classification was a handicap. We now wanted to present ourselves as a fully developed nation, capable of accepting all the obligations of full membership of the EEC. Indeed, for a time, the fact that we had been in the less developed country grouping in the Free Trade area negotiations was a handicap for us. We were now trying to destroy the image of ourselves which we had tried to project in the Paris negotiations, so it was a disappointment when, in 1963 the United Nations put us into this category.

DR: Were there any advantages in being classified as underdeveloped in 1963?

SL: I suppose there were arguments in favour of accepting some differentiation in our situation as compared with the developed countries as when the United States imposed restrictions on capital, we would have liked them to exempt us from these restrictions. There was also a tax on American investments for which we were trying to get an exemption.

DR: In a sense, the speeches are the political part of the task?

SL: In the general election, I spoke on practically nothing else but Common Market membership. I avoided getting involved in political conflicts with Fine Gael and the other parties. We won the election on EEC membership. I felt, if I had got involved in the normal type of inter-party slanging at that time, it would have caused us to lose votes and it was very much to the advantage of Fianna Fáil, as the government in office, to emphasise and, if necessary, exaggerate the magnitude of the task facing the government in adjusting the country for the EEC. And to therefore leave an idea that the only people capable of doing this were those who knew what was involved – which were ourselves. This was very deliberately done and I did not deviate from the decision at the time. There may have been an odd aside here and there. I remember, a year later, soon after we had applied for membership, somebody said we should have gone to the country, that the country had not voted to go into the EEC. I had spoken about nothing else during the election.

There was the actual suggestion in the Dáil, after we had applied for membership, that it was undemocratic to bring the people into this when we had not asked the people to vote for it. I had asked them to vote for nothing else. Once we are in the area of common political policies, we must have a common defence policy. I, personally, would not at all disagree with de Gaulle that Europe must be capable of an independent defence, if this is feasible, because there is a great deal of sense in his contention that when the chips are down, America would not commit suicide for the sake of Europe. This was demonstrated to a great degree during the Suez crisis. The Russians were rattling their bombs and America was afraid of this situation and was hostile to the whole Franco-British policy. Suez made it clear that if Russia did no more than sabre-rattle, America was not going to be involved. America was not going to commit herself to entering a war just because Britain and France had become involved in one.

DR: I thought that the Polaris business was the most significant single fact which de Gaulle felt indicated their non-European attitude.

SL: Yes, de Gaulle recognised that you cannot have a European state without a European defence. It has to be independent, yet the British entered into this defensive arrangement with the Americans. I am quite certain they thought of themselves as having a special relationship with America and with the Commonwealth countries, and special obligations and responsibilities around the world. Europe was, in their minds, a nuisance on their doorstep and they had to endure it, merely because they had not succeeded in breaking down the vision of European unity. But I think they have now learned their lesson. I think it is true to say that the present British government has now developed the right attitude in that respect. Whether the British public has done so I do not know.

The son-in-law

'I would say Charlie Haughey would be the nearest example. I see him in much the same situation, reproducing my life all over again in himself.'

Seán Lemass's daughter Maureen, born in 1925, was his eldest child and her parents stretched themselves to give her an education at Muckross Park College, which her mother had also attended. Maureen Lemass then went to University College Dublin (UCD) to study commerce. There she met a scholarship student, Charles Haughey, the third of John and Sarah Haughey's seven children.

Haughey's parents were from Swatragh, County Derry. Both were involved in the War of Independence: he in the IRA, she in Cumann na mBan. Commandant Johnny Haughey joined the National Army and fought on the pro-Treaty side in the Civil War. He operated in an environment where the civilian population was 'almost entirely hostile to the army', according to his pension file in the Irish Military Archives. In March 1928 Johnny Haughey bought a 100-acre farm at Dunshaughlin, County Meath, but developed multiple sclerosis and was unable to farm it. The family moved to Donnycarney, Dublin and they lived on his disability pension.

Charles Haughey went to St Joseph's Christian Brothers school (Joey's) in Marino and won a scholarship to study for the Leaving Certificate. He then won a scholarship to study commerce at UCD. Both the Leaving Certificate and a university education were usually only the preserve of those with means in 1940s Ireland. Maureen Lemass was the daughter of arguably the most powerful man in Ireland at the time, given her father's role as Minister for Supplies, though she did not grow up in a wealthy environment.

Given his father's background (he kept a portrait of Michael Collins in the house), Charles Haughey might naturally have gravitated towards Fine Gael, but he saw them as a privileged caste and two of his friends from school, George Colley and Harry Boland, were sons of Fianna Fáil politicians.

Haughey joined Fianna Fáil in 1948. He was unsuccessful in four elections before entering the Dáil in 1957 as a TD for the Dublin North-East constituency. At the same time he qualified both as a barrister and an accountant and founded the firm Haughey Boland & Company with Harry Boland. Haughey first met his famous father-in-law at Maureen's twenty-first birthday party in 1946. The couple married on 18 September 1951 and had four children.

SL: By the time I became taoiseach the political situation had changed. We no longer have the first generation – anti-treatyites – at all. The present Fianna Fáil party consists of a lot of people who are sons of those who opposed the Treaty and a lot of people who are not. Charlie Haughey, my own son-in-law, his father was a Free State Army officer in the Civil War. These people are there because of an intellectual decision, their own decision to join Fianna Fáil. They didn't come there by inheritance or any similar route and therefore in the handling of this new party there is a much more difficult problem. We have now got to work at this business of handling the party, meeting them and bringing them along with you. Then we didn't have to work at it at all.

When Seán Lemass became taoiseach in 1959, the status of his ambitious and able son-in-law became an issue for him. Matters came to a head in 1960 when the ailing Minister for Justice Oscar Traynor, then aged 73 and another veteran of the revolutionary generation, requested a parliamentary secretary (a minister of state) to help him manage the department. While the taoiseach had sole responsibility for cabinet appointments, the cabinet agreed to parliamentary secretaries.

SL: The taoiseach must not allow the question of ministerial appointments ever to pass from his own hands. If he allows it to go to the cabinet he is ceasing to be taoiseach. The parliamentary secretaries are appointed by the cabinet. This is also a difficulty because when I was forming the government in 1961, I brought in people and told them that I wanted them to be parliamentary secretaries, but I could not guarantee that they would be appointed. I could only put them forward to the cabinet, but the appointment did not rest with us.

There was a natural tendency on the part of the cabinet to challenge my judgement, if for no other reason except to assert their right to make the appointment. Oscar Traynor was Minister for Justice and when he became ill, I wanted a parliamentary secretary in Justice to take over and do the work on the understanding that he would be appointed Minister for Justice when the time came. I proposed that Seán Flanagan[6] be made parliamentary secretary, but the cabinet wanted Charlie Haughey. I will admit my judgement was not completely objective because Charlie Haughey was my son in-law and I felt from his own personal point of view that he would be very unwise to give up all his business associations to be parliamentary secretary. I brought him in and told him that the cabinet was offering him this job and that it was my duty as taoiseach to ask him to take it and my duty as a father-in-law to tell him not to be a fool. Once he had broken through there was no question of any restraint in further promotions for him. He went right to the top post. His ability justified my choosing him. If he had not the requisite ability I would have advised him to stay out of politics.

Haughey took over the Justice portfolio when Traynor retired in 1961. He proved to be one of the best politicians ever to hold the position. He brought in a succession of bills that would help modernise Irish society, the best known of which was the Succession Bill of 1965. Prior to that a wife in Ireland had no automatic right to inherit from her husband, resulting in the not uncommon scenario of a husband leaving his farm or land to the Catholic Church and not to his widow. Lemass consulted the hierarchy before pressing ahead with the bill.

SL: As taoiseach I found a number of aspects of some bills had to be cleared with them, particularly the Succession Bill. In such matters I had to meet with the hierarchy and be satisfied I wasn't going to have any trouble with them.

In October 1964 Lemass faced a rare internal crisis when his veteran Minister for Agriculture Paddy Smith[7] resigned. Smith had been a stalwart of the Fianna Fáil party since its foundation. As a rural TD from County Cavan, he felt Lemass was too fixated on urban issues. Smith's unhappiness led to his resignation, sparked by Lemass settling a construction workers' dispute by granting them a pay rise, which Smith felt was unjustified. In his rather intemperate resignation speech, he described the offer to construction workers as 'not only a tyranny, but a dishonest, incompetent one'. Lemass immediately appointed Haughey to be Minister for Agriculture. There was much consternation among the farming communities that Haughey, an inner-city Dublin TD, would take over the Agriculture portfolio, but Lemass stood by him. It may have been a way to prepare Haughey for leadership of Fianna Fáil by getting the farmers onside, but

it had the opposite impact as Haughey engaged in a long and difficult stand-off with farmers that was only resolved just before Lemass left office in 1966.

DR: On 8 October 1964, Paddy Smith, Minister for Agriculture, resigned.

SL: Yes, Smith's resignation. Well, for a long time before that he was becoming quite a difficult person to deal with … extremely argumentative about government matters; non-co-operative with other ministers on certain matters that impinged on the Department of Agriculture, and generally showing signs of being disgruntled on basic matters of policy. I suppose it would be true enough to say that it was some concession we made to the trade unionists which was the final straw which drove him into resignation. He had, of course, threatened to resign at various times before. On one occasion he had resigned, and I accepted his resignation, but he withdrew it again. I could not say that I was surprised when he resigned, in the sense that there was always a possibility that he would argue himself into a position upon some matter where this would be the inevitable outcome.

On this particular occasion, though, when his resignation was actually effective, he had not intimated it to me. I had heard word that he was going around saying he had resigned and I had heard that he was summoning a press conference to announce it and to give reasons for it, at a time when he had not told me about it. But I had enough warning of it to be able to act immediately on it. And when I ultimately got his letter of resignation, I accepted it, by return, and I appointed Charlie Haughey to be Minister for Agriculture, all in a matter of a few hours.

DR: Smith was becoming almost impossible as a member of the government?

SL: Yes, one could not really get effective discussion at government level because of his unreasonable interventions in debate, and because of his reluctance to co-operate in matters where co-operation was necessary because of the agricultural interests involved. It did not interfere with the party at all – indeed the surprising thing is that his resignation was, if anything, accepted with relief by the party. There was not the slightest sign of regret, which surprised me, from members of the party.

But, of course, Smith was also in this situation which may never arise again – that he was 'one of us'. I mean, he was a Civil War man; he had been saved from being executed by the 'ceasefire' order. He would never argue reasonably. He would proclaim his point of view, you know, and state it strongly, and at very great length not enabling the meetings to be harmoniously conducted.

This helped me in my speedy decision to accept his resignation. The effect was minimal in the party ... none at all; and outside the party it was forgotten inside a couple of weeks. The Minister for Agriculture ultimately falls out with every farmers' organisation; they are always looking for something you cannot give them. There is always the hope that if somebody else comes in he will give them more than his predecessor was able to provide. So that there is not and never has been any great difficulty in changing the Minister for Agriculture.

Lemass lived a frugal life in comparison with Haughey. Haughey bought Abbeville, a large Georgian house in Kinsealy, County Dublin in 1969 and hosted Lemass's seventieth birthday party there. Lemass was amazed at the extravagance of it all and asked Haughey how much it cost. Haughey told him it cost £200 and Lemass was astonished. 'I hadn't the heart to tell him that it actually cost £2,000,' Haughey told friends.

SL: This is the life I had to lead and I have no sense of having suffered anything either in my relations with my family or myself personally. I should think this is probably true of most ministers. I would say Charlie Haughey would be the nearest example. I see him in much the same situation, reproducing my life all over again in himself, although he does much more in the way of social entertaining, social occasions, than I ever did. He would be different in the sense that, on the whole, he would prefer not to have to stay at home; he is a restless type of person and would never stay at home reading a book as I would. If he found he had nothing to do at home, he would go out.

People will turn to the person who appears to be completely trustworthy, even if this trustworthiness arises from the fact that he is not clever enough to be crooked. I think probably I had that handicap. I think Charlie Haughey has it now, of appearing too much on top of the job, too professional and that a lot of de Valera's support was due to this fervent honesty, his capacity to be able to stand in the rain and talk for an hour on the simplest terms to [people], which I could never do. Paying no attention to the rain or anything else, spelling everything out in the simplest terms to them, going back over it again and again if he thought they hadn't understood it. Now this extraordinary loyalty and enthusiasm that he engendered was partly due to this – simplicity, I suppose is the word for it. Lack of sophistication, anyway.

CHAPTER 14

REBUILDING IRELAND

'There will always be a very high need for housing and I do not think that any country in the world can say that it has satisfied all its housing needs.'

Lemass took over when Ireland was about to go through the most difficult decade since independence. As the economy continued to improve from the trough of the 1950s, Lemass began to ponder seeking his own mandate as taoiseach.

SL: 1960 was the first full year in which I was taoiseach, and I was conscious of the fact that I had obtained the position by inheritance and not by public selection or decision. My main problem was whether I had been accepted by the country and the party as taoiseach. I realised that I would never have proper authority or status as taoiseach until I got this as a result of a general election. During 1960 I decided I would call a general election in 1961. One of the problems of a government ruling with a majority is to justify an election when the time seems ripe and when it is required by law. In 1961 there was not much difficulty because an election would have to be held in 1962, and I had made it clear that I was not going to wait until the last moment and that the election would be held at any time from the beginning of 1961 to the beginning of 1962. Nobody could claim that he was being taken unawares and left with no freedom of action.

Buoyed with opinion polls showing that the public overwhelmingly backed EEC membership, Lemass decided the time was right for a general election. The background to the election was a two-week strike by ESB electricians, which began on 21 August and was not resolved until 7 September. Though independent contractors managed to maintain the power supply, there were real fears that the electricians who went on strike could bring the country to a complete standstill. Lemass called the general election a day after the strike was resolved; polling day would be 4 October.

Lemass sought a mandate based on the party's record in government. The economy was improving, but with rising expectations came rising demands, and the country was beset with industrial problems in the early 1960s as construction and dock workers were among those seeking better wages and conditions. The number of Dáil seats was reduced by three because of the falling population. The general election was the first for Fianna Fáil with a leader other than de Valera. Fianna Fáil ended up with 70 seats in the 144-seat Dáil. Its share of the vote fell from 48.3 per cent to 43.8 per cent. Fine Gael, under James Dillon, made gains, increasing its seats from 40 to 47. The Labour Party, under new leader Brendan Corish, gained four seats, from 12 to 16. Though Fianna Fáil lost its overall majority, Lemass was re-elected comfortably as taoiseach with the help of independents.

Domestically, the first economic programme had been more successful than anybody had expected, with annual growth averaging 4.5 per cent. Industrial investment had more than doubled and industrial wages increased by 35 per cent between 1958 and 1963. Most important, emigration, which peaked at 43,100 in 1960, was only half that, 21,900, in 1963. The population began to increase again for the first time since the Great Famine.[1] Lemass's government, in a short period of time, had persuaded many more would-be emigrants to stay in Ireland.

The first programme, scheduled for five years, was due to run out in 1963. Lemass and his advisers set about building on its success with a second programme to cover the years from 1964 to 1970. It envisaged an economy that would be 51 per cent bigger in 1970 than in 1960, a goal that would only be achieved with average annual GNP growth of 4.3 per cent. Tariffs were to be reduced by a third in the lifetime of the programme to prepare Irish industry for entry into the EEC, even if that entry was not guaranteed. In return the Lemass government promised tax incentives and grants for export-oriented businesses. The programme identified the importance of attracting large-scale foreign businesses to Ireland and promised to invest in power, transport and communication facilities to facilitate such businesses.

DR: An outline of the second programme was published in August 1963. Are you satisfied with the progress made towards the projected targets and what, in your opinion, was the main cause of our failure to meet some of the projections?

SL: One of the main problems of setting targets was that we had – quite deliberately – understated the targets in the first programme. This was done for the purposes of boosting public morale when we did better than we had [with the first] programme. The 2 per cent, which was the annual rate of progress, conceived in the first programme, became 4 per cent actual achievement and [that] did have this effect on morale. I saw a recent criticism of the second programme on the grounds that the average rate of progress was only 3.3 per cent. Now, this was less than we had programmed for. It was a big increase on what was achieved in the 1950s; and one of the factors that influenced us in putting in the 2 per cent annual rate of growth in the first programme was the understanding that if we did better than this, we were going to stimulate an encouraging public response to it, whereas if we did less than that we would have despondency by doing less than we had set a target for. This, I think, was the mistake we made in the second programme.

It involved the consequence when we came to the second programme that we had either to state a 4 per cent per annum target or appear to be lowering our sights, aiming to achieve less than we had already actually attained. It was recognised that there was a reasonable doubt as to whether or not 4 per cent in our annual rate of growth was going to be achievable in the light of the international circumstances and of the British difficulties[2] and the probably diminishing returns which could be got from effort here. There was, however, no alternative, apart altogether from the nature of internal conditions. The OECD had stipulated a 4 per cent rate of annual growth for Europe as a whole, and we could not appear to be striving for less than what was said to be possible for every other country.

We had reservations on the question of achieving our aims, and what the consequences of failure to reach our target might be. In the end, these doubts were resolved for me by various studies which showed that while there would be variations from year to year, it could be done over the whole seven-year period, perhaps 3 per cent in one year could be offset by 5 per cent in another year, so that we could achieve our average growth rate of 4 per cent. There is no doubt it would have been achieved if things had remained as stable for us as they were during the period of the first programme. Things were favourable to us then, the world trade situation was improving, public morale had been revived, efforts were being expanded. But I thought it might be unduly optimistic to expect that these very favourable conditions would continue indefinitely. The possibility of another world recession was there, and it was bound to affect us, perhaps even more than other countries, because of our heavy dependence upon exports. We could be hit harder than most other countries in circumstances where world trade tended to contract – the impact here would be relatively higher than in other countries which were less dependent on exports.

DR: Could you say why targets were not reached in 1965/66?[3]

SL: The specific reasons why the actual achievements fell below 4 per cent in 1965/6 were the downward turn in British trade, the imposition of the special levies, and the credit restrictions which were necessitated here as well as elsewhere. We were unable to expand exports at the rate we had assumed, mainly because of the British situation. The whole international financial situation made it necessary for us to assume that the inflow of capital would not be very great. Then there was this constant pressure for wage increases, with inflationary consequences.

DR: Would you think there is general agreement on programming now?

SL: The concept of programming is now fully accepted. In 1958, the idea of trying to forecast what this country could do in five years was a revolutionary concept, but now it is accepted. And I suppose there will be a much more critical approach to the details of any new programming that there was before. The great achievement of the first programming was its complete acceptance by all the organisations of the country … the trade unionists, the farmers and industrialists. They all said, 'Yes, accept this. We will try to make it work.'

Housing was an issue that had challenged every government from the inception of the state. Fianna Fáil prided itself on its record on housing in the 1930s and 1940s. Slum clearance saw the rise of suburbs in Dublin, including Cabra, Crumlin and Drimnagh. Between 1932 and 1942 82,000 homes were built in the state, of which 41 per cent was public housing provided by local authorities. The war saw a significant slowdown in house building, which did not recover until the late 1940s. Despite the declining population, the 1950s and early 1960s saw another 140,000 homes added to the national housing stock, the state being the prime provider. Now, the rising population and rising expectations presented a major challenge to the Lemass government. Slum conditions in Dublin were blamed for the collapse of two separate tenement buildings in June 1963, in which four people were killed. This provoked a national debate on housing. In addition, a new entity, the National Building Agency (NBA), was established in 1960 as a semi-state body to tackle projects that were regarded as too big for the local authorities. Unfortunately, it was not a success and was responsible for many housing developments that soon became synonymous with bad planning, such as Ballymun in Dublin, Rahoon in Galway and Southill in Limerick.

SL: The National Building Agency was set up by the government to make up for the shortcomings of the existing institutions concerned with housing. The traditional method of dealing with housing for the working classes was to get the local authorities to build [it]. The government would lend them the money, give them grants and all powers necessary to undertake building. We found the ability of the local authorities to meet housing needs was not developing as rapidly as we had hoped. I saw there were other categories of housing with which the local authorities could not deal. One of the problems of decentralising industry is the need to provide houses for executives as well as for workers in the areas where the new industries are located. In this connection I remember a request from a coalmine in Slieveardagh.[4] I wanted 100 homes for their workers. The local authority could build 100 houses, but they would have to go to the people most in need of them. In other words, they could not guarantee them to workers and even where they did, they could not guarantee that if they lost their employment, the worker would be put out of his house.

***DR:** How about the problem of providing public servants, such as Gardaí, for example?*

SL: This was another problem which the NBA tackled. Local authorities could not build houses and reserve them exclusively for Gardaí. The National Building Agency could and did. But the biggest operation of the agency was to supplement the efforts of the Dublin, Cork and Limerick local authorities by initiating large-scale housing schemes. This was not intended to replace what the local authority was doing, but to supplement it. Initially the National Building Agency showed a great deal less drive and initiative than I had hoped. They were also slow getting into their stride, in a great many respects, and I am not at all that sure we were wise in appointing civil servants as the executives of the National Building Agency. They had the usual cautious approach of the civil servant to financial expenditure.

However, they are now moving at a steady pace. For a long time to come, I think we will need both the local authorities and the NBA. We should hope that the day will come when the housing needs of the country will have been met. From that day on, it will be necessary only to replace houses which have fallen into disrepair and to build for any shift in population which might occur. But this is some time ahead yet, although I think the planners would say it is only about ten years ahead. Shortly after I became taoiseach, I met the trade unions and Dublin Corporation about the housing programme. A peculiar situation had arisen in Dublin in that, under the coalition government, the corporation was told to stop planning for housing, as there would be no money for it. And by the time I came in, in 1959, this mistake had not been repaired; there were insufficient plans for new houses. It takes about five years for an initial decision to build to the time when the houses are ready to be occupied.

The estimated housing need in Dublin at that time was about 5,000. The Corporation had 1,500 houses vacated by people who had subsequently left them, so there did not seem to be a great housing shortage.

DR: Why has the housing need in Dublin increased since then?

SL: First, because of the increase in the population of Dublin.[5] Second, Dublin Corporation had to condemn a lot of houses after some houses had collapsed.[6] The collapse of these houses brought to light an enormous need which had not been anticipated earlier. Also as a result of this, some thousands of people who were moved out of condemned houses were given first priority for new houses, thus increasing the waiting list to the present ten or twelve thousand.[7]

DR: Will the day come when all our housing needs will have been met?

SL: There are three reasons why house building must go on: one is the constant need to replace old housing, the second is the increase in population, and the third will be the continuing demand for higher standards in housing accommodation. It is true that there are many people living in council houses who could afford to live in better houses. These are people whose incomes have moved far beyond the limits that the council houses were intended to cover. However, in time, these people will become conscious of their higher social status and will want to move to a purchase house in some other area. This will also tend to keep up the demand for housing.

There will always be a very high need for housing and I do not think that any country in the world can say that it has satisfied all its housing needs. Part of the problem in France during the recent trouble was the bad housing situation.[8] Even in Sweden, which is the wealthiest country in the world, you have to wait two or three years before you get a licence to own a house.

CHAPTER 15

THE KENNEDY VISIT

'I met Eisenhower and Kennedy as presidents and each time I was very conscious of the fact that I was talking to the most powerful man in the world. Even if he was an idiot, he was still the most powerful man in the world and on his decisions rested the fate of mankind.'

President John F. Kennedy's visit to Ireland in June 1963 was undoubtedly a highlight, if not *the* highlight, of Seán Lemass's time as taoiseach. The ascent of the great-grandson of a famine emigrant who left Ireland in 1848 to the office of the leader of the most powerful nation on Earth was an immense source of pride for the Irish at home and the Irish diaspora across the world.

Kennedy's ancestry was wholly Irish on both sides: his father's family originated from County Wexford; his mother's, the Fitzgeralds, from counties Limerick and Fermanagh.

Lemass saw Kennedy's visit as a chance to show that Ireland was advancing economically and socially after the grimness of the 1950s, but any hope that Lemass could persuade the first Irish-American president to back an end to partition was confounded by the realpolitik of the Cold War. No American president was going to interfere in the internal affairs of an ally as staunch as the UK.

While the first visit of a sitting US president to Ireland preoccupied the country, Lemass had an acute political crisis to deal with first. His minority Fianna Fáil government proposed the introduction of the turnover tax – an early forerunner of value added tax (VAT). Lemass's government recognised that the Irish tax base was too narrow, with 40 per cent of all revenue coming from excise on alcohol, tobacco and petrol.

The tax applied at a relatively modest rate of 2.5 per cent on the monthly turnover of retailers, yet it was met with fury and was seized upon by the opposition as a potential means to defeat the government. Lemass was faced with the prospect of losing a vote in the Dáil, thus precipitating a general election, on the eve of the Kennedy visit. In the end Lemass's government passed the bill in a packed Dáil by a single vote, 72 to 71, with the help of two independents, Joseph Lenehan and Frank Sherwin.

SL: Kennedy arrived on the day of this vote, the day on which we survived. When he got off the plane, he said: 'How did that vote go?' I told him we won by one vote. He said: 'One of how many?' I replied: 'One out of 140' and he said: 'That's a bigger majority than I had. I only had a small percentage margin.' I went on to explain the position with regard to the independents. Once they saw the government in danger they rallied to us straight away.

DR: Did you consider President Kennedy's visit to Ireland a great boost to the country?

SL: I think Kennedy's coming to Ireland was a tremendous boost in many ways. National prestige was enhanced, morale was raised and we gained in international influence by reason of the fact that he came here. I must confess I got a tremendous personal satisfaction when he, the president of the United States, laid the wreath on the graves at Arbour Hill.[1] He was the first president or head of state to do this. Since then there have been several others, but you would have had to be alive in 1916 to realise the real significance of this event – the head of the greatest state in the world coming to pay honour and respect to the men who had been shot at that time.[2]

DR: Did you notice any special qualities or weaknesses in President Kennedy?

SL: It is very hard to answer what qualities or weaknesses in him I noticed. We did not have any problems to settle, and therefore I did not have an opportunity of forming any very definite opinion about his qualities, but I had many discussions and conversations with him, all of which showed what everybody knows, that he had a very clear mind and a very wide vision of things. But we spoke mainly of generalities and never got down to details of the international situation except, perhaps, in regard to his thinking on the gold situation. We had no problem in the matter because we had no interest except to see that some general solution was worked out. Kennedy was a likeable person, but then, every American politician is a likeable person. This is partly a product of training and partly a product of the public image built up by public relations officers. It takes a long time to find out what the real man behind the public image is like. Every American politician lives behind a facade, but in Kennedy's case, I would say that the facade was less artificial than in most other cases. He had a capacity to see humour in almost any situation and to make some amusing comment, which made him very easy to travel with. I think the test of any man is how one would like to travel with him in the back of a car for 500 miles. Would one be bored before one got to the end of the journey or could one maintain the conversation all the way? With Kennedy I have no doubt it would have been an interesting conversation. I had no problem of adjustment. Indeed, I cannot remember that anyone here had.

DR: Was he asked to lay the wreath at Arbour Hill?

SL: Yes, he was invited to do this.

DR: There was no problem?

SL: Oh, no problem at all. There may have been some discussions in American circles as to how the British would react, but I feel sure Kennedy would have no hesitation in saying he was going to lay the wreath anyhow.

DR: Was Kennedy impressed by the ceremony?

SL: Very much so. Indeed, he felt that our ceremonial procedures [were] more inspiring than the corresponding American ceremony. He got the whole military ceremony done again by cadets and filmed for the purpose of bringing it back to America to try and introduce changes in the corresponding American ceremony.

I think this is what led to the request of Mrs Kennedy for a contingent of cadets to go over to his graveside,[3] after he was assassinated. He must have spoken very often to her about the Irish cadets.

At that time, I did not know what authority she had to make this request, so I was a little dubious about granting it. It would have been an embarrassing situation if the American government had not wanted it or had resented it, so I did not agree immediately. I asked Matt McCloskey, the ambassador here, whether Mrs Kennedy, even as the widow of an assassinated president, had the authority to make this request, and whether the American government endorsed it. He said not only did they endorse it, they were sending a special plane for the cadets. That satisfied me. If the Americans went to this trouble to get them over, then obviously, we would not be imposing. I had thought it just possible that the American Army could resent this contingent of a foreign army being brought up. The special plane decided it for me. I did not want to say 'no' and yet I did not want to say 'yes' until I was satisfied there would be no resentment, of their presence there, either by American officialdom or by the American people.

President Kennedy addressed the Dáil on 28 June 1963. He spoke at length of his pride at being the first American president to visit Ireland. Though never mentioning Lemass by name, he praised the country's efforts to modernise itself.

> And it is the present and the future of Ireland that today hold so much promise to my nation as well as to yours, and, indeed, to all mankind, for the Ireland of 1963, one of the youngest of nations, and the oldest of civilisations,

has discovered that the achievement of nationhood is not an end, but a beginning. In the years since independence, you have undergone a new and peaceful revolution, an economic and industrial revolution, transforming the face of this land, while still holding to the old spiritual and cultural values. You have modernised your economy, harnessed your rivers, diversified your industry, liberalised your trade, electrified your farms, accelerated your rate of growth, and improved the living standard of your people.

DR: What did you think of Kennedy's speech in the Dáil?

SL: Kennedy's speech in the Dáil was prepared by someone else, but he himself changed a fair amount of it. Indeed, on the way down from Áras an Uachtaráin to Arbour Hill, he was correcting the speech. Certainly, when he delivered the speech he did not look like a man reading a script. He had developed this technique of delivering a speech spontaneously.

In the course of that speech he quoted Lord Edward Fitzgerald, who said: 'Nothing good ever came out of Leinster House.' Afterwards he went up to Áras an Uachtaráin and Dev, who had been listening, said: 'Mr President, you did no good to Irish politicians by using that quotation, "Nothing good ever came out of Leinster House".'[4] Kennedy called his press officer and said: 'Kill that,' and it died. It never appeared anywhere afterwards. It has not appeared in the official published report of the speech. An enormously efficient organisation immediately sprang into action to kill the quotation, so that it does not exist anywhere. When Telefís Éireann sent me a 16mm film of the Kennedy visit, which included the whole of his speech, this quotation was missing.

How they did it I don't know, but the sentence is not on any film, in any handouts, or even in the Dáil Éireann reports.[5]

DR: Which impress you most – those who create or those who implement policy?

SL: I have often been asked before what people impressed me most. It is very hard to really make a valid judgement upon other people. First of all, statesmen are international figures. By the time you meet them they are going to have a place in world history. To judge them as individuals is not an easy task because they are coloured with the glamour of their international fame and the high offices they hold. This applies particularly to the president of the United States of America. I met Eisenhower and Kennedy as presidents and each time I was very conscious of the fact that I was talking to the most powerful man in the world. Even if he was an idiot, he was still the most powerful man in the world and on his decisions rested the fate of mankind. But in fact both Kennedy and Eisenhower are extremely attractive personalities, very easy to get to like, Eisenhower even more than Kennedy. I don't think Eisenhower was a great president, I don't think he had the highest intellectual qualities, he was slightly out of his element as president, but you could not help but like him. I met him again when he had ceased to be president and he still was the same very attractive personality to whom you were drawn immediately; there was a warmth there.

He was the type of person you would call by his first name after a dinner together. He had this type of personality. He was not an aggressive protagonist of any particular point of view and this helped to draw people towards him. Kennedy also had charm and was a strongly attractive personality. I always felt, however, that he had a motive for everything he did. There was a certain noticeable reservation in his attitude, a mind working away behind the outward facade of the charming personality. One could detect that his mind was working but one could not know what it was producing. Kennedy's eyes were the most striking, they were almost expressionless; even when he was joking or laughing, he was coldly calculating the effect he was having on listeners.

But I liked Kennedy very much and I think he had an enormous impact on the world and could have had enormous influence on the future of the world because of, first, the originality of his approach to matters of public policy, and second, his intellectual capacity to argue his point of view. When I was taoiseach, I said several times we were not neutral, although we were not a member of any military alliance. In any conflict between the East and West, we will be on the side of the West. Ireland will side with democracy against any socialist or totalitarian system. But we consider we could give more service to the West outside a formal alliance.

This whole policy got confirmation with the visit of John Fitzgerald Kennedy, when he came here and said this, in effect, in the speech to An Dáil. He said we were of more help to the West outside a formal arrangement. His statement defended our argument here as well as everywhere else. But much that was said at the time in Ireland, was really directed towards embarrassing the government, by people who did not understand the situation or did not want to understand it. However, I never had slightest anxiety that we would be presented with the proposition that we went into Europe only provided we joined NATO. But I recognise that once there is a European state with political institutions, we cannot refuse to commit ourselves to participation to whatever extent it is feasible for us in the defence arrangements. What these defence arrangements would be I cannot tell. The idea of nuclear bases here died an early death, because now static nuclear bases have become obsolete. The only nuclear defence now is one which is constantly moving, such as the Polaris submarine and the aeroplane in the air. The static situation with the rockets ready to go would be the first targets because they are vulnerable; they are a source of danger.

During the Cuban missile crisis of 1962, Lemass found himself in Berlin at a meeting with the German chancellor Konrad Adenauer.

SL: While we were discussing the general situation at the chancellor's residence, an aide came in with a message. Adenauer then told me that Kennedy had made an announcement to the effect that Cuba was to be blockaded. Later that afternoon when I met him at dinner he said he had sent a message to Kennedy supporting him in the action he was talking. He had also been in touch with de Gaulle, whose reaction was that, had he been in Kennedy's place, he would have forcibly occupied Cuba. He would not have contented himself with rather modest efforts at blockade. De Gaulle said he would have his army and his air force in to occupy Cuba rather than take the risk of having the Russian missiles there.

I think this was interesting because the only country which was hesitant in supporting what Kennedy did was Britain. The British press was reluctant to show support for America. The only suggestion emanating from the British press was that a deal should be made by which the US would give up bases in

Turkey in return for Russian withdrawal from Cuba. The British government was stronger than the British press probably, but in sharp contrast to this pussyfooting attitude was the firm support from Adenauer and from de Gaulle. There is a certain irony in all of this in the light of the situation which developed later, when de Gaulle kept Britain out of the Common Market because [they claimed] a special relationship with the United States.

DR: How did you feel about the Cuban crisis? What would you have done had you been in Kennedy's position?

SL: I think Kennedy handled that situation very well. He wanted to avoid an immediate threat to the United States which was – it must be remembered – a very real threat. The missile gap on which the US was relying would be undermined if the Russians were to have missile launching sites in Cuba. I think Kennedy was wise to play it in the way he did, rather than to force a showdown straight away. After all, he did succeed in his objectives. How far he would have gone if the Russians had persisted, I do not know, but he could not, under any circumstances, have allowed Russia to establish missile bases in Cuba. I think the Russians underestimated the American reaction to what they were trying to do. They made the mistake in thinking they might get away with it.

DR: On the other hand, supposing the Russians had sent their ships on, and the Americans had sunk those ships, the Russians would have been in a very strong moral position.

SL: The Russians would have said: 'We are face to face, and, if you strike the first blow, then it's war.' They made the correct decision to withdraw and they have never attempted anything on the lines of what they were doing in Cuba ever since. They have built up their forces in the Mediterranean, in the Middle East, and in places which are sufficiently close to their borders to give them the opportunity of manoeuvre. On the other hand, they have not attempted to establish themselves as far away from home as Cuba. If there is to be peace in the world for, say, the next 100 years, it must be on the basis of some unofficial acceptance of spheres of influence. For example, if any problem arises within the Russian sphere of influence, it will be their prerogative to resolve it. Russia is becoming more and more conservative and I believe, where one bureaucracy or one totalitarian party runs a country for a long time, it tends to become completely conservative and hidebound by traditional procedures. As a result, it will fall behind the rest of the world in making changes, and one can see this already happening in Russia. Not to change. If it is not necessary to change, it is necessary not to change. That's the classic definition.

I doubt very much if many of the Russian communists, even way back, had any other idea than to establish a dictatorship of their party which would give them complete power over the whole Russian people. They established their power with the utmost brutality. They shot millions of people and completely disregarded any human rights to further their conception of this centrally controlled state.

Lemass's attempts to project his status as a moderniser was bolstered after the Kennedy visit when he featured on the cover of *Time* magazine in July of that year. The cover juxtaposed the Ireland of leprechauns and shamrock with that of a thrusting nation of industry and enterprise, the one Lemass was championing at home. The magazine's flattering portrayal depicted Lemass emerging from de Valera's shadow while labouring 'single-mindedly for decades to break the vicious circle of declining living standards and dwindling population that threatened Ireland's very survival as a nation. Though he has little of the personal magnetism of Old Spellbinder Dev, the Quiet Man's drive to get Ireland into the world's markets and forums has attracted some of the bright, restive young Irishmen who are showing a revival of interest in politics.' His status was bolstered in the United States when President Kennedy reciprocated the invitation to Ireland, and Lemass visited the US at his invitation in October 1963. The ten-day trip was celebrated at home and abroad as a measure of the ancestral bonds between Ireland and the US that go back centuries. Lemass received a 19-gun salute on arriving in the White House. On his arrival he said:

> You can imagine what a proud moment it is for me to come to your country as the leader of an Ireland that has a government of its own, which is resolutely dedicated to the same ideals which motivate this great democracy and is determined to provide for its people opportunities for well-being and happiness such as you provide for yours.

Lemass was told not to raise the issue of partition with Kennedy. Politically, the trip is best remembered for a speech Lemass gave to the National Press Club in Washington in which he railed against partition, drawing a rebuke from the Northern premier Terence

O'Neill: 'Co-operation certainly does not stem from derogatory speeches in another country. It is notable that when President Kennedy came to Dublin he was a model of circumspection, not a mention of Northern Ireland came from his lips.' Lemass's visit was cherished by both himself and his wife. It was given added poignancy by President Kennedy's assassination in Dallas just a month later.

CHAPTER 16

LEMASS GOES NORTH

'I therefore began to talk about unity as a spiritual and not a political conception – something which would only follow upon the removal of these misunderstandings, these bigotries, these historical animosities.'

As a minister Lemass rarely spoke on the issue of partition, leaving de Valera to articulate Irish government policy on the issue. That changed when he became taoiseach. The unification of Ireland was a prime goal of the Fianna Fáil party. Lemass could never resile from the fundamental belief shared universally among Irish nationalists, north and south, that partition was a great injustice and a united Ireland a historical inevitability, however long it took. Ireland was one nation – even many British figures such as Winston Churchill and Herbert Asquith said as much, he told the Oxford Union in October 1959 in his first major speech on partition. The fundamental problem, he believed, was not the British government, which could be persuaded to give up the North if the majority demanded, but the 'Carsonite' unionists who had threatened to rise up before the advent of Home Rule and would do so again if a united Ireland was forced on them. In that he differed from his predecessor, Éamon de Valera, who, in and out of office, was singularly fixated on partition, but was at a loss as to how to bring it to an end. The British had created partition and they should end it. De Valera refused to acknowledge the legitimacy of successive Northern governments and made no attempts to reach out to them. There was no meeting between the two leaders of partitioned Ireland from 1925 until 1965.

Lemass took a different approach. He believed only persuasion could bring about an end to partition, but it could only be achieved from the bottom up. During his time as taoiseach Lemass focused on improving relations in areas of common concern such as agriculture, waterways and tourism. His attitude towards the British government and partition was coloured by de Valera's experiences during the war when British prime minister Winston Churchill offered an end to partition in return for Ireland's participation in the war. The offer made in extremis by Churchill was not taken seriously by de Valera and created bad feeling between the two leaders.

SL: There might well have been a situation brought about in Great Britain where, with the advent of a war, and the desirability from the British point of view that they should have the Irish with them during the war, we could have had some formal arrangement regarding partition at that time. Now, this did happen – after the war started, the British did try to raise this issue, on the old basis of coming into the war and then promising a united Ireland after the war. But we could not fall for that trick twice. That was the very thing they had tried in the First World War[1] and got away with, so we could not accept this. We said, 'All right, we are prepared to consider the idea of formally coming into the war as a united Ireland but not otherwise – the unity of Ireland.' It was Malcolm MacDonald[2] who was over here some time in 1940, trying to get this idea over, i.e. that we would join them in the war and declare war on Germany, and they promised us the unity of Ireland after.[3] It was not in their power to do this.

This was an unrealistic attitude towards partition, which we ourselves had helped to foster – that it is solely a matter for a decision of the British government. In fact, there is no end to partition unless the people in the North are prepared to accept whatever arrangements are made, because, in the last resort, you could have another Carsonite rebellion and doubtless the British government would not be expected to coerce people who are asserting their loyalty to Britain. It would have made a situation in which the ending of partition would be even worse than the partition situation; it would have to be done by military force with all the legacy of bitterness and hate that would result from it – a permanent and perpetual sore for the Irish people.

There was a time in 1957–1958 when I was over in London, and Lord Longford began to play around with the idea of our coming back into the Commonwealth on the basis of ending partition.[4] He went to Macmillan with this idea and he thought Macmillan was prepared to buy it. I told him, however, that the people in Belfast were not going to come into a united Ireland just because Macmillan told them to do so. Anyhow, we got nowhere. Macmillan began to talk to a few people who knew something about it and then learned the facts of life about the North. I went to him, and he said that the basis of the partition question was in the North and had no connection with the British association. Well, I suppose there is a belief that the Six Counties have commercial advantages within the Commonwealth, but even these are beginning to wear very thin, and there is a lot of disillusionment about them now, too.

When Lemass took office in October 1959 the IRA's unsuccessful border campaign (Operation Harvest) was still active, albeit at a much lower level than it had been when it started in 1956 and in the following year.

DR: Under the coalition government the IRA became active again – would you attribute this to weakness on its [the government's] part?

SL: Mac Eoin was Minister for Justice, and when we left office in early 1948 the IRA were dead – they had no organisation, no activity, no sign of movement at all – but Mac Eoin let them build up again because he did not want the political unpopularity of internment with them.[5] So they built up to the stage where they were able to start that border campaign later on. Peadar Cowan was allowed to march his army up and down the streets, and the guards were ordered not to interfere, which caused considerable frustration among the guards.[6] They knew these things were happening; they could have nipped them in the bud, but they were not allowed to do so. This was Mac Eoin's peculiar approach to it; he was completely irresponsible in this field, and a lot of trouble was caused by his weakness during that period.

The violence on the border started during the period when we were in opposition, and there was no effort by the coalition government to do anything about it. In the first coalition government, John Costello said that they were going to take the gun out of politics. They were reluctant afterwards to admit that they had done nothing of the sort during either coalition government period. They were aware that the extremists were organising and yet there were no positive orders issued to the Gardaí to prevent them doing so. Mac Eoin was Minister for Defence at the time.[7]

Mac Eoin wanted to avoid trouble. He did not want to admit that the problem existed, and this meant that the Gardaí were completely frustrated in their whole approach to it. By the time the second coalition came into being the earlier mistakes were beginning to bear fruit.

The first obvious change in policy in that regard was the ambushing of an RUC patrol near the border. Shots were fired from the Republican side of the border with no purpose other than to kill.[8] The incident decided us to take more vigorous measures to curb it. Those who were picked up were at first charged in the District Court and sentences of six months, three months, and so on were passed on them. Considerably later on, before my time as taoiseach, we took the decision to set up the Special Military Court, which brought the campaign to an end. [9]

The shooting of an RUC man in 1961 on a by-road near the border was just a brutal, unorganised local effort.[10] I was due to go to Belfast to speak in Queen's University on the day after this happened, but they called off the function in Belfast and a QUB professor told me they feared that feelings might be running high. There was some doubt in my mind that this may have been the real reason for the murder. I feared that if I accepted other invitations to go to Belfast, the murder might be repeated.

I believed it was necessary to come out strongly against the campaign. The Gardaí knew where they were operating from, but, often, by the time the Gardaí went to the training camps, they had broken camp and gone. They were operating from sanctuaries and were trying to work on the basis of the minimum risk to themselves;

hop over the border, shoot somebody and back in. If we were to catch any of these people and hand them over to the Six-County government, it would have stopped these raids. However, this course of action would have been politically impractical.

The Special Court came into existence in 1959, but it rarely had to sit. By that time the campaign was dying out. It had already degenerated from the spectacular raids on military barracks to the placing of time-bombs by people who were miles away before they went off, and an occasional shooting from behind hedges. This was a cowardly business and, as a means of ending partition, it was ludicrous. It was the sort of thing that was keeping North and South apart.

The border campaign eventually petered out, ending on 26 February 1962 with the IRA citing a lack of public support for the campaign. After the threat of violence had receded, Lemass returned to the issue of ending partition by negotiation. Lemass refers here to a speech he made in Tralee on 29 July 1963 in which he recognised 'that the government and parliament [in Northern Ireland] exist with the support of the majority in the Six-County area – artificial though that area is.' This was far as he was prepared to go to recognise the reality of the North's existence. He went on in his Tralee speech to acknowledge the 'genuineness of the fears which have influenced the religious minority in the North ... We have in effect said to our separated countrymen, "What safeguards do you need in a reunited Ireland? Whatever you may in reason ask we are prepared to give."'

SL: I said [in Tralee] we were prepared to leave aside the question of *de jure* recognition; but we had to recognise the facts that the government there existed; that partition had persisted for 40 years; that there was no immediate prospect that the situation would end; and, basing our policies on the recognition of these facts, we had to think in terms of a new approach to the situation that might ultimately result in unity in some form.

It would be true to say that up to that time, the problem of partition had never secured any deep study down here. There was a vague idea that we could end this by some sort of pressure, by physical force, by economic pressure, by international pressure through the United Nations or otherwise. I had long been convinced that this was an unrealistic approach that would never succeed; we would never be able to exercise enough pressure or command enough force to do so, and even if we forced them unwillingly into a united Ireland we would have a problem for a hundred years of keeping them there by force.

We would have to turn the North into a police state to prevent various movements from breaking out again and I could not see this being helpful to Ireland. I could see it as almost a disease which would ultimately destroy the nation, and I therefore began to talk about unity as a spiritual and not a political conception – something which would only follow upon the removal of these misunderstandings, these bigotries, these historical animosities, and so forth. This was, I think, the first full expression of an idea I had been developing in speeches before.

The prime mover in the first meeting of the leaders of divided Ireland was Northern premier Terence O'Neill through his private secretary Jim Malley, who delivered a personal message to Lemass on 4 January 1965 suggesting that a 'fresh approach should be made in the matter of co-operation between the two parts of Ireland'. Lemass immediately agreed. His first visit to Belfast as taoiseach was conducted with utmost secrecy on both sides of the border. Members of his cabinet were informed but were told to say nothing if asked. O'Neill only told his cabinet colleagues shortly before Lemass arrived in Belfast. The caution was necessary given the opposition that it would have generated in loyalist circles had they known Lemass was travelling north.

DR: On 14 January 1965, your first meeting with O'Neill took place at Stormont. Following this, Mr O'Neill said you had shown courage in accepting his invitation. Were there any political problems for you in your decision to go to Belfast?

SL: So far as I was concerned, I could see then no political problems for me. All the problems seemed to me to be on his side. I know our people would think of it as a first breakthrough – a first step in our coming together – and regard my meeting him as the beginning of something that was going to develop into the realisation of our ideal of a united Ireland. I knew this was the interpretation they would put on our meeting down here, but for him, that very interpretation of the meeting was going to cause political upheaval. I did not hope for very much from this. While there was talk of co-operation – and some practical co-operation has developed – the scope of this has not proved to be as great as I expected. As far as I was concerned, it was nothing more than a recognition of the fact that there were problems of an all-Ireland kind which an all-Ireland effort could more easily solve than separate efforts. In the political sense this was a new approach to the whole problem of partition; after so many years we were coming together again and beginning the process of at least talking with each other.

The problem for O'Neill that I saw was the back bencher vote, and this had in fact developed in one form or another. We have had a number of recent events which show how deep-rooted are the prejudices and hostilities to any idea he had of improving community relations up there; until the old bigotries, suspicions and hostilities disappear there can be no real progress. Immediately after my meeting with O'Neill, I received an enormous flood of letters from Protestant and Presbyterian clergymen in the North expressing their satisfaction at the turn of events and expressing a sense of release from old compulsions not to consort with Catholics.

A new era of community relations was heralded up there, and for a time it looked very much as if there was going to be a complete change. I am quite sure O'Neill, for example, got a similar volume of correspondence and was greatly encouraged by it; then the Paisley element came on the scene and the backbench people began to feel that they might have been jeopardising some of their support by these approaches. As we dug down deeper, of course, we came upon the bare, hard-rock prejudices which have always been there.

So far as we were concerned nobody who was interested in this question of partition could possibly raise objections to what appeared to be the first breaking down of the barriers between the Six Counties and here. This is what it looked like here and this is what it was. No, I did not anticipate any problems down here, nor were there any problems. I could see the possibility of trouble for O'Neill. I did not know to what extent we had taken steps to minimise this trouble. After I had met him, I met all the members of his government. I was studying them to see to what extent they regarded it as 'supping with the Devil' when they were having a cup of tea with me; it would have been hostility to O'Neill's policy not to meet me. I could see no sign of it, so I assumed he had taken some preliminary measures to deal with the matter, although he had not said so. Some of the members of the government I met at tea after the meeting said that they did not know I was there until they were summoned to come along and meet me, so I suppose they were also a bit in the dark as to the public reaction in the North.

I would say O'Neill was very much concerned with the ugly image the Six Counties has in the world, and with the deterioration in community relations which it should be his job as head of the government to improve.[11] They were getting a very bad press at that time, as bad as they are getting now, and I would think they are not going to solve any other problems in the North until some improvement in community relations is brought about. In his view, this was a step towards that, and he could have been right. As you know, in recent months they are back again to square one. I would say he knew that the Six-County situation could not really be put right until there was a greater harmony between the two elements in the population and an acceptance of the need for co-operation in the Six Counties, including the nationalists.

There was no love lost between Lemass and the Northern nationalists' political representatives. Lemass had a jaundiced view of all Northern politicians, considering them tribal and unreasonable. Nationalist Party leader Eddie McAteer felt Southern politicians saw them as the 'bastard children of the Republic, generally speaking they try to keep their distance'.

I met Eddie McAteer[12] and we talked about the role of the nationalists up there. I tried to sell him the idea that we envisaged the unification of Ireland as taking a form which would leave the Six-County government or parliament in existence – in other words, a federal solution. If he accepted that idea as the solution to partition this would enable him to take a fairly active role on a logical basis in the working of the Northern parliament. A Six-County parliament in a federal system would make laws for its own area and a person living in the area would have an interest in making good workable laws.

I tried to give him a logical basis for political action up there, which he had not got before that. You see, before that their attitude was 'We are against it.' That was a basis perhaps for a programme of action outside parliament, but it was not a basis for action by a parliamentary party. On the basis that a United Ireland would leave a Six-County parliament in existence, they had a framework within which to operate. Mind you, he accepted this and the nationalists became the official opposition party shortly afterwards and participated in the working of parliament to a greater degree than before.[13]

DR: When did you first consent to go up?

SL: Well, there had been talks between [T.K.] Whitaker and [Jim] Malley, who was O'Neill's private secretary. Now a private secretary to the prime minister in the North has a different role, a more important role than a private secretary down here. He is also secretary to the government, and Malley has since moved up in the hierarchy to a more important position as secretary to the Department of Finance. As a result of the talks, there came an informal suggestion that O'Neill was prepared to have me up. Now I could have said to O'Neill that the first meeting must be in Dublin, but I felt that this would be all wrong, because it would appear to be capitulation on his part. In a sense, we were the fellow courting the girl, and the girl could not go to the fellow; the fellow had to come to the girl. I felt therefore that I should go there first since it was impossible for him to come to Dublin first. Once I had gone there, there was no problem for him to come back here. O'Neill's visit to Dublin[14] was only a follow-up, it was only a reciprocal gesture – there was in fact nothing discussed in Dublin that had not been covered in Belfast and the visit to Dublin was, to a large degree, a social occasion rather than a business occasion because all the things we could talk about in relation to co-operation between government departments in each area had already been discussed.

DR: Did you see the preceding visits of lord mayors and the discussions about state visits? Did you see this as leading up to ...

SL: Oh no, no connection really. There was never any real discussion about a state visit. From time to time occasionally some British minister would talk in terms of a royal visit to Ireland – somebody who had no understanding of the real situation at all and ... with no authority to make a proposal. But there had been no formal approaches in that regard and there would be no sense in it since it would only create further misunderstandings. I couldn't see this ever happening until the whole partition situation had been ended, but that does not affect individuals.

The Queen Mother was always fishing for a visit to the Dublin Horse Show. She is keen on horses and has always regarded the show highly. Indeed, on one occasion she threatened our ambassador in London that she would set off for Belfast and have her plane break down on the way so that she could get into Dublin and visit the Horse Show, in circumstances where we could not very well keep her out.[15] Of course, Princess Margaret's visits from time to time were just a headache – that's all they were, a headache.[16] There was no possibility of stopping her, barring a very formal action saying we didn't want her to come. We felt this would be misunderstood, but we certainly didn't encourage her to come – not for any reason other than recognition that we were going to have a security problem on our hands when she was here.

She could have come as the wife of a man who had a residence in Ireland and wanted to visit his family without any ceremony attaching to the occasion. There would have been no question at all in that case – that is, if she was coming as Mrs Snowdon. There was no official character to her visit and she got no official reception. At least no one could possibly allege that it was a royal visit and because of this there would be no political repercussions either here or in Britain.

DR: You said a moment ago, in a very philosophical way, 'we seem to be back to square one'.[17]

SL: Well, this is perhaps too sweeping a statement, because I think there is no question but that there is a much healthier approach to the whole situation amongst the younger generation in the North – I am talking about university students and similar people. They are apparently much more conscious than the older generation of the very defective image they present to the world, very much more concerned to do something about rectifying the situation. The older type of unionist up there would not give a damn about this; he would be the type of person who would not know what we were talking about, and he would stick to his point of view anyway. But there is amongst the new generation up there a surge of feeling which is quite useful and healthy, but it is so easy to get back to square one. All the politicians in the North, on both sides I suppose, are to blame for this.

I said, when I was speaking in the North a couple of years ago, that the unhealthy aspect of the northern political situation is the fact that political and religious demarcations are identical.[18] In this regard it is as true of one side as the other that you could not conceive of a Protestant being nominated as a nationalist candidate or a Catholic being nominated as a unionist candidate. One side was the same as the other. Economic issues, social issues, normal political debates can be suppressed by raising the old battle cries again and so long as that's there, the temptation to resort to this tactic in the last instance will be very strong and will be used.

DR: You don't feel that your visit to Belfast indicated an approach to the solution of partition through peaceful federal-type means, rather than through external pressures?

SL: No, I didn't see it as an end to partition. I saw the development of a situation where contact between people on both sides on practical issues could ultimately lead to discussions of political issues but only in the long run. There was no signpost on the road that the next step was a political agreement; this wasn't there. There was an outlook there in the mid-'50s which made it possible for the ministers of the Belfast government to come to Dublin to negotiate agreements, but this was wrecked by the IRA campaign, which again raised the old Adam in the Orange people. We were only getting back to a situation we had been in before, and now that we are back again, it seems to me to be upset by these recent disturbances; but perhaps there has been some advance in the meantime. I wouldn't know; only history will tell.

The talks between Lemass and O'Neill occurred against the background of improving Anglo-Irish relations in the 1960s. The prime reason for this was the coming to power in 1964 of the Labour government, led by Harold Wilson, which would be in power for the rest of the decade. Wilson and Lemass forged a productive relationship based on mutual respect.

DR: What did you think of Wilson's personal qualities and abilities? Did you think he was extremely able?

SL: His outstanding personal qualification was his enormous confidence in himself. He faced the world without any doubt about his capacity to deal with any situation the world could bring him. I would like to meet him now, to see whether his self-confidence has been shaken by recent events. He has been quiet recently, and this leads me to think that he could be losing his confidence. If he does, he is finished. This was his great quality. He was afraid of nothing. There is no problem which he did not feel he could handle. It is true to say that in administration he often saw the short-term solution of any problem. He did not think beyond the next week or the next fortnight. This would be, I think, a result of the attitude … 'Well, if the situation does prove difficult, I can handle it too.' He did not feel the necessity for thinking of all the options, because he felt he could take any of them. I would say he is a man of high intelligence. I have no doubt of this. His record shows it. He was placed first in all his examinations, and he never had a failure. In everything he went into in life he emerged on top. When he went for a university fellowship he emerged first; when he applied for a professorship at Oxford, he was the youngest man to get it. When he went forward for election first, he was elected to a seat that was formerly Conservative with an increased majority. He never failed in anything he did.

DR: How would he compare with Kennedy in your mind?

SL: Ah, there would be no comparison between them. Kennedy had the capacity to see events as a whole, the capacity to speak in terms which the ordinary man could grasp in terms of events as a whole. Kennedy looked at the world as a whole and was able to talk about every problem in the context of the world situation. If Wilson had this quality, he never used it. His main characteristic was to deal with this problem when it arises. And if he created another problem, he would say 'OK, I will deal with that problem too.'

And this, I suppose, was his weakest point, really, that he did not tend to stand back, as Kennedy would, to see the whole historical trend of events. He was not concerned with this. When I talked about the EEC, I could not get a spark out of him, I remember. He was completely inert on the subject. He seemed just not to have a thought about it and had no sort of plan about the EEC. He knew he had a split cabinet on this issue. In many ways he had a kind of surprising xenophobic attitude. He was very much the Britisher. 'These bloody foreigners are just a bloody nuisance' was the attitude, you know, although he never used those words to me.

Nevertheless, Wilson was determined to forge a better relationship with Ireland and an early opportunity arose to demonstrate goodwill. The repatriation of the remains of Sir Roger Casement was a point of contention between the British and Irish governments for decades after Irish independence. Casement was the only leader of the Easter Rising to be executed outside Ireland. He was convicted of treason and, after a very public trial, hanged in Pentonville Prison in August 1916. One of Casement's last requests was to be buried in the old churchyard in Murlough Bay in County Antrim. The British government refused his request. The law only allowed for executed people to be buried within the walls of the prison where they were killed. The desire to have his remains repatriated never abated. A grave was chosen for him in Murlough Bay and de Valera, then leader of the opposition, visited in 1953. Winston Churchill, in his last term as prime minister, was minded to grant the repatriation, but was eventually dissuaded because of the opposition of the Northern government.

Harold Macmillan rejected Lemass's request to return the body in 1959. Harold Wilson's election in 1964 finally ended the impasse, something that he recalled in his memoir: 'The refusal to return [Casement's] body had soured Anglo-Irish relations for almost half a century and I felt the time had come for us to set it right.' In January 1965 the British cabinet agreed the repatriation of Casement's remains, but not to Northern Ireland because the unionist government would have objected. Instead, he would be repatriated and buried in Glasnevin Cemetery in Dublin. His

remains were flown to Ireland on 23 February 1965 and the oration over his grave was given by President de Valera six days later.

SL: We had been asking various British governments for a long time about the possibility of the remains of Roger Casement being restored to Ireland. There was even the idea that he could be bought back and buried in the Six Counties. That, I think, was always unrealistic, but the Conservative government kept opposing any move very vigorously, not on the grounds that they didn't want to do it, but on the grounds of legal and other practical problems. They said it would require an Act of Parliament to give up the dead body of a convicted criminal; that there was no dead body; that it had been buried in quicklime and had disappeared. They even said that the place where he was buried was not recorded and that nobody could be certain that it was Casement's body that would be dug up, if there was any body there when they started digging. They raised a variety of problems of that kind which all ended up in a refusal to restore the remains, but when I went to Wilson, all the problems disappeared. There was no Act of Parliament required.

The Labour government and Wilson came to power in 1964. If he did not understand our problems, he certainly knew much about them. He was very conscious of the fact that he represented a constituency with 60 or 70 per cent population of Irish origin.[19] He professed his desire to have the most friendly relations with us. He expressed his contempt of the Northern government in the Northern situation, as strenuously as you could expect he would. Yet I never felt he would do anything that was not politically advantageous to him in Great Britain, nor did I expect it. But he did do things he could over the return of Casement's remains and those who shot General [*sic.*] Wilson.[20] These things required something more than a political decision.

I liked Wilson. There was no personal animosity between us at all. The chemistry of people sometimes reacts adversely, but Wilson and I did get on very well. We got to first-name terms very quickly, but I did not feel he was doing it for the purpose of placating me. I naturally fell into the same situation with him, without any sense of being 'phoney' about it, so there was a very happy personal relationship between himself and myself. Wilson's problem was not reluctance to return Casement, but avoidance of political trouble over it. That is why we concocted an arrangement that nobody knew about, until the remains had actually arrived in Dublin. You can see from Wilson's point of view this was an important consideration. Nobody was going to start an agitation to get the remains back to England again.[21] You could see an agitation starting in England about the removal that would bring the whole question of Casement and what he did and all the rest of it to the forefront again, so this was handled very well. There was not the slightest leakage of news on the matter; nobody anywhere knew that there was an aeroplane in the air carrying Casement's remains to Dublin Airport until we announced that the plane had landed in Dublin and the army was told to go out and take charge.

Wilson, on these trivial matters, had no hesitation, apparently, in meeting the various requests that were made. You remember the 1916 flag that was flown from the GPO and some other material, all of which had been either refused or would have been refused by a Conservative government? To Wilson these were no problem and he was, of course, very much aware of the fact that he was not losing political support by conceding these things to us.[22]

The Conservatives would have been worried about the possibility of losing political support from their right wing. They would have been worried about the anti-Irish sentiment, still fairly strong amongst their supporters, and the criticism they would have encountered from any concession to ex-rebels, but Wilson had no problem and never had.

There was pressure for the Casement diaries, but I did not press for these at all. First, I think that legally these diaries are the property of the Casement relatives and not of the Irish government and, second, I did not want to open the issue of the bona fides of the diaries. I felt this was completely wrong, that our attitude should be to honour Casement for what he did as an Irish national leader regardless of whether the diaries are phoney or genuine.[23] The issue of whether they were true or false was used at the time to swing public opinion in Britain and the USA in order to justify the judicial murder of Casement.

CHAPTER 17

ONE MORE ELECTION

The talks with Sir Terence O'Neill and the repatriation of the Casement remains created a positive atmosphere in the country, which led Lemass to call a general election for 14 April 1965. Lemass had managed between 1961 and 1965 to run a successful minority government, but he lost two by-elections in 1964 and a third early in 1965 when the Labour Party's Eileen Desmond succeeded to her late husband Dan Desmond's seat in Cork Mid. Lemass warned that a third by-election defeat would lead to a general election. He was not bluffing. Lemass again stood on his record and the campaign was personalised with the Fianna Fáil slogan 'Let Lemass Lead On'. He defended the rising tax burden by stating that if the public wanted more money for education, health and social welfare spending they would have to pay for it. Lemass won exactly half of the 144 seats. The Fianna Fáil share of the vote increased by almost four percentage points from 43.8 per cent to 47.7 per cent. But for a couple of hundred votes in some constituencies, Lemass could have won an overall majority. Lemass actually got more first preference votes in 1965 (597,000) than de Valera in 1957 (592,000). It was the first time since 1933 that an incumbent Irish government actually increased its vote.

DR: Were you satisfied with the 72 seats?

SL: Yes, as far as any politician is ever satisfied with 72 seats; but 72 seats is a working majority. I would have felt quite secure in a parliament of 74. It was in theory a working majority of one, because Hogan[1] was still the Ceann Comhairle. In practice, it was of course, much stronger and, as you know, the government has added to their strength ever since by reason of the fact that Paddy Norton[2] left the Labour Party and is now with the government and by reason of victories at by-elections ever since then. If they get 72 at the next election they will be very happy. You can in theory be defeated on some issues when all members are present and voting. In practice it doesn't happen. There were a number of new deputies elected and I still couldn't say what the significance of this was in relation to the future – there is no question of its significance in relation to the management of the Fianna Fáil party.

DR: Now, about the long count in Dublin North-East[3] and Longford–Westmeath?[4]

SL: Well, of course this is one of the factors which make people say we will have to get rid of this system of PR altogether. This was a farcical situation, as you know. The government got 72 seats in the end; whether we were going to get 70 or 74 depended altogether on whether they could detect an almost invisible stamp on a ballot paper which had been handled already over 20 times during the course of the count and the temptation of the counter to rub it out if it is going to affect the result, is very strong. I made a speech shortly afterwards at some function in Jury's Hotel, and I said that this showed the unsuitability of the system of electing deputies, and this was the first hint I gave that we could in fact be thinking in terms of going back again for a constitutional referendum.[5]

We lost a seat in Dublin North-East by four; we lost a seat in North Mayo by 14; we won a seat in Longford/Westmeath by 12; we won a seat in South Kerry by 20 or so. While the element of luck is very strongly involved it nevertheless works one way as much as the other. Why we did not demand a recount in North Mayo I haven't got a clue; that was the most stupid business in the world.

Lemass brought new members into the cabinet. George Colley became Minister for Education, Patrick Hillery Minister for Industry and Commerce, Micheál Ó'Móráin Minister for the Gaeltacht, Donogh O'Malley Minister for Lands and Brian Lenihan Minister for Justice. It was the most significant change in the make-up of the government since Fianna Fáil first took office in 1932. In December 1965 Lemass added another significant achievement to his time in office with the signing of the Anglo-Irish trade agreement in December. The agreement was a realisation that the UK's and Ireland's applications for membership of the Common Market had failed and there was no certainty as to whether or not it would ever succeed.

In March 1963 he began trade talks with the UK about a free trade agreement. Matters took a step forward when Harold Wilson came to power. The two countries agreed free trade terms in July 1965 and the Anglo-Irish Free Trade Area Agreement was signed on 15 December 1965. Britain agreed to abolish all import duties on Irish goods from 1 July 1966. Ireland agreed to cut import duties on all British goods by 10 per cent, and by another 10 per cent each successive year until all industrial duties eventually disappeared in 1975. The agreement allowed unrestricted, duty-free access to the British market for Irish store cattle, store sheep and store lambs, while the Irish undertook to export at least 638,000 head of cattle per annum. For Lemass the agreement was not just about free trade with Ireland's biggest market by far, but a further step in weaning Irish industry away from protectionism and towards an export-driven free trade economy.

DR: The free trade agreement was signed in December 1965. Were the advantages anticipated realised in practice?

SL: It would be wrong to suggest that this was an idea which was born for the first time in 1965. This had been debated in various ways over a number of years on various occasions. The idea of some type of trade agreement with Britain was urged in the Dáil by spokesmen of various parties. I had myself discussed it with British governments on a number of occasions following the breakdown of the European Free Trade Area talks. I went over to London after these talks broke down to try and ascertain their thinking on the subject. At that time they were organising the European Free Trade Area and I hinted that we were not interested in this at all, but would be interested in a corresponding arrangement between them and ourselves. That would be about 1959 or 1960.

Our argument against EFTA is that we would be giving access to our markets to all the Scandinavian countries and so forth with which we had no possibility of getting corresponding reciprocal trade, and therefore we did not want this, but we wanted it with the British, where we would have the possibility of reciprocal trade. Then the British, of course, began to turn their own thinking to membership of the Common Market and that killed the idea of a separate arrangement for both of us, for once that happened, we did not want to tie ourselves up with any prior arrangement. The matter only came back to life again after the breakdown of the British effort to get into the Common Market. At that time I went over to the British government and outlined this idea in broad principle to Macmillan and to Heathcote-Amory[6] – who was then Chancellor of the Exchequer – and they all said that it was an interesting idea and must be examined. No one said no, we won't examine it, but they did not; at least nothing happened. We went over a couple of times and each time I raised the idea again, and they always appeared to accept it, but did nothing about it. It was when I went over to see Wilson in 1965 concerning the special import duties[7] and arising out of their inability to meet us on our request for special treatment on import levies, I referred to the possibility of these discussions. I told him my experience, that we had been hawking this idea to London several times and getting nowhere. I said I wouldn't do it again unless he gave me an assurance that he was serious about it. He said he was serious about it and we got down then to real practical work. After I returned to Dublin, the committees sat on both sides and began to hammer it out. They brought it as far as they could at official level, but there were a number of points outstanding that had to be settled at the final meeting over in London.

DR: Was that before your visit on the levies? I cannot remember whether it was before or after that.

SL: The levies came into operation at the end of 1964,[8] and these discussions were arranged when it was clear we were not going to get anywhere on the basis of special treatment on the levies. We began to talk about this and it was then that Wilson said he was quite serious about negotiations for an Ireland/Britain free trade area, and we recorded that we had agreed in principle to negotiate an agreement. The trade agreement we made with the British in 1962/63 provided for periodic meetings between officials on both sides to review the workings of the agreement and at this committee on several occasions the idea of the Free Trade Area Agreement had been discussed, but it was never clear that any British officials had been authorised to negotiate for it until after my talk with Wilson.

You must remember that apart from any immediate benefit to the country from such an agreement with Britain, foremost in my mind were the ideas that we were going to become members of the Common Market, and that the drive behind our preparation for Common Market membership had been losing its strength by reason of the fact that the date of membership was receding rather than advancing. The various measures which had been adopted to try and bring Irish industry into line for Common Market competition were not working very well, because many people did not see any prospect of our entry. I felt then that if we could bring free trade into operation under some international agreement, even with the British only, it would help us in our preparations for Common Market membership. There was also an idea in my mind that we could perhaps negotiate with Britain a free trade area agreement which would contain safeguards for our interests which we could carry into the Common Market.

I could see us, assuming that Common Market membership became feasible in the end, going to Brussels and saying: 'Here is a free trade agreement we made with Britain. We are prepared to make the same agreement with you with all the safeguards and tariff-dismantling provisions and time schedules in the British agreement.' I had considerable hope that we could get this accepted en bloc, by the Common Market members, and that it would be useful in our negotiations at that stage to have an agreement in existence. I saw our negotiations with Brussels – after we had completed successfully our agreement with Britain – taking place when they were all tired of the process of negotiations with Britain. I recognised that Ireland and Denmark and Norway would be quite willing to short-circuit the negotiations, and the remainder might agree if we could produce an already signed, already functioning agreement between ourselves and Britain. So there were a number of considerations which seemed to me to make it worthwhile entering into Free Trade Area negotiations with Britain at that time, and I see no reason now to change my mind as to their value, even if it is true that Common Market membership is still as far away as ever.

CHAPTER 18

1916 AND ALL THAT

'If ever a generation is born which says we are satisfied with all our fathers did for us, that is the end of progress; that nation would just wither and die.'

With Anglo-Irish relations in a good position, Lemass was free to participate in the fiftieth anniversary commemorations of the Easter Rising as one of the few veterans still involved in active politics. The main commemoration took place on 10 April 1966 in O'Connell Street. Some 900 veterans marched past the viewing stand where Lemass and his fellow Easter Rising veteran President Éamon de Valera stood. The president opened the Garden of Remembrance on Easter Sunday 1966. RTÉ Television, now coming into its own, aired the drama-documentary series *Insurrection*. There was much talk of how much Ireland had progressed or not progressed in the intervening 50 years since the Rising. Lemass emphasised many times in various speeches during 1966 that marking the fiftieth anniversary was not about the past but about building on the freedom won as a result of the Rising. He used the word 'patriotism' repeatedly to stress that the best way forward was through economic and social development and not through narrow sectional interests. He outlined his thoughts in a speech he gave in Tralee, County Kerry in April 1966: 'For the next 50 years the symbol of patriotism is not the armed Irish volunteer, but the student in the Technical College, the planning officer, the busy executive of industry and trade union, the progressive farmer, the builders and workers on whose skills and enthusiasm the country's future depends.'

DR: At the time of the 1916 commemoration, did you look back on the 50 years?

SL: I did not. I had to write various articles and make many speeches about it, but I did not sit at home and ask where we had gone in the last 50 years. Many people have asked me that question since. I gave an interview to *The Kerryman* and this was the particular point of the interview.[1] I had no hesitation in saying that the progress made in the country in the last 50 years would have been inconceivable in the circumstances of no national freedom. There would have been some progress anyway, because the whole world was going ahead, but we could never have achieved anything like what was done – the intensification of the industrial effort, the creation of employment opportunities, the rise in the standard of living and social conditions – if there had not been an Irish government.[2]

The fact that there was an Irish government free to examine in detail what the social and economic problems were and free to adopt its own policy made this progress possible. I think it is probably true to say that the young people of today do not appreciate what this progress has been. They are not capable of looking back and visualising Ireland 50 years ago, with foreign troops, English government and most appalling social conditions, particularly as far as housing was concerned. After the conclusion of the 1914 war, there were literally no employment opportunities at all when the wartime industrial boom ended. Indeed, I suppose most people looking objectively at the situation, certainly if they looked with the economic knowledge that people have nowadays, would have been convinced that it would be almost impossible for the country to develop an independent existence building on that basis.

I am talking about young people who are saying we did not do a lot, but young people must always say that. If ever a generation is born which says we are satisfied with all our fathers did for us, that is the end of progress; that nation would just wither and die. There must always be a new generation saying their fathers didn't do enough and we can do better than that, providing they are expressing their criticism on the basis of the facts, and recognise what can be done. I would not be at all upset by the fact that young people are critical of the past generation's achievements, so long as they do not think they have a right to be born into a world there are no problems left to be solved.

Men must always have this sort of divine dissatisfaction with things as they are, which is the source of progress in all directions. We could all retire into a monastery, but if you want to live in the world you have to be thinking in terms of future development. Further development, of course, is facilitated by scientific discovery and scientific discovery is always accelerating because it works from the basis of what is known to what is unknown, and what is known is always growing. The rate of progress into the unknown is always increasing and this opens up new opportunities and creates new problems, particularly in the social areas. I am not at all sure that the problems of increasing affluence in countries like Sweden – the social problems arising from it – are not more intractable, far harder to deal with than the social problems arising from endemic poverty. The world has got to think in terms of a whole new set of social problems which did not exist before, when everybody was poor anyway. I am quite certain that there will always be social tensions, strains and dangers in every country.

On 18 February 1966 Lemass gave a speech at the Law Students' Debating Society of Ireland at King's Inns in Dublin in which he admitted that the Irish revolutionary generation had not really thought about the economic consequences of Irish freedom. Ireland was one of the first small countries to gain its freedom and there was no precedent to follow.

DR: At King's Inns you said: 'Patriotism in its finest sense appears today to have so little influence on individual and sectional behaviour' and referred to 'the pursuance of self-interest'. Can you tell me what you specifically had in mind?

SL: Well, I was talking about the pressure groups that were exercising and voicing their demands in the interests of their own sectional welfare and I suppose that is something that always has to be said. There is a demand on individuals over and above seeking their own self-interest and that is to serve the interests of the community as a whole. That would specifically apply to wage demands. There is no question but that the country would be better off if we could develop a system relating wage increases to the requirements of expanding total output. But can you do this? Can you impose a demand for patriotism on the individual worker?

Patriotism may demand that you should look for a 3.5 per cent increase in wages this year, not 5 per cent, but you may get this 5 per cent if you fight hard enough for it. You would be better off by getting it, but the country as a whole would be less well off. I said somewhere recently that the choice between national welfare and individual welfare is always arising. In the area of labour it takes the form of increasing the total number of jobs or increasing the salaries of those in jobs. This question has often been answered in favour of the standard of living of those in jobs; let the unemployed go where they will. If you could get the trade unions to agree for a period of three, four or five years to maximise employment, to get rid of unemployment altogether and accept that this means curbing wages demands, unemployment could disappear.[3] This could be done and is what a dictator would do whether he be a fascist or a red.

Patriotism, had, in fact, become a dirty word. Somebody said that patriotism was the last refuge of a scoundrel[4] and politicians were getting somewhat chary of using the word in trying to appeal beyond self-interest to a wider emotion. I think this was a phase in our national history which has ended. It is true to say that people respond more readily than a few years ago to a patriotic appeal based upon national consideration and not self-interest.

When Eisenhower was going for election as president of the United States, he was no politician, and his political advisers said the American people always respond to a demand for a sacrifice. This is what the American people respond to; they like to think of sacrificing themselves for some public good, and, if that is true, if this sentiment prevails in America, it certainly is a healthy sign that people will respond to a request for its leaders to sacrifice something for a greater good than their own personal living conditions. Ten years ago, this would have fallen on deaf ears in Ireland, but I would not consider this true now. I think you could get an emotional response, and it looks as if we are getting it.

In July 1966 de Valera, at the age of 83, sought a second term as president of Ireland. Charles Haughey was appointed de Valera's election director. Fine Gael tasked Tom O'Higgins with finding a suitable candidate. O'Higgins was a former Minister for Education and a member of the O'Higgins family who included his uncle Kevin who was slain in 1927. Tom O'Higgins nominated himself when no other suitable candidate could be found. Lemass lent his personal prestige to the de Valera campaign. De Valera's re-election, he said, would be 'an affirmation by the people that the aims for our country which have directed him throughout his life remain constant, and that patriotism is as relevant in the island of 1966 as it was in 1916'.

The fact that Fine Gael sought to challenge an incumbent president and an icon of revolutionary Ireland irritated Fianna Fáil. The presidential campaign was marked by an extraordinary level of complacency on the part of Fianna Fáil. Lemass advised de Valera that as head of state he could not campaign to retain his position. Fianna Fáil emphasised his association with the Easter Rising in subtle and unsubtle ways, making him central to all the main events. No television debate between the two candidates was allowed.[5] De Valera did not canvass at all while the relatively young O'Higgins (49), modelling himself on President Kennedy, travelled around the country projecting himself as the youthful candidate standing against the elderly incumbent. Fine Gael highlighted 'the need for a youthful, forward-looking president to personify the real Ireland and what it can best contribute to modern civilisation'. Still, the received wisdom in the days before polling was that de Valera would win comfortably. The end result confounded that expectation. The big winner was apathy; more than a third of the electorate stayed at home. De Valera won with just 50.5 per cent of the vote (558,861 to 548,144), a margin of 1 per cent.

DR: De Valera was elected president in 1966 by a very small majority. Did this have any bearing on your decision, which was taken within a year, to resign?

SL: I was disappointed with de Valera's majority, but it was a relief when he was elected, because it looked at one stage as if he might not be elected. This result was, no doubt, attributable to the fact that he was old and certainly that he had not been able to campaign on his own behalf. Also, there was a very successful and rigorous campaign by the opposition.

They did a really good job on organising that campaign for him, using him to a much greater extent than de Valera could be used. Also, I suppose it is true to say that a lot of young people now look on de Valera as a figure of the past. Whether a lot of those who did not vote would have voted against him and really wanted him defeated I cannot say; I would be surprised if this were so. There is one point regarding the bearing of the presidential election on my decision to resign. I was looking for a time to resign when there would be no problem as to a successor. There was, at that time, also a need for us to define more precisely our objectives as the government party. I tried to do this in a memorandum which was published shortly after the election, but I had the feeling during that campaign that there was not so much hostility to the policy of the government as lack of certainty as to what the policy was. We had not defined our policies in a comprehensive way for some time. We had dealt with individual aspects of the policy, but we had made no attempt to restate it in a comprehensive way. However, it was very hard to get people to pay attention to this restatement of policy, which I attempted that year. I think it is true to say that we did not put enough effort into the presidential election campaign. There was an assumption that de Valera's re-election was certain and therefore that we did not work too hard. If people had known that the majority was going to be so small they would have put much greater effort into campaigning.

The proposal to introduce free secondary schooling was the most significant announcement of Lemass's last government and had a dramatic and long-lasting impact on Irish society. Minister for Education Donogh O'Malley ambushed his cabinet colleagues on 10 September 1966 by publicly announcing that free secondary education would be available to every pupil from the following school year. Did Lemass know about the speech in advance?

Lemass regarded 'kite-flying' as a legitimate tactic in testing public opinion about dramatic changes. O'Malley was a maverick politician who, calling attention to the fact that a third of children left full-time education after primary school, described it as 'the dark stain on the national conscience'.

Irish Times journalist John Healy, a long-time friend of O'Malley, stated that Lemass had read and approved the speech in advance. In the original draft O'Malley proposed a means test for students who wished to pursue a Leaving Certificate education. Lemass deleted any suggestion of a means test.

Lemass delivered a gentle admonition to O'Malley for keeping his colleagues, particularly Minister for Finance Jack Lynch, in the dark about his proposals, but this may have been a white lie to placate both Lynch and the secretary-general of the Department of Finance, T.K. Whitaker, who were furious such a decision was made without consultation. As it turned out, Lynch introduced the scheme on time after becoming taoiseach. Between 1966 and 1969 the number of secondary school pupils increased from 104,000 to 144,000.

In 1967 O'Malley appointed District Justice Eileen Kennedy to examine the reformatory and industrial schools system. It was an early indication of a more progressive and critical approach to the problems of institutionalisation in Irish life. The industrial school system had been criticised as far back as 1946 by Fr Edward Flanagan, the founder of Boys Town in Nebraska, as a 'national disgrace', yet nothing was done about it until O'Malley got involved. O'Malley was spoken of as a future taoiseach, but tragically he died in 1968 from a heart attack at the age of only 47.

SL: De Valera's great strength was that he could provoke amongst the people intense personal loyalty or intense personal hatred. Indeed, this is true of any really successful politician. Donogh O'Malley could have done this. You had people who were prepared to die for him and were prepared to kill him too. O'Malley often broke the tapes in announcing projects that had not been considered at all, much less finally decided upon. Perhaps he thought he was committing the rest of us by making announcements without authorisation. This is a continuous problem for a taoiseach.

I used to lay down rules that ministers were only entitled to speak in public on matters relating to their own department, and if they were to talk about other departments they had to obtain my prior consent. The duty in controlling wanderers rests on the taoiseach. Once or twice I had to do this. Ministers talked on general policies in a way that implied decisions had been taken, or disclosed an attitude that had not been adopted.

The big thing in the past ten years was the growth of interest in education – the demand which has arisen in the country for better and wider educational services, the public interest in seeing these services provided and the general recognition of the importance of education in the whole national situation. I think it is true to say that this began to coincide with the rise in living standards. When living standards rise, one of the most immediate manifestations of the improvement is the desire of everybody to give his own children a better education than he had himself, and you get individual people in every walk of life anxious to see a wider education for their children. If they cannot afford to pay for these facilities themselves, then they expect the community to provide them. This is what is happening because a large proportion of the vote for the increase in these services in recent years has been, obviously, set aside for education. This is most important because even still nobody can contend that our educational services are fully developed, or will ever be, or will be fully developed to the extent that you can say there is no more to be done. But social policy at that time was confined to ensuring that each year some contribution was made to the improvement of the social welfare services.

CHAPTER 19

RETIREMENT

'I had succeeded in having a fairly long and active political life and that was the end of it, the feeling that I had enhanced rather than damaged my reputation in that period.'

The economy had prospered between 1960 and 1965, growing by an average of 3.6 per cent per year, and unemployment reached a post-war low of 5.6 per cent in 1965. In 1966 a bank strike, over pay, from 7 May to 30 July had a serious impact on economic activity, with 7,600 workers involved on both sides of the border. The latter half of 1966 was also punctuated by a protracted stand-off between the government and the farmers' organisations. The National Farmers' Association (shortly to become the Irish Farmers' Association) began a series of protests in October 1966, involving a march from as far away as Bantry, that escalated into a 20-day siege outside Government Buildings. The farmers demanded more of a say in agricultural policy and criticised the lack of effort being made to market Irish beef worldwide. Against this background, in the autumn of 1966 public speculation began about Lemass's retirement.

He was 66 going on 67 and had no intention of following the example of de Valera, who was 76 when he finally stepped down as taoiseach. Lemass made light of his health issues, but in 1952 he had been laid up for two months with gall bladder problems, and his prodigious pipe-smoking habit had left him with an ashen pallor. He was prone to blackouts and breathlessness and his wife began to fret about his health. Lemass never regarded himself as indispensable in the way de Valera had. 'All political careers end in failure, is a maxim attributed to Enoch Powell, but Lemass was an exception. He would get to retire at a time of his choosing without any external pressure from political colleagues or the media.

After the Easter Rising commemorations, Lemass began looking for a time to announce his retirement. Another general election was not due until 1970. His successor would need at least two years to make his mark as taoiseach before going in front of the people. Events may have concentrated his mind. The *Irish Press*, effectively the house newspaper of the Fianna Fáil party, ran a story on 1 November 1966 that Lemass's resignation would happen in a matter of days.

SL: I don't know at what stage in my political life I began to think of retirement. I had the idea of retiring voluntarily, not being just put out, but retiring by my own decision at a time when I selected to do so, and when I still had enough vitality left to enjoy the experience of being out of public life. I could not say when – it was something that grew very imperceptibly over the years; perhaps soon after the 1965 election, with the realisation that the next election would be in 1970 and I would by then be 70 years of age. In this period, I felt it must happen, and I began to think in terms of when it should best happen. 1965 and 1966 and the early part of 1967 were rather difficult. I thought as soon as the upswing came, as soon as I could put my successor in on the upswing, I would be very satisfied to go, but again, this was merely the fulfilment of an idea that had been born many, many years before and I could not put a date or even a year on when it began. When I decided to resign as taoiseach, I felt that the outlook was good, and that the new taoiseach would come in on this rising note and get down to it. That was the end of 1966, and we could see that things were beginning to turn up right again. That is why I resigned then, so that [my successor] would come in in good times and be able to claim, if he so wanted, the benefit of all the improvements and achievements.

Lemass's pending retirement created the first succession crisis in Fianna Fáil since its foundation in 1926. Lemass was de Valera's obvious successor, but there was no obvious successor to Lemass. Jack Lynch would appear to have been Lemass's choice. Lynch was a popular figure in the party who entered Dáil Éireann in 1948 and entered the cabinet in March 1957. Much of his popularity was due to his prowess as a sportsman – he won five All-Ireland hurling titles and an All-Ireland football title with Cork in a career that lasted 14 years. In September 1966 Lemass asked Lynch if he was interested and he said no. Lemass then asked Minister for Labour Patrick Hillery, who also declined to put his name forward. This left Charles Haughey, George Colley and Neil Blaney, but all had weaknesses. Haughey was not trusted by the party's older TDs; Colley was considered to be too inexperienced at cabinet level; and both men, being 41, were viewed as potential future taoisigh, not Lemass's immediate successor. Neil Blaney was seen as too much of a one-issue candidate, that issue being partition. Lemass then approached Lynch again and after talking it over with his wife, Lynch put his name forward as taoiseach. Blaney and Haughey withdrew, leaving Colley to contest the leadership. Lynch won comprehensively by 52 votes to 19.

SL: Take the circumstances which arose when I made it known I was going to retire. George Colley had made up his mind that he was going for the job. He was genuinely convinced that he could do a good job, and considered he had the intellectual capacity and the personality to do it. I encouraged this. I want you to understand that I encouraged George Colley to think of the possibility of being my successor. He took it quite seriously and did genuinely, I think, try to get himself equipped to do the job properly. I encouraged Charlie Haughey in the same way, and Jack Lynch also. Charlie Haughey did not try to prepare himself to the same extent. Charlie Haughey allowed himself to go forward only because people said he was the man for the job. When, in the end, it became obvious that there were differences of opinion and it was indicated that he would have to stand down, he did so without a moment's hesitation.

He did not then give me the impression of a man who was abandoning his life's ambition. Probably he said to himself. 'I am a young man and it will come to me in the course of time.' George Colley did not stand down. Even though he knew he was going to be beaten in the party, he still went on. Then other people were suggested. Neil Blaney rather surprised me, because it never occurred to me that he had any idea of ever being taoiseach and when he said he was going to be nominated by the party, I was taken aback. I know he decided, quite genuinely, to go forward, so that it would cease to be a two-man confrontation. He wanted to put a third man into the field, because he thought that damage could be done to the party if there was a two-cornered contest. When Jack Lynch said he was prepared to accept the job, Neil Blaney pulled out. I would say that personal motivation was no part of his decision at all.

I encouraged George Colley. I said to him: 'I have no doubt whatever, George, that you are fully eligible to be taoiseach when I retire, fully qualified from every point of view and I am encouraging you to aspire to this post when the time comes.' He was in America when I made the announcement of my retirement, and I sent him a cablegram telling him so, and suggested that he might come home, which he did. Whether I was right or not is another question, but he came home. I made it quite clear to him that, as far as I was concerned, he was fully acceptable to me, as were the others who were mentioned, and that I regarded it as his duty to prepare himself to take the post if it came to him. In the end, when I saw there was going to be a contest and a division in the party and when Jack Lynch agreed to stand, I tried to persuade him [Colley] to stand down. I was not very surprised when I found he was not going to do so. As I say, I do not know to what extent this was due to pressures on him, or who the pressures were from. We were in an upswing again. I did not want my successor to have this problem. I wanted to say to him, 'It's yours – keep things going as they are and you are going into a good year,' and so 1967/68 was. Now I became taoiseach when Dev retired by unanimous vote. I had reached that stage where there was no alternative to me, there was nobody else and this of course simplified my position a great deal. Jack Lynch didn't have as easy a route. He had opposition, and other people seeking the office, and this is going to be more and more so in the future.

Seán Lemass finally resigned on 10 November 1966. It was a political decision to resign, he told a packed press conference, and there was no question about his health being a factor. The fiftieth anniversary commemorations of the Easter Rising had demonstrated to him that he had been on active service for his country for all those years, including 30 years in government and seven as taoiseach. It was time for the post of taoiseach to pass to a younger man, he told the nation.

DR: Was there anything painful about it?

SL: No, nothing at all.

DR: A lot of people don't like giving up power?

SL: I had no such experience at all. On the contrary, the only sense I experienced when I was out, was relief – free at last of all the responsibility. I had succeeded in having a fairly long and active political life and that was the end of it, the feeling that I had enhanced rather than damaged my reputation in that period. I am better off now. This is something that had been in my mind for quite long time – the question of when I was going to retire. I had been talking about it to my colleagues in the government for some time back. But as is usual in such circumstances, the reaction against my retiring was strong. Everybody was against the idea. The party did not want to face up to the problem of finding a successor and nobody was anxious to have the situation changed. I recognised that this was just the normal disposition in most people's minds, to wish that the clock would stand still, so such a situation would never end. I had to publicly announce that I was retiring in order to get everybody to face up to the fact that it was going to happen and that there was nothing they could do to prevent it happening.

DR: How far ahead of the time when you publicly announced a date had you, in fact, stated that you intended to retire shortly?

SL: I did not publicly state it at all. I allowed the press to speculate on it. I let the idea be developed in newspaper commentary as a possibility. But, in fact, there was no statement by me until I announced when it was going to happen. Once you say you are going, the sooner you go the better, otherwise everybody gets the impression that everything is at a standstill until the next man takes over. I believe that chances of that kind should always come quickly, thus minimising the time available for the exercise of pressure of any sort, and for the development of personal ambitions. This would be true whether it involves minister or taoiseach. The less time there is between the announcement of the intention to make the change and the actual completion of the change, the better.

DR: Do you think there is any particular age at which one should retire from politics?

SL: Jack Lynch used always say that a man could be a top-class hurler or footballer for six years. He could start at 18, pass his peak at 24, and stay in the top class until he was 30. But there you are.

DR: Should you retire after six years at the top in politics?

SL: There are a limited number of years in which you can carry the top responsibility in government and it really does not matter when you start or when you finish. You will have the same endurance capacity. Konrad Adenauer[1] started at 70 and, to my mind, was still very nimble and active at 84.

DR: The extent to which Jack Lynch – everybody likes him …

SL: It is accepted that he is not penetrating enough.

DR: You feel critical of him because one group is not condemning him?

SL: You see, you will not get people to come out and defend you unless they think you need defending, that you need help in defending yourself, and once you produce that, you have no great problems at all. Until the time when I became taoiseach and became the symbol of the party, I could never rouse a public meeting with the enthusiasm that de Valera could. But I'd be convinced that the speech I made was twice as good as his. It would be accepted and people would no doubt be influenced by what I'd say, but in the end it would be, 'Ah, that's a good speech,' whereas in Dev's case it would be hats up in the air, which I could never engender at all. I've seen this capacity to get this type of enthusiasm provoked by people whom I knew hadn't got anything like the intellectual capacity of other people who were lucky in being elected as deputies. I think Jack Lynch has it, as a matter of fact – this capacity to provoke the feeling of trust rather than admiration.

Although he had resigned as taoiseach, Lemass remained a TD until the general election of June 1969, when he stepped down from politics. Whatever reservations Lemass had about Lynch were confounded by the result of the election, which saw Fianna Fáil get an overall majority, increasing its Dáil representation by three seats. The 1969 general election was the last before the Troubles dominated politics on both sides of the border for much of the following three decades. Lemass had one last service to perform for the state when he left the office of the taoiseach. He set up an informal committee for a review of the Irish Constitution in September 1966. He became a member of the committee following his resignation as taoiseach. According to committee member Michael Kennedy, a Fianna Fáil TD, barrister and future minister, Lemass never missed a meeting and was the 'driving force' behind its deliberations.

The committee reported in December 1967 and was farsighted in its recommendations, many of which eventually came to fruition. The committee looked at amending Article 3 of the constitution, which states: 'Pending the re-integration of the national territory, and without prejudice to the right of the parliament and government established by this constitution to exercise jurisdiction over the whole territory, the laws enacted by the parliament shall have the like area and extent of application as the laws of Saorstát Éireann and the like extra-territorial effect.' This eventually happened following the Good Friday Agreement in 1998.

It recommended ending the prohibition on divorce, but only for those who were members of a religious denomination where divorce was allowed. The divorce referendum in the state was eventually passed in 1995. The committee recommended that the principle of equal pay for equal work should be enshrined in the constitution.

DR: You referred in Limerick to the desirability of regular reviews of the constitution. It is not possible to know from the report of the constitutional committee what items you, personally, feel should be reviewed. What are they?

SL: I avoided specific matters for review, but suggested that there should be an automatic review of the constitution every quarter of a century or so. My reason for making this suggestion was my belief that any constitution can become outdated in relation to current needs, as time goes on.

The American Constitution is a written constitution also, but it has, in effect, been changed from time to time, not merely by specific constitutional amendments enacted by plebiscite, but by varying interpretations of it by the Supreme Court of America. This court plays a vital role in keeping the constitution up to date in accordance with the needs of the times.

In Ireland it is not generally accepted that the Supreme Court should have this sort of role in relation to the constitution. It is true that at that time there were a number of changes in the constitution which I, myself, would have liked to list for examination. Most of them were considered in one form or another by the constitutional committee. Anyway, I did not want to commit myself to any particular set of changes, but rather to sell the idea of a periodic review of the constitution.

The review was started on the basis that nobody, not even a

member of the committee, was committed to any point of view expressed there. They were not committing their parties nor were they committing themselves. They would not be bound in any subsequent proposals in the Dáil to support an amendment that they had accepted in the committee. It had to be on this perfectly free basis, otherwise the other parties would not have agreed to it.

It was a free committee, the members of which were entitled to express their views freely, and they were not bound by these views in any subsequent public attitude which they might adopt. Certainly, their views were not binding on their parties and this was made quite clear.

There were many things which could have been done to improve the constitution, but none of them were vitally important. There have been cases where the Supreme Court did interpret the constitution in a way which was at odds with the intentions which were present when drafted. But again, these were not terribly important. One of the big disappointments to me was that although I tried to get the purely legal aspects of the situation examined by a committee under the attorney general, for some reason he never got this committee functioning. He said he would do it, but apparently he did nothing about it. I do not know what his objection to it was.

DR: Many people were surprised that the arguments in favour of the actual amendment which came up afterwards, from the single seat and the straight vote, were not listed.

SL: That proposal was not considered in the constitutional committee. The question of single-seat constituencies was not raised, but it was debated in the context of the straight transferable vote. This, possibly, was my fault since I did not at that time think it was feasible to review the idea of the straight vote in single-seat constituencies. Consequently, I argued for the single seat without any change of the voting system for the purpose of trying to ascertain to what extent there might be support for this among the parties.

Eventually I found it very hard to get any indication of what their final attitude would be. Insofar as I did form a conclusion, it was that it would not be opposed very strongly by the Fine Gael people.

The committee could reach no consensus on the thorny issue of amendments to the electoral system. Lemass once again put forward the issue of single-seat constituencies elected by first past the post, but no consensus could be reached. In 1969 the Lynch government introduced two referendum proposals. The first was to abolish proportional representation in favour of a single-seat, first-past-the-post system. It also proposed amending the constitution to give greater representation to rural constituencies. As in 1959, the Fianna Fáil government was accused of trying to rig the electoral system in its own favour. The proposals were resoundingly rejected by the electorate, with 61 per cent in favour and 39 per cent against. The issue has never been revisited.

The committee recommended the deletion of Article 44.1.2 of the constitution, which stated that the 'State recognises the special position of the Holy Catholic Apostolic and Roman Church as the guardian of the Faith professed by the great majority of the citizens.' Article 44.1.2 was seen as problematic in the context of aspirations towards a united Ireland. The issue was put to a referendum in December 1972. With all the main political parties in support and the Catholic Church unopposed to the change, it passed with nearly 85 per cent in favour of repeal. This was the first time the constitution was amended by plebiscite.

CHAPTER 20

LEGACY AND DEATH

'You must never be satisfied with what you have done, never be satisfied with the way you progress; you must always be arguing that more could be done, more can be done, and more must be done.'

Seán Lemass's good standing following his resignation saw him offered various directorships of different businesses. At that stage he was worried that he might die without making sufficient financial provision for his wife Kathleen. He became a director of Waterford Glass and other blue chip Irish companies, including Cement Roadstone and Wavin Pipes. After 50 years of service in the cause of Ireland, going back to the Easter Rising, he was able to get some financial reward for his efforts. He managed in the four and a half years of retirement to return to the simple pleasures he had enjoyed before becoming taoiseach. He began to attend race meetings again, and rugby matches. He retained his interest in politics by having regular lunches with the younger TDs, especially Brian Lenihan.

'The historians have no interest for me. In 50 or one hundred years' time they will be judging the events of this period with completely wrong standards.'

DR: One of the problems of a leader is the extent to which he has to try to get ahead of the people he is leading, not to get too far ahead. Now, with regard to the Irish people generally, as distinct from sectional interests, we have as a community various attitudes which could be regarded as conditioned by our geographical situation and our history. Where were the areas where you had to watch yourself in trying to bring about things which were unacceptable to the people?

SL: I don't know that I had to watch myself. In a sense I don't have inside me a desire to do things that would have this conflict with the basic sectional interests, the basic interests of the Irish people. I don't think this arose at any stage and I suppose this is what anybody who becomes as absorbed in politics as I was must develop a capacity to keep in tune with the public sentiment, so that in fact you don't have to be watching yourself to prevent yourself stepping too far out of line.

DR: At retirement, what did you consider to be the greatest problem you had faced?

SL: Several people have asked me such questions. I suppose the person concerned is the least able to answer this type of question. It is not possible to have a really objective judgement of the most important matters in order to define the problem which gave you personally the greatest difficulty. These could have been matters which nobody ever heard about. I think it is sometimes forgotten that about 50 per cent of the business of government is preventing bad things happening, organising good things, and the more you are successful in preventing bad things happening, the more you are doing work that the public never hears about and doesn't have to hear about, because the very measure of your success is the fact that nobody has heard about it. Some of the greatest difficulties were of that kind; you saw a danger emerging; a threat appeared somewhere and you successfully averted it, and having averted it you forgot all about it. You did not then try to assess the size of that difficulty compared with the one you had last year or the one you are going to have next year. Indeed, this was part of the protective process of preventing a disclosure that the crisis had to be dealt with at all. So it is very hard to know what was the greatest difficulty. If you asked me what were the greatest achievements, you could no doubt look back over time and name the things that you thought gave you personally the greatest satisfaction, but these need not be necessarily the greatest achievements at all; in other words, you have a standard of judgement which varies from one person to another. When you ask if all the progress that took place was as much as I had hoped for, politically the answer to that is no. You must never be satisfied with what you have done, never be satisfied with the way you progress; you must always be arguing that more could be done, more can be done, and more must be done, but that aside you may say, we did better than we might have done, than we originally were entitled to hope for.

I regard it as the function of government to promote national growth, national economic growth, and to ensure that this is reflected in social benefits. You could undoubtedly set out to prove that it would be feasible to achieve a growth rate of 6 per cent, 7 per cent, or 8 per cent per year, which would be spectacular in relation to what other countries are doing, but you could only do this by seeking the complete co-operation of every sector of the community; by eliminating any conflict of personal or sectional interests which, of course, it is not possible to do in a democratic society.[1] If you could get the fullest co-operation from organised labour, from employers, from all the people who are concerned with national economic growth, you could achieve 7 per cent or 8 per cent in the year. You know that you cannot, so you settle for 4 per cent and ultimately, if you achieve 4 per cent you know it is quite an achievement, because other countries with similar problems to ours are achieving less.

DR: You could still go on and it could disimprove or it might improve more. Churchill spoke himself of the judgement of history, and [Lyndon B.] Johnson seems very concerned with the great society idea, to go down as a great president. You talk about your reputation.

SL: This reputation I am talking about is only of importance so long as I am alive. I never did feel anything about a judgement later, but now, in 1968, two years after I retired from office, people still say he was not a bad fellow when he was in office. It is this type of reputation that earns you a certain amount of public respect and goodwill.

The historians have no interest for me. In 50 or one hundred years' time they will be judging the events of this period with completely wrong standards. They will be applying to this period the tests of a hundred years hence and they will be looking at our inadequacies, our scientific ignorance to see the obvious, or rather what would then be obvious. They would see the problems we were not able to cope with, just as we nowadays judge the people of a hundred years ago, who had not our capabilities.

It is impossible to do it, put ourselves into their shoes and try to judge their problems in the light of the limited knowledge they had of events and the lack of foreknowledge of what was going to happen. I would never be really worried about the judgement of historians. The only possible way that their judgement might affect me would be if it was likely to damage my children or my grandchildren. If they can say my old grandfather was not too bad a guy when he was in it and feel that this is some advantage, so much the better. If I had ended up in jail it might have been a different story, and this is a terrible handicap for children whose ancestors did get themselves into public disapproval for some social misbehaviour of some sort.

***DR:** You felt a feeling of relief when it ended. You were glad to have that phase of your life over, your whole political life, glad to have it over ...*

SL: Perhaps there is one final test I had to pass. I had to bring it to an end without anybody being able to say I had let them down at any time. You could walk out of a political job at any time, but to walk out in circumstances where people could say you let down your associates, your colleagues, your party, your government, [that] would have been something very hard to live with later on. So I had to end this in such a way that when people came to accept the fact that I had gone they would also say that he had gone the right way. It leaves a bad taste anyway.

It is a great deal more comfortable for me in 1968 because the general feeling is I did a good job in government and that makes life more tolerable for me. If people said, 'It is about time you went and we are glad you are gone', life would be different, at least you would feel a desire to vindicate yourself. To be able to retire in an atmosphere of approval for what you have done is something I am very glad to have achieved. It could have worked out otherwise and this is why, having cut the tape and having retired, I can honestly say I have never regretted the decision and certainly have not the slightest wish to return.

DR: Well, now, what I am saying is that when you do recognise the importance of people's opinions over the years, particularly while in office and when actually making decisions, have you found it painful to have people put constructions on your behaviour?

SL: In politics you regard this as part of the business in which you are. If people misrepresent you, you have got to fight this misrepresentation; if people attack you, you have got to attack back; this is part of politics. In fact, at the Fianna Fáil ard fheis a couple of years ago we had a half dozen pickets outside. I felt that the party was dead if it could not provoke sufficient irritation to want to picket the ard fheis. I always regarded the picket as a status symbol and when some of the Fine Gael people would say something about it, I would say there is no danger of someone picketing your ard fheis, they don't care; they do care what happens to ours. I was never perturbed by this evidence that we were a source of irritation to some people.

Lemass's interviews with Ryan ended in January 1969. In August of that year the Troubles began. The work that he had tried to do in bringing about a better atmosphere between North and South was destroyed by events.

In 1970 Charles Haughey was a chief protagonist in the Arms Trial, which almost tore the government and Fianna Fáil apart. Haughey and Neil Blaney were suspected of illegally smuggling arms into the Republic. Both were sacked by Lynch. When Lynch attended the family home in 1971 to pay his respects following the death of Lemass, Maureen Haughey turned her back on him. Lemass is reported to have given Lynch no advice on the Arms Crisis other to tell him, obliquely, to do what he had to do as taoiseach. The case against Haughey collapsed, but his career was severely set back and he did not rejoin the cabinet until 1977. He was finally elected taoiseach in December 1979.

In February 1971 Lemass was admitted to the Mater Hospital, complaining of difficulty breathing. He was diagnosed with pyopneumothorax, a collapsed lung. He died on 11 May 1971 at the age of 71.

Actually, most people would prefer to die. If they could come back to earth after death for one hour, this is what they would do. This was the life I had and now …

DR: What do you mean, this is what they would do?

SL: They would not regret dying if they could come back and say they had a good life, a satisfied life, a happy life, or whatever life they wanted. That is the feeling I had when I left off; that is the end of my active political career; it is finished. Now I could look back over it and say, whatever else could be said about it, I enjoyed participating in it. I did not damage my personal reputation; I never did anything without some amount of public goodwill for the work I had done.

Lemass died, as he had lived, with a minimum of fuss. His dying wish that he not be interred in the republican plot in Glasnevin Cemetery was granted. He was buried instead in Deansgrange Cemetery. A simple headstone makes no claim to his profound impact on Irish life. He left an estate worth €55,000 (€821,646 at 2025 prices), much of it wrapped up in the value of his home at 53 Palmerston Road. Having enriched his country in so many ways, he did not die a rich man.

ACKNOWLEDGEMENTS

I am grateful to the Lemass family for entrusting this material to me. I would especially like to thank Seán Lemass's great-grandson Aidan O'Connor who initially approached me eight years ago about making these tapes public. The Lemass Tapes were published as a supplement in *The Irish Times* on 2nd of May, 2018. I am grateful to Mark Hennessy, the then *The Irish Times* news editor, now the newspaper's Ireland and Britain editor, for commissioning and bringing the supplement to fruition.

Seán Lemass's grandson Seán Haughey has also been very supportive of helping turn these transcripts into a book format. Rory O'Connor supplied some of the photographs for this book.

The Ryan family has also been helpful and I would like to thank Natasha Ryan, Dermot Ryan's granddaughter, for her cooperation in the process of writing of this book. Dermot Ryan lived long enough to see The Lemass Tapes published in *The Irish Times*. It is with some regret that he did not live long enough to see this book being published. Nevertheless, I hope it goes some way to vindicate his vision of a book featuring Seán Lemass in his own words.

Thank you to UCD archives and especially principal archivist Kate Manning for providing copies of the hard copy transcripts and for providing the transcripts to me in digital form. Without the copies, it would have been very difficult to bring this book to fruition.

Historian and fellow journalist Dr David McCullagh provided salient commentary to the early drafts of this book as did historian Dr Cormac Moore. And Prof Gary Murphy provides a foreword to this book.

Dr Martin Mansergh agreed to review this draft but died suddenly last year before he could do that. I would like to acknowledge the immense debt we all have to the late Dr Mansergh for his knowledge and input into Irish histography.

I would like to thank my agent Faith O'Grady and Deirdre Nolan, the publisher of Eriu for believing in this project. Thanks to Lisa Gilmour, assistant editor of Eriu for her diligent editing. Thanks to Declan Heeney, Helen McKean and Simon Hess from the Gill Hess team, and thanks to Sophie Raoufi of Bonnier Books UK for her help also.

Eriu has published Eoin O'Malley's *Charlie vs Garret* and this book should contribute to the store of knowledge about our previous taoisigh as should Iain Dale's *The Taoiseach: A Century of Political Leadership* published last year.

My grandfather John Francis McGreevy was an IRA veteran of the War of Independence and a founder member and former secretary of the MJ McManus Fianna Fail cumann in Carrick-on-Shannon. He named my father Eamonn, who died in 2024, after Éamon de Valera.

I would like to dedicate my work on this book to their memory and also to the memory of my aunts, Phyllis and Margaret, who died recently.

Ronan McGreevy, January 2026

ENDNOTES

Foreword by Gary Murphy

1 Ryan to Haughey, Haughey papers, Dublin City University, C7/114 (1), 1 June 1971.

2 Haughey to Ryan, Haughey papers, C7/114 (1), 4 June 1971.

3 Interview with Maureen Haughey, 14 March 2014.

Introduction

1 *Sunday Independent*, 3 April 2022 www.independent.ie

2 *Irish Times*, 1 December 2023 www.irishtimes.com/ireland

3 Ibid

4 Correspondence between Seán Haughey and Dermot Ryan seen by author.

5 The Lemass Tapes

6 *Irish Times*, 2 May 2018, The Lemass Tapes

7 Ibid

8 Oireachtas reports, 11 May 1971 www.oireachtas.ie

9 Fianna Fáil Europe Day speech 9 May 2024 www.fiannafail.ie

10 *Sunday Business Post*, 11 August 2019 www.businesspost.ie

11 www.doublebandfilms.com/sean-lamass

12 The Lemass Tapes

13 Ibid

14 *Irish Times*, 17 February 1951.

15 J.J. Lee, *Ireland 1912–1985: Politics and Society,* Cambridge University Press, 1989, p.359

16 Brian Girvin, *Between Two Worlds; Ireland since independence,* Barnes & Noble Books, 1989.

17 www.magill.ie/archive/sean-lemass-profile

18 Tom Garvin, *Preventing the Future: Why was Ireland so poor for so long?,* Gill & MacMillan 2004, pp. 278.

19 *Irish Times*, 29 April 2017.

20 *Irish Press* 21 January 1969

21 John Horgan: *Seán Lemass; Enigmatic Patriot,* Gill & MacMillan, Dublin, 1997 p.43

22 Stanley Lyon (1882–1975) was director of statistics in what became the Central Statistics Office (CSO) from 1931 to 1947.

23 Edward J. (EJ) Riordan.

The early years

1 www.geni.com/projects/Huguenots-of-Ireland/12955

2 *Time* magazine, 19 July 1963

3 John Horgan, *Seán Lemass: The Enigmatic Patriot,* Gill & MacMillan, Dublin 1997, p.6

4 Christopher Todd Andrews, *Dublin Made Me*, Lilliput Press, 2001, p.56

5 Ibid

6 Ibid

7 *Irish Press*, 20 January 1969

8 Horgan, p.8

9 Horgan, p.10

10 *Irish Press*, 20 January 1969

11 Ibid

12 *Sunday Independent*, 30 January 1916

13 Bureau of Military History, witness statement by Joseph O'Connor, www.bmh.militaryarchives.ie

14 *Irish Times*, 20 July 2013

15 Conversation with author and Seán Haughey

16 Iain Dale (editor), *The Taoiseach: A Century of Political Leadership*, Swift (London).

17 *Irish Times*, 20 July 2013

18 Royal Dublin Fusiliers archive www.iar.ie/archive

19 Dr Martin Mansergh, *The Political Legacy of Seán Lemass,* Etudes Irlandais, 2000, pp.141–172

20 *Irish Press*, 20 January 1969

21 The *Studies* article written by Lemass: www.magill.ie

22 *Irish Press*, 20 Jan 1969.

23 Seán Lemass: Military Service Pensions File MSP34REF2078

24 www.bloodysunday.co.uk

25 Ernie O'Malley notebooks, UCD Archives, P17b

26 Matt McDonnell Military Service Pensions collection File MSP34REF21416

27 James 'Jimmy' Brennan Military Service Pensions Collection File MSP34REF943

28 Lemass Military Service Pensions Collection File MSP34REF2078

29 Patrick Moran was executed on 14 March 1921 along with five other men. He was one of the 'forgotten 10' executed during the War of Independence who were reburied in Glasnevin Cemetery with full military honours in 2001.

30 Horgan, p.20

31 *Irish Press*, 30 January 1969

32 *Irish Press*, 22 January 1969

33 *Irish Echo*, 16 August 2023 www.irishecho.com

34 *Irish Press*, 22 January 1969

35 Ronan McGreevy, *Great Hatred: The Assassination of Field Marshal Sir Henry Wilson MP*, Faber, London 2022, p.296

36 *Irish Press* 22 January 1969

37 *Dictionary of Irish Biography*: Kevin O'Higgins www.drb.ie

38 Ernie O'Malley, *The Singing Flame*, Anvil Books, Dublin 1978, p.84

39 Ibid, p.102

40 Horgan, p.18

41 Horgan, p.26

42 *Irish Times*, 28 July 1923

43 *Irish Times*, 2 May 2023

44 Dictionary of Irish Biography: Joseph McGrath

Chapter 1 Accidental politician

1 Mary MacSwiney (1872–1942) was the sister of Terence MacSwiney, the former Lord Mayor of Cork, who died on hunger strike in Brixton Prison in 1920. Mary MacSwiney was regarded as a hardliner who refused to countenance any co-operation with the Irish Free State. She lost her seat in the general election of 1927 as Sinn Féin was wiped out by the new Fianna Fáil party.

2 The IRA, post-Civil War, consisted entirely of anti-Treaty forces.

3 The Second Dáil was elected on 24 May 1921, during the War of Independence. The British had set up two legislatures through the Government of Ireland Act (1920) and separate elections were held in Northern Ireland and Southern Ireland. No actual election took place in the South as all 124 Sinn Féin MPs were returned without a contest. Five of the six seats Sinn Féin won in the North were won by candidates who were also elected in the South. The Second Dáil, therefore, consisted of 125 Sinn Féin MPs (TDs). In republican theory this was the last 32-county Dáil and therefore the only legitimate one.

4 Comhairle na dTeachtaí was established by de Valera in 1923. It comprised members of the Second Dáil and those elected to the Third Dáil who did not take their seats. It sat until 1926 and the foundation of Fianna Fáil.

5 Frank Aiken (1898–1983) was, along with Lemass, one of the most significant political figures in Ireland in the twentieth century. He was the chief of staff of the IRA when the 'dump arms' order came. He went to become a long-serving Minister for Foreign Affairs in various Fianna Fáil governments.

6 Gerald Boland (1885–1973), another significant figure in Fianna Fáil, served in many ministries. He was noted for the hardline position he took against the IRA during the Second World War.

7 Seán MacEntee (1889–1985), a founder member of Fianna Fáil, had long stints as Minister for Finance in Fianna Fáil governments. He clashed repeatedly with Lemass on fiscal policy.

8 James Ryan (1892–1970). A medical doctor by profession, Ryan took the anti-Treaty side in the Civil War and went on hunger strike in the Curragh. He was a founder member of Fianna Fáil.

9 Séamus Hughes (1881–1943), Irish revolutionary and trade unionist who became the first general secretary of Cumann na nGaedheal.

10 Lemass got 17,297 votes against 16,340 for Hughes, a margin of 957.

11 Michael Colivet (1884–1955) was de Valera's cellmate when de Valera made a daring escape in 1919. Colivet was elected to both the First and the Second Dáil. He did not join Fianna Fáil.

12 https://historyireland.com/the-secret-ira-soviet-agreement-1925/

13 Article 17 of the Free State Constitution states: 'The Oath to be taken by

members of the Oireachtas shall be in following form: I ______________ do solemnly swear true faith and allegiance to the Constitution of the Irish Free State as by law established, and that I will be faithful to H. M. King George V., his heirs and successors by law in virtue of the common citizenship of Ireland with Great Britain and her adherence to and membership of the group of nations forming the British Commonwealth of Nations. Such oath shall be taken and subscribed by every member of the Oireachtas before taking his seat therein before the Representative of the Crown or some other person authorised by him.'

14 The IRA repudiated the authority of the Provisional Government at a convention in Dublin on 26 March 1922.

Chapter 2 New party, new beginnings

1 Labour leader Thomas Johnson, de Valera (on behalf of Sinn Féin), the Independent and Farmers' Party TDs all met in the Shelbourne Hotel on 8 December 1925 to discuss the London Agreement. Those present also included a deputation from northern nationalists that included Cahir Healy and T.J. Harbison. De Valera was leaned upon to end abstentionism and vote against the agreement, but he refused.

2 The vote was 71–20. If Sinn Féin had participated it would have been 71–68.

3 After the First World War, the UK debt pile reached 160 per cent of GDP. The British estimated that the Irish share was £155.75 million, amounting to a repayment each year of £6.25 million, a quarter of all tax revenue raised in any given year. The write-off amounted to 80 per cent of Irish GDP for 1925.

4 The land annuities were bi-annual payments made by Irish farmers to the British Land Commission for government loans used to purchase land under the various land acts from 1881 to 1923. They amounted to £4 million a year (the equivalent of €3.15 billion today) and were resented by farmers.

5 Mary MacSwiney (1872–1942) was the sister of Terence MacSwiney, the former Lord Mayor of Cork, who died on hunger strike in Brixton Prison in 1920. Mary MacSwiney was regarded as a hardliner who refused to countenance any co-operation with the Irish Free State. She lost her seat in the general election of 1927 when Sinn Féin was wiped out by the new Fianna Fáil party.

6 Art O'Connor (1888–1950), the former Sinn Féin MP for Kildare North, became titular president of the Republic when Éamon de Valera resigned in 1926. O'Connor resigned a year later.

7 Sinn Féin got only 3.6 per cent of the vote in the March 1927 general election and did not contest either the November 1927 or 1932 general elections.

8 The party had £8,663 12s 2d (€682,000) in funds, which were frozen by the High Court in February 1924. The money was the subject of protracted legal proceedings in the 1940s.

9 Robert Farnan (1898–1962), a wealthy doctor, was one of de Valera's best friends and a founder member of Fianna Fáil.

10 De Valera made fundraising trips to the United States between December 1927 and February 1928 and also between December 1929 and May 1930. This was partially to raise money for Fianna Fáil but also to raise money for the *Irish Press*, a pro-Fianna Fáil newspaper which was launched in 1931.

Chapter 3 Entering the Dáil

1 James Joseph Walsh (1880–1948), from Cork, served in the GPO in 1916 and was sentenced to death, but the sentence was commuted. He was also involved in an attempt to assassinate the Lord Lieutenant to Ireland, Lord French, on 19 December 1919. He was elected as a Sinn Féin MP in the 1918 December general election and took the pro-Treaty side. He served in government as postmaster general (1922–1924) and then as Minister for Posts and Telegraphs (1924–1927). He retired at the September 1927 general election.

2 Major Bryan Cooper (1884–1930) was from an Anglo-Irish unionist family who owned Markree Castle in County Sligo. He was elected as Unionist MP in the 1910 British general election. During the First World War he served with the 10th (Irish) Division in Gallipoli and Salonika, and wrote an acclaimed account of the division, which was published in 1917. He was elected as an independent TD for the Dublin County constituency in 1923 and then joined Cumann na nGaedheal in 1927, winning a seat in the general election of June that year. Cooper opposed the motion of confidence as he believed a coalition involving Fianna Fáil and Labour would lead to an increase in taxation and undermine the creditworthiness of the state. He later stood successfully for Cumann na nGaedheal. A heavy man and most likely an alcoholic, he died at the age of 46.

3 John Jinks (1871–1934), born in Sligo, was a member of the National League Party elected in the June 1927 general election. He left the party after absenting himself from the motion of no confidence and was never re-elected to the Dáil again. He denied that he had been kidnapped or drunk. In fact, he said, he had absented himself because he didn't want Fianna Fáil in government.

4 The Ceann Comhairle, Michael Hayes, voted in favour of the government when the vote was tied. Jinks returned to Sligo on the midnight train.

5 James Joseph (J.J) Walsh (1880-1948: A Cumann na nGaedhael TD, Walsh was Postmaster General (Minister for Posts and Telegraphs) in the Irish government from 1923 to 1927. He resigned from Cumann na NGaedheal in 1927.

6 The Army Mutiny of 1924 was provoked by the decommissioning of the National Army after the Civil War.

7 Ernest Blythe (1889–1975) was a Northern Protestant who had dual membership of the Orange Order and the Irish Republican Brotherhood (IRB). He was in jail at

the time of the Easter Rising. Blythe was Minister for Finance in the early Cumann na nGaedheal governments and was notorious for cutting the old age pension by a shilling in the 1924 budget. He lost his seat in the 1932 Irish general election.

8 There was a bank raid in Tipperary by the IRA in April 1929 and in June 1929 Detective Garda Tadhg O'Sullivan was killed by an IRA bomb in Tullycrine in West Cork.

9 Patrick Hogan (1885–1969) was an IRA volunteer who was elected as a TD in 1923 and held his seat until 1938.

10 George O'Brien (1892–1973), Professor of Political Economy at University College Dublin from 1921 to 1961, was an independent senator representing the National University of Ireland (NUI) from 1951 to 1965.

11 Frederick Sterling was the first United States representative (effectively ambassador) to the Irish Free State. He was appointed in 1927, marking the beginning of formal diplomatic relations between Ireland and the United States.

12 James Fitzmaurice (1898–1965) made history when he and the German crew of the *Bremen* made the first successful transatlantic flight from east to west, which was initially planned to take three days. The plane took off from Baldonnel Aerodrome on 12 April and crash-landed a day later in a bog in Greenly Island, Canada, off the coast of Newfoundland.

Chapter 4 1932: From guns to government

1 Patrick Reynolds (1887–1932) was a Cumann na nGaedheal politician who was elected as TD in the September 1927 general election. He was shot dead on 14 February 1932, two days before polling, by a constituent named Patrick Leddy. Reynolds claimed to have got Leddy, an ex-RIC officer, a pension for Leddy's service to the IRA during the War of Independence. Reynolds accused Leddy of canvassing for his rivals and struck him, then went to get his shotgun and killed both Reynolds and Detective Patrick McGeehan. The shooting was regarded as unrelated to political tensions at the time and more as a spontaneous act of violence.

2 Rather than have a by-election, it was decided to run the whole election again in the seven-seat Sligo-Leitrim constituency. The results were the same as the general election, except that Mary Reynolds replaced her late husband. She was one of only two women TDs in the seventh Dáil, the other being Michael Collins's eldest sister, Margaret Collins-O'Driscoll.

3 Blythe wrote an article in the Cumann na nGaedheal newspaper *United Ireland* in which he said, 'It might happen that the army would be bound to subdue a political people for the welfare of the people in general.'

4 Patrick Hogan (1891–1936), a minister in all the Cumann na nGaedheal governments from 1922 to 1932, died in a car crash in 1936.

5 Paddy Daly (1888–1957), a member of Michael Collins's squad, was associated with some of the worst atrocities of the Irish Civil War. Daly, who commanded the pro-Treaty Dublin Guards in Kerry, ordered the extrajudicial killings of 17 republican prisoners in March 1923. At Ballyseedy, he ordered eight IRA prisoners to be tied to a landmine; seven were killed.

6 The Army Comrades Association (ACA) was founded in August 1932 by former Free State soldiers to oppose the IRA and to protect Cumann na nGaedheal (later Fine Gael) meetings.

7 Charles Gordon Campbell (1885–1963), second Baron Glenavy, was the son of the Irish Lord Chancellor and was appointed secretary (the equivalent of secretary-general) of the Department of Industry and Commerce in September 1922. He was an energetic secretary but thought the civil service culture was lacking in ambition. He resigned before the chance of government came.

8 Patrick McGilligan (1889–1979), born in Derry, was appointed Minister for Industry and Commerce in 1924 and held that post until 1932. He became Minister for External Affairs from October 1927 after the death of Kevin O'Higgins.

9 John Leydon (1895–1979) was crucial to the Lemass story. He was an outstanding civil servant in the British administration before independence and transferred to the Department of Finance in 1923. He became secretary (the highest position) of the Department of Industry and Commerce when Lemass became minister, and followed Lemass to the Department of Supplies during the Second World War. He was chairman of Aer Rianta (1936–49), Aer Lingus (1937–49), Irish Shipping (1941–49), the Insurance Corporation of Ireland (1955–73), Aerlinte Éireann (1958–61) and Cement Ltd.

10 Stanley Lyon (1882–1975) was director of statistics in what became the Central Statistics Office (CSO) from 1931 to 1947.

11 Edward J. Riordan.

12 John Bernard Connell was the father of Archbishop Desmond Connell. In 1936 he became managing director of the Irish Sugar Company.

13 The Irish Sewing Cotton Company was established in Westport, County Mayo in 1935 under a reserved commodity order (RCO) which gave it guaranteed access to the Irish market. The town had a long tradition of cotton manufacturing. The company produced thread at a higher price than British imports. The factory closed in 1980.

14 William Norton, along with being Labour Party leader, was also the General Secretary of the Post Office Workers' Union. Hence Lemass's reference to postmen.

15 The Unemployed Assistance Act 1933 was introduced during the Great Depression.
It provided a register of unemployed people and means-tested assistance.

16 Leydon joined the National Bank as chairman in 1963.

Chapter 5 The Munich bother

1 The Coal-Cattle Pact of 1935 allowed the export of Irish cattle to Britain and the import of British coal on a like-for-like basis. It was the first step towards resolving the Economic War.

2 Correspondence between de Valera and Chamberlain is in the UCD archives and can be accessed at www.ucdculturalheritagecollections.com.

3 Thomas Inskip (1876–1947) was Minister for Coordination of Defence in the Conservative pre-war government between 1936 and 1939. He was regarded as not very good as his job. Winston Churchill said of him: 'He had the advantage of being little known and knowing nothing about military subjects.'

4 The British developed the Allied Submarine Detection Investigation Committee (ASDIC) between the wars to detect enemy submarines.

5 Malcolm MacDonald (1901–1981) was Secretary of State for Dominion Affairs between 1935 and 1938.

6 The de Valera government was defeated on an opposition motion in May 1938 calling for mandatory arbitration in disputes between the government and civil servants. Sixteen Fianna Fáil TDs missed the vote. The suspicion is that de Valera was looking for a pretext to call an election and got one.

7 Lemass would appear to be incorrect here. Both Fine Gael and Labour voted in favour of the agreement in the Dáil in 1938.

Chapter 6 Second World War: Minister for Supplies

1 In the Dáil on 16 April 1943, Lemass said, 'I have often expressed the opinion that, if the scarcity of textiles made it necessary for the Government to prepare an Order prohibiting individuals from wearing trousers, nobody would unduly complain about it unless and until he saw one person with a pair of trousers.' www.oireachtas.ie.

2 The Irish government's fears were well founded. The IRA had begun collaborating with the Nazis in 1934 when Seán Russell, its chief of staff, met a German agent named Oscar Pfaus in Ireland. In April 1939 Russell went on a fundraising campaign to the United States. In early 1940 he travelled secretly to Germany with a view to getting Nazi support for IRA activities. In May 1940, while the Wehrmacht was invading the Low Countries and France, Russell was being trained by German secret service agents in sabotage. Russell requested Frank Ryan, his IRA comrade who had fought in the Spanish Civil War against Franco's nationalists, be released from prison in Spain. Russell died on the German submarine while being returned to Ireland. Frank Ryan returned to Ireland.

3 The Emergency Powers Act 1939 allowed for the use of military tribunals and suspended habeas corpus. It gave scope for severe censorship and near total government control of the economy.

4 Lemass is not correct about this. Denmark had an army of 14,000 men and a navy of 3,000 men at the outbreak of the war, but the country never tried to build up a military strength sufficient to resist a German invasion.

5 The 250,000 figure was given by Joseph Walshe in a secret memorandum from May 1941.

6 Lemass was reappointed Minister for Industry and Commerce in August 1941 along with his portfolio as Minister for Supplies.

7 Britain supplied all of Ireland's cotton in 1940. It halved exports to Ireland in 1941 and then to 15 per cent of pre-war levels in 1942.

8 According to the Department of External Affairs, 34,000 Irish emigrants went to the UK (including Northern Ireland) in 34,000; 52,000 in 1942; and 38,000 in 1943. Emigration to the UK fell to 13,000 in 1944 and 23,700 in 1945.

9 The Limerick Clothing Factory was established in 1850. It began by making uniforms for the British during the Crimean War, and it also became world famous for producing uniforms for the Confederations during the American Civil War. During the Second World War it produced uniforms for the Irish, British and American armies.

10 *NUI Maynooth: Rationing in Emergency Ireland, 1939-1848* by Ciarán Bryan. https://mural.maynoothuniversity.ie/id/eprint/9130/1/CBryan_66665772_PhD_Thesis.pdf

11 The Emergency Scientific Research Bureau was set up in February 1941 to address industrial problems faced by agriculture and the food, clothing, building and engineering industries.

12 Lemass is wrong in his recollections. The 'Hitler has missed the bus' quote is from a House of Commons debate on 3 April 1940. Six days later Nazi Germany invaded Denmark and Norway. Chamberlain resigned as prime minister on 10 May 1940 and was replaced by Winston Churchill.

13 Lemass may be referring to a visit he made to London in October 1945, which was mostly concerned with aviation.

14 UCD History Hub, author Bryce Evans: https://historyhub.ie/lemass-marine

15 Irish Maritime History and Lemass: https://lugnad.ie/isl_lemass/

16 It was originally called the *Vassilios Destounis*. It had been badly damaged during the Spanish Civil War in Aviles. The government paid £120,000 for it, and repairs cost another £15,000.

17 *Irish Alder* (January 1942), formally *Piret* (Estonian), *Irish Rose* (January 1942) (*Mall*, Estonian), *Irish Willow* (October 1941) (*Otto*, Estonian). Latvia produced two vessels, *Ramava* and *Everoja*.

18 *Ramava* (Latvian) moved to Britain; *Everoja* transported Irish goods.

19 The Italian ship *Caterina Gerolimich* was trapped in Dublin during the war and was acquired by the Irish government after the surrender of Italy in June 1943. It was sent back to Naples after the war.

20 The British cut the tea exports to Ireland in January 1941 to 85 per cent of normal requitements, to 60 per cent in February, 50 per cent in March and 25 per cent in April. Ireland had 25 per cent of its normal tea requirements while British consumers had 85 per cent.

21 Tea Importers Éire was founded on 8 June 1941.

22 Normal consumption of coffee in the state before the Second World War was 672,000 pounds (304 tonnes) annually. By March 1943, 9 million pounds (4,000 tonnes) or the equivalent of 13.5 years' supply had been imported into the state, mostly from Brazil.

23 Known as COFF-O-ERA, it was made from barley and herbs.

24 Thomas Wheeler (1899–1962), the state chemist, was involved with the Emergency Scientific Research Bureau. They synthesised penicillin from Irish sea moss. It was available to the public from 1944.

25 Costello raised the issue in the Dáil twice, first on 20 May 1942 and then on 26 June 1942. Doctors, he said, were the 'sport of this department [Supplies] ... the medical profession has been subjected to a system of spying and snooping on the part of the Department which should not be tolerated in public ... It should be recognised that the professional men of this country are a class who can be trusted.'

26 Lemass would appear to be wrong about the dates here. He is referring to Christmas Eve 1940, not 1941. In the Dáil in January 1941, he made no mention of a tanker being sunk but merely stated that the distribution company in London had told his department that a situation had arisen where it was too dangerous to supply Ireland.

27 Eddie McGuire (1901–1992) founded the Federated Union of Employers in 1942 to represent the interests of small businesses.

28 Fr Thomas Burbage (1879–1966), who was the son of an RIC man, was interned by the British during the War of Independence. He was strongly anti-Treaty during the Civil War.

29 Pádraig de Brún (1889–1960) was a professor of mathematics who became president of University College Galway in April 1945, an office he held until 1959. He was a writer of Irish poetry and translated Homer's *Iliad* and *Odyssey* into Irish.

30 Dr John Charles McQuaid (1895–1973), a colossus of the twentieth century in Irish religious and social life, was Archbishop of Dublin from 1940 to 1972. He was a tireless campaigner for the poor and sick, but also possessed of an arrogant and dominating streak.

31 Cardinal John Francis D'Alton (1882–1963): D'Alton was appointed Archbishop of Armagh in 1946 and then a cardinal by Pope Pius XII in 1953.

32 The commission reported in 1959.

Chapter 7: Post-war malaise

1 The Turf Development Board became Bord na Móna in 1946. The first turf-fired power station was opened in Portarlington in 1950.

2 The Irish had one of the best diets in Europe during the Second World War, with an estimated average daily intake of 3,000 calories. By the end of the war most of occupied Europe was subsisting on 1,500 calories a day.

3 Oliver J. Flanagan (1920–1987) was one of the longest-serving TDs in Irish history, representing Laois-Offaly from 1943 to 1987. He was noted for his conservatism, especially in his latter years.

4 Pope Pius XII thanked the Irish government when the Irish representative (ambassador) to the Vatican, Joseph Walshe, met him on 13 June 1946.

5 The International Wheat Conference was held in London in May and June 1947.

6 In 1946 an Anglo-Irish agreement gave Aer Lingus a monopoly on all British–Irish routes in return for the British Overseas Airways Corporation (BOAC) and British European Airways having a 40 per cent stake. The two airlines merged to becoming British Airways (BA) in 1974.

7 The Rural Electrification Scheme, which began in 1946, was a big success. Over the next 20 years 300,000 homes were connected. By 1975, 99 per cent of Irish homes were connected to the grid.

8 The Arterial Drainage Act 1945 led to a scheme to improve land for agriculture. By the 1990s arterial drainage schemes covered 20 per cent of the country.

9 The Customs-Free Airport Act 1947 made Shannon Airport the first duty-free airport in the world.

10 The Korean War lasted from 1950 to 1953. Both the United States and the United Kingdom were involved. The first significant conflict of the Cold War ended with an Armistice in July 1953.

11 The Industrial Relations Act 1946 became law in August 1946.

12 The Standstill Order 1941 sought to mitigate wage rises rather than freeze them completely. Between 1939 and 1944, wages rose by 13 per cent, while prices rose by 70 per cent. As a result, the living standards of Irish workers fell dramatically.

13 There was a 60-day bus and tram strike in Dublin in 1947.

14 Bread rationing was introduced on 18 January 1947, as a direct result of the poor harvest of 1946.

15 The International Wheat Agreement of 1946 sought to stabilise wheat prices. Large exporters including Australia, Canada and the United States agreed a maximum price for export and countries like Ireland agreed a minimum price for imports.

16 Between 1942 and 1947, over half a million tonnes of hand-cut turf was transported to Dublin by canal, by train and by army lorries. It was stored in high mounds of up to 30 feet on the Fifteen Acres and along Chesterfield Avenue in the Phoenix Park, also known as the Long Straight.

17 The Dáil was dissolved on 12 January 1948.

18 There were no opinion polls in Ireland until the 1960s.

19 James Everett (1890–1967), a trade union official, was one of the longest-serving TDs. He represented the Wicklow constituency from 1923 to 1967, first as a Labour TD and then as a National Labour Party TD. National Labour and the Labour Party reunited in 1950.

Chapter 8 Out of office

1 Magill magazine, https://magill.ie/archive/profile-mrs-lemass

2 Patrick McGilligan was the Minister for Finance in the first inter-party coalition. Lemass does not acknowledge that Fianna Fáil had opposed the Shannon scheme proposed by Cumann na nGaedheal in 1920s as being too expensive.

3 The five Lockheed Constellations bought by the Fianna Fáil government were sold off at a profit by the inter-party government to the BOAC. According to a letter in the *Irish Times* some years later, the Labour Party was so against retaining these aircraft that they made their sell-off a condition of entering government.

4 The London Declaration of 1949 made it possible to be a republic and yet remain within the Commonwealth. India became a republic in 1950.

5 The anti-partition rally took place on 10 May 1949 in O'Connell Street, Dublin. The catalyst was the British government's Ireland Act.

6 The Ireland Act 1949 confirmed that Ireland had left the Commonwealth, but the common travel area between Ireland and Great Britain was retained.

7 When India and Pakistan declared independence in 1947, they also repudiated the British monarch as head of state. Under the London Declaration of 1950, they were allowed to remain within the Commonwealth, though they had a president as head of state.

8 This isn't entirely correct. The Health Act 1953 included a means test, which Browne's bill did not include. Mothers could only get free care for up to six weeks. Historian Dr Daithí Ó Corráin has stated that the 1953 Health Act killed any prospect of Ireland having a national health service on British lines.

Chapter 9 Lemass: The man with the plan

1 Browne joined Fianna Fáil in 1953, but lost his seat at the 1954 general election. He resigned in 1957 when he did not get a nomination from the party.

2 There were nine by-elections during the 14th Dáil – a record. Fianna Fáil held four of the seats and lost two.

3 Fianna Fáil's share of the first preference vote fell from 46.3 per cent to 43.4 per cent, a drop of almost three percentage points, or 6 per cent in their vote share.

4 In the early 1950s the percentage of tax taken by the Irish state was only about 20 per cent of national income. Today it is around 37.5 per cent of GNI* (gross national income), the most reliable method of measuring the Irish economy. Ireland only introduced PAYE in 1960 and VAT in 1973, after joining the European Economic Community (EEC). Irish state spending was very low in 1951 compared to the UK (33.82 per cent), France (29 per cent) and Sweden (22 per cent).

5 Lemass is wrong about this. Mac Éoin was Minister for Defence, not Minister for Justice, in the second inter-party government.

6 According to the *Irish Times*, he replied 'no comment' when asked about the operation of the IRA's border campaign.

Chapter 10 De profundis: The First Programme for Economic Expansion

1 This was seen as a major mistake by de Valera. Had de Valera supported the Fine Gael proposal whereby single-seat constituencies would have an alternative vote, it might have passed. The proposal would have involved No. 2 transfers until a candidate got a majority of the votes.

Chapter 11 Portrait of a taoiseach

1 This story was told by Lemass's daughter-in-law Eileen Lemass to Tom Garvin in 2008.

Chapter 12 Into the sixties

1 Macmillan sacked his Chancellor of the Exchequer Selwyn Lloyd.

2 The first Minister for Transport, Fuel and Power was Erskine Hamilton Childers Jr, the son of Erskine Childers, who had been executed by pro-Treaty forces in 1922, during the Civil War. Erskine Childers went on to be President of Ireland, succeeding de Valera as president in June 1973, but he died in office after just 17 months in the job.

3 Noel Huggard was a hotelier who bought Ashford Castle in 1939 and turned it into a hotel. Parts of *The Quiet Man* (1952) was filmed there.

4 Spellman, the Irish-American head of American Catholicism, was furious about the Irish decision and told Aiken he would 'raise the devil' if he voted to admit China.

5 Ireland had sent 50 unarmed observers to Lebanon in 1958 as part of the United Nations Observation Group in Lebanon (UNOGIL).

6 Patrice Lumumba (1925–1961) was the first prime minister of the Democratic Republic of the Congo and the leader of the Congolese National Movement. He was executed by the separatist Katangan authorities in January 1961.

7 Jack McQuillan (1920–1998) was elected as a Clann na Poblachta TD in 1948. He left the party in 1951 and held the seat in Roscommon as an independent until 1965.

8 Irish troops were sent on a UN peacekeeping mission to Cyprus in 1964.

9 Moïse Tshombe (1919–1969) was the first President of Katanga. He went on to become President of Congo, serving in office for just over a year, and died in exile in Algeria at the age of 50.

10 Irish troops left the Congo in 1964.

11 Frederick (Freddie) Boland (1904–1985) was an Irish civil servant who became Ireland's ambassador to the UN in 1956. He became president of the General Assembly of the United Nations for the 1960–1961 session. The notorious incident when Soviet Union leader Nikita Khrushchev banged his shoe off the podium at the UN happened while Boland was presiding.

Chapter 13 The European dream

1 The Anglo-Irish Free Trade Agreement was signed in 1965 and took effect in 1966. It was agreed in the absence of the failure of both the UK and Ireland to be admitted to the Common Market. It allowed for preferential access for Irish agriculture and the gradual scaling down of trade barriers between the two countries.

2 The UK Board of Trade and the EEC entered into negotiations about forming a free trade for goods, excluding agriculture, but the talks broke down.

3 Reginald Maudling (1917–1979) was a Conservative MP and Minister for the Board of Trade (1959–1961). Maudling was opposed to any proposal to join the Common Market on the basis that it would end Britain's right to make commercial agreements with New Zealand and Australia. He is most famous in an Irish context for having been punched in the House of Commons by Bernadette Devlin after Bloody Sunday in 1972.

4 Denmark applied in 1961 for membership, Norway in 1962. Both countries' applications also failed when the UK was refused entry.

5 James Charles Brendan McCarthy (1908–1990). McCarthy was assistant secretary at the Department of Industry and Commerce and then secretary from 1956 to 1972. He was closely involved in the setting up of the Industrial Development Authority (IDA).

The son-in-law

6 Seán Flanagan (1922–1993) was the captain of the Mayo team that won back-to-back All-Irelands in 1950 and 1951 and a TD for Mayo from 1951 to 1977. He was associated with Haughey and Brian Lenihan as one of the 'men in the mohair suits'.

7 Paddy Smith (1901–1982), the youngest IRA officer commanding in the War of Independence, was sentenced to death by the British but released under the terms of the Truce. He joined the anti-Treaty side in the Civil War and was a founding member of Fianna Fáil.

Chapter 14 Rebuilding Ireland

1 The population increased by 2.3 per cent between 1961 and 1965 from 2,818,351 to 2,884,002. It was the first increase in population in the area covered by the Republic of Ireland since the Great Famine, aside from a tiny increase of 5,000 between 1946 and 1951 brought about by Irish emigrants returning home after the Second World War.

2 The British were forced to devalue the pound in 1967.

3 According to the World Bank, Irish GDP grew by 3.8 per cent in 1964, 1.9 per cent in 1965 and just 0.9 per cent in 1966, but the economy rebounded strongly after that.

4 Slieveardagh, County Tipperary had been the location of a coalmine for more than 400 years, but the mine was regularly in financial trouble and finally closed in 1973.

5 The population of Dublin increased from 666,000 to 771,000 between 1961 and 1971.

6 In 1963 Dublin Corporation rehoused 759 families living in dangerous accommodation following the tenement collapses in the city.

7 Between 1964 and 1965 some 1,200 of Dublin's Georgian terraced houses and mews were deemed to be unfit for habitation and were knocked.

8 Lemass is referring to the May 1968 riots across universities in France – though housing was not a prime grievance.

Chapter 15 The Kennedy visit

1 Fourteen of the 15 executed leaders of the Easter Rising, the exception being Sir Roger Casement, were buried in the grounds of Arbour Hill Detention Centre after they were shot. They were buried in the order in which they were executed.

2 This is one of the few times during the Ryan recordings that he refers to the Easter Rising.

3 The Irish Army Cadet School performed a series of drills, which impressed President Kennedy. Just five months later they were invited by Kennedy's widow Jackie and his mother Rose to perform a drill at his funeral in Arlington Cemetery.

4 The exact quote is: 'Lord Edward, however, did not like to stay here in his family home because, as he wrote his mother, "Leinster House does not inspire the brightest ideas." That was a long time ago, however. It has also been said by some that a few of the features of this stately mansion served to inspire similar features in the White House in Washington.'

5 Lemass is mistaken in this assertion. It did appear in a number of newspapers, for instance the *Munster Express* of Friday 5 July 1963.

Chapter 16 Lemass goes north

1 Lemass is most likely referring to an offer by British Minister for Munitions David Lloyd George in May 1916 for the immediate introduction of Home Rule in the 26 counties with the fate of the Six Counties to be decided after the war. Irish nationalism rejected the compromise as it believed partition would be permanent.

2 In a Dominions Office file from 27 June 1940, Secretary of State for the Colonial Office Malcolm MacDonald told the taoiseach over lunch that if the plan was accepted 'a united Ireland would come into actual being within a comparatively short period of time'.

3 Churchill's offer was that, in return for Irish participation on the side of the Allies, the British government would immediately accept the principle of a united Ireland and would take steps to merge the northern and southern administrations. De Valera rejected it.

4 Lord Longford (1905–2001), born Frank Packenham, was an Anglo-Irish peer, a biographer and confidant of Éamon de Valera and a well-known penal campaigner. In 1956 Longford was appointed a mediator to try to negotiate for many of Hugh Lane's paintings to be returned to Ireland. This he successfully did. Lemass may be referring to a meeting that Longford had with Macmillan in August 1957.

5 Mac Eoin was Minister for Justice in the first inter-party government and Minister for Defence in the second.

6 Cowan, a radical left-wing politician who was expelled from the Labour Party in 1945, founded Vanguard, a short-lived socialist/republican organisation.

7 Lemass is incorrect; Mac Eoin was Minister for Defence at the outbreak of the border campaign.

8 On 30 December 1956 RUC Constable John Scally was shot and killed at Derrylin RUC barracks on the border.

9 The Special Criminal Court, composed of military officers, was set up in November 1961, when the Border Campaign was nearly over, by Minister for Justice Charles Haughey.

10 RUC officer William Hunter was killed in a gun battle in south Armagh on 12 November 1961. He was the last fatality of the border campaign.

11 Lemass is referring to the notorious Divis Street riots, which began on 27 September 1964, during that year's British general election campaign. The republican campaign office in Divis Flats had an Irish tricolour in the window. Under pressure from Rev. Ian Paisley, the RUC raided the offices, leading to three days of rioting. The rioting spread to the Falls Road and images of police using armoured cars, guns and water cannons were shown on television, attracting worldwide condemnation.

12 Eddie McAteer (1915–1986) was a long-time nationalist politician and anti-partition campaigner who became leader of the nationalist bloc in the Stormont Assembly in 1964. He was suspicious of all Southern politicians, Lemass among them. However, he did agree to become the official opposition in Stormont in February 1965.

13 The Nationalist Party became the official opposition in February 1965.

14 O'Neill made a reciprocal visit on 9 February 1965.

15 The Queen Mother also angled for an invitation to the Dublin Horse Show a year after her grandson Prince Charles visited in 1995, but it was regarded as too much of a security risk.

16 Princess Margaret married Antony Armstrong-Jones (1st Earl of Snowdon) in May 1960. Armstrong-Jones's mother, Anne, had divorced his father Ronald in 1934 and a year later had married Michael Parsons, 6th Earl of Rosse, becoming the Countess of Rosse. They lived in Birr Castle, County Offaly. Princess Margaret made her first visit to Birr Castle on New Year's Eve 1960, creating huge excitement. She made further visits in 1962 and 1965, but a visit in 1968 was called off because of security concerns.

17 This exchange is from the twentieth tape, which was recorded on 28 November 1968. The civil rights march in Derry, which had been baton-charged by the RUC, occurred on 5 October 1968 and is widely viewed as one of the events that triggered the Troubles.

18 McAteer took exception of Lemass's views that both sides in the North were equally intransigent.

19 Wilson represented the constituency of Ormskirk in Lancashire, north of Liverpool. It had been a major centre of Irish immigration during the Great Famine, when its population doubled in the space of a decade.

20 The remains of Reginald Dunne and Joseph O'Sullivan, the men who shot dead Field Marshal Sir Henry Wilson MP on 22 June 1922, were repatriated to Ireland in 1967, though the Irish government wanted nothing to do with the repatriation. See my book *Great Hatred: The Assassination of Field Marshal Sir Henry Wilson MP* (Faber, 2022).

21 Lemass and Wilson announced in the Dáil and House of Commons on 23 February that the remains would be repatriated. The remains were flown that day back to Ireland where they lay in state for four years. Casement was given a state funeral on 1 March, 1965. A graveside oration was given by President Éamon de Valera.

22 The Irish Republic flag that flew over the GPO during Easter Week was captured by the Royal Irish Regiment during the Rising and became part of the royal collection. It was sent back to Ireland in March 1966 as a gesture of goodwill by the British government.

23 The notorious *Black Diaries* were used to discredit Casement before his trial for treason in 1916. They purported to portray Casement as a homosexual and sexual deviant during his time in Peru and Congo. To this day they remain a matter of controversy. In 2002 forensic scientist Dr Audrey Giles, working from handwriting analysis, declared the diaries were 'genuine throughout' and not forgeries.

Chapter 17 One more election

1 Patrick Hogan (1885–1969) was elected as a Labour TD for Clare and became Ceann Comhairle in 1951, a position he held until 1967.

2 Patrick Norton (1928–). A son of the former Labour leader William Norton, Patrick succeeded to his father's seat in 1965. He did not like the leftward turn of the Labour Party and joined Fianna Fáil in 1969.

3 The last seat in the Dublin North-East constituency was won by Denis Larkin, the Labour candidate, over the Fianna Fáil candidate Eugene Timmons.

4 In Longford-Westmeath Patrick Lenihan, the father of the Minister for Justice Brian Lenihan, won a seat over General Seán Mac Eoin on the last count by 13 votes. He was a very good friend of Lemass.

5 Lemass is referring to a speech he made a few days after the election in which he stated that the closeness of so many seats meant that the electoral system was not fit for purpose.

6 Derick Heathcoat-Amory was a British Conservative MP who served as Chancellor of the Exchequer between 1958 and 1960.

7 A 15 per cent import duty was imposed in October 1964 on all imports into Britain with the exception of foodstuffs, raw materials and tobacco. It was introduced to rebalance Britain's balance of payment duties. The tax affected more than 20 per cent of Irish imports to Britain and had a serious impact on trade between the two countries.

8 They lasted until November 1966.

Chapter 18: 1916 and all that

1 *Kerryman*, 12 April 1966.

2 The paper delivered by Oxford University's Professor of Economics Kevin O'Rourke at the Easter Rising National Conference in 2016 at the University of Galway gave a detailed outline of Ireland's economic performance since independence. In essence, Ireland remained relatively as poor as it was before independence until joining the EEC in 1973. The gap closed rapidly after that and Ireland became wealthier than the UK per capita in the early 2000s. (See www.ora.ox.ac.uk/objects)

3 This was a proposal similar to the social partnership pioneered by his son-in-law Charles Haughey as taoiseach. Unions and employers agreed to wage restraint in return for tax cuts as the economy improved. The Programme for National Recovery was a success and paved the way for the Celtic Tiger era, which began in the mid-1990s.

4 Samuel Johnson (1709–1784) is credited with coining the phrase in 1775.

5 This changed in 2018 when President Michael D. Higgins became only the second incumbent to face a contest. He participated in three debates, two on television and one on radio.

Chapter 19 Retirement

1 Konrad Adenauer (1876–1967) was the first chancellor of West Germany, a position he held from 1949 to 1963. Lemass spoke admiringly of him many times in the Ryan tapes.

Chapter 20 Legacy and death

1 In fact, Lemass's son-in-law Charles Haughey achieved that as taoiseach in 1990 during the First Programme for National Recovery. The Irish economy achieved an 8.5 per cent growth in GDP that year.

BIBLIOGRAPHY

- Brian Farrell, *Seán Lemass*, Gill & MacMillan (Dublin) 1991
- Michael O'Sullivan: *Seán Lemass: A Biography*, Blackwater Press, 1994
- John Horgan: *Seán Lemass: Enigmatic Patriot*, Gill & MacMillan (Dublin), 1997
- Brian Girvin and Gary Murphy: *The Lemass Era: Politics and Society in the Ireland of Seán Lemass*, UCD Press, 2005
- Tom Garvin *Judging Lemass*, Royal Irish Academy (RIA), Dublin 2009
- Bryce Evans, *Lemass, Democratic Dictator*, The Collins Press 2011
- Robert Savage *Seán Lemass* (Life & Times series) UCD Press, 2014
- Iain Dale (editor), *The Taoiseach: A Century of Political Leadership*, Swift (London), 2025
- JJ Lee, *Ireland 1912-1985: Politics and Society*, Cambridge University Press, 1989,
- Brian Girvin, *Between Two Worlds; Ireland since independence*, Barnes & Noble Books, 1989
- Tom Garvin, *Preventing the Future: Why was Ireland so poor for so long?*, Gill & MacMillan 2004
- Christopher Todd Andrews, *Dublin Made Me*, Lilliput Press, 2001
- David McCullagh, *Rise & Rule, De Valera Volumes 1&2*, Gill Books, 2017
- Gary Murphy, *Haughey*, Gill Books, 2021

ABOUT THE INTERVIEWER DERMOT RYAN (1928-2023)

Dermot Ryan was born in Dublin and was the founder of the tourism and leisure business The Ryan Group. He was also a member of the Fianna Fáil national executive and TACA, the party's fundraising arm. He moved to London in the 1970s and worked in computer and video technologies until he retired.

INDEX